In Harness

Judaic Traditions in Literature, Music, and Art
Ken Frieden and Harold Bloom, *Series Editors*

In Harness

YIDDISH WRITERS' ROMANCE
WITH COMMUNISM

Gennady Estraikh

 Syracuse University Press

First Edition 2005
05 06 07 08 09 10   6 5 4 3 2 1

The paper used in this publication meets the minimum requirements
of American National Standard for Information Sciences—Permanence
of Paper for Printed Library Materials, ANSI Z39.48–1984.∞™

Library of Congress Cataloging-in-Publication Data
Estraikh, G. (Gennadii)

  In harness : Yiddish writers' romance with communism / Gennady Estraikh.— 1st ed.

    p.   cm.— (Judaic traditions in literature, music, and art)
  Includes bibliographical references and index.
  ISBN 0-8156-3052-2 (hardcover (cloth) : alk. paper)
  1. Yiddish literature—20th century—History and criticism.   2. Yiddish literature—Soviet
Union—History and criticism.   3. Authors, Yiddish—Soviet Union.   4. Jewish
communists—Soviet Union.   5. Jews—Soviet Union—Intellectual life.   6. Communism in
literature.   I. Title.   II. Series.

PJ5120.E88   2004
839'.1309947—dc22

2004021013

Manufactured in the United States of America

Contents

Illustrations

Gennady Estraikh is currently the Rauch Visiting Associate Professor of Yiddish Studies at New York University. He is the author of *Soviet Yiddish: Language Planning and Linguistic Development* and *Intensive Yiddish,* and coauthor (with Mikhail Krutikov) of *Yiddish and the Left.* He has also coedited *The Shtetl: Image and Reality* and *Yiddish in the Contemporary World.*

Preface

IN HARNESS, or *In shpan* in Yiddish, is the name of a literary journal founded in 1926 and phased out the same year after only two issues. The short-lived Yiddish periodical was inspired by the prominent prose writer David Bergelson, who was living in Berlin at the time after escaping from the revolution-riven Russia. *In Harness* marked his sensational transformation from an opponent of the Bolshevik regime into a vociferous supporter of the Soviet Union. Bergelson was one of hundreds of East European Yiddish intellectuals galvanized by the Communist dream. Inspired by the Soviet Union's large-scale projects of Jewish colonization and cultural development, these Jewish intellectuals, scattered throughout the world, began to believe that Soviet society represented the only environment in which their brainchild, a secular, Yiddish-speaking nation, could find its secure habitat.

This book traces the formation of this cadre of Communist Yiddish writers, both within the Soviet Union and elsewhere. It concentrates primarily on Yiddish literary life in such cities as Kiev, Moscow, Kharkov, Minsk, and New York, covering the period between 1900 and the mid-1930s, when Yiddish Communist literary activities reached their climax.

People not involved in studies of Yiddish culture rarely have any idea of the scale and intensity of Yiddish literary life in the Communist circles of the 1920s and 1930s. These circles, scattered all over the world, were linked through the network of the Communist International, or Comintern. Although a similar extraterritoriality generally characterized Yiddish writers who were not Communist, hardly any other Communist literary milieu had such a broad geographic distribution and such mobility within its cadre as that of Communists writing in Yiddish. As a result, it is sometimes difficult to define a writer as, for instance, Soviet, Argentine, or American. Therefore, I use the term "Comintern writers" to emphasize their loyalty to the Moscow-based ideological center.

Within the Soviet Union proper, Kiev was the main breeding ground: scores of Yiddish writers and critics began or developed their literary careers there. This fact explains the central place occupied in the book by the Kievers, most notably David Bergelson, Der Nister (Pinkhas Kahanovitch), David Hofshtein, Leyb Kvitko, Peretz Markish, Itsik Fefer, Moshe Litvakov, Yekhezkel Dobrushin, and Nokhum Oislender.

My own interest in Yiddish literature initially developed under the influence of my father, Yakov Estraikh (1909–1982). After graduating from the Yiddish Department of the Zhitomir Teachers Training Institute in 1931, he worked for a decade in the Nayzlatopol (Novozlatopol) Jewish National District in Ukraine. Yet he could not imagine that later in my life I would become a Yiddish story writer—still less that in 1988 I would give up my "secure" profession of computer engineer (which, indeed, helped me survive during my refusenik years) to become managing editor of the Moscow Yiddish literary monthly *Sovetish heymland* (Soviet homeland).

Between 1988 and 1991, all the members of the editorial staff and many of the journal's authors contributed to my Yiddish literary education, but my best teacher was the poet and historian of Yiddish literature Khaim Beider (1920–2003). When I was at Oxford working on my doctorate in the early 1990s, I was lucky enough to meet Professor Khone Shmeruk (1921–1997), who regularly spent a month or so in England. The last Yiddish scholar-polymath, he was also a historian of Soviet Yiddish literature. My doctoral study, devoted to Soviet Yiddish sociolinguistics, involved reading numerous works by Soviet writers. Because of my own writing, I met a few of these writers or their kin.

I am particularly indebted to my friend and colleague Mikhail Krutikov, with whom I discussed this project numerous times. I also wish to thank Mordechai Altshuler, Boris Budyanski, Valery Dymshits, Hillel Kazovsky, Marion Neiss, Chana Polack, Ingedore Rüdlin, Boris Sandler, Joseph Sherman, Howard Spier, and Arkadi Zeltser, who provided not only editorial suggestions and advice but also books, copies of other material, and illustrations. Another source of help has been the colleagues and students who listened to my lectures on the topics in this book at various conferences and seminars; their questions and comments have proved invaluable at various stages of the work.

I would like to thank the Memorial Foundation for Jewish Studies and the British Academy for supporting my studies. My spring 2003 visiting fellowship at the Potsdam-based Moses Mendelssohn Center gave me a chance to deepen my knowledge of Yiddish literary life in Germany after the First World War. I bow down before librarians in Berlin, Helsinki, Jerusalem, London, Moscow, New York, Oxford, Paris, St. Petersburg, and Urbana-Champaign, but particularly before Oxford librarian Elena Estraikh, my ever-patient wife.

Some material in this book represents revised versions or fragments of my previously published articles:

"A Touchstone of Socialist Realism: The 1934 *Almanac* of Soviet Yiddish Writers." *Jews in Eastern Europe* no. 3 (1998): 24–37.

"From Yehupets Jargonists to Kiev Modernists: The Rise of a Yiddish Literary Centre, 1880s–1914." *East European Jewish Affairs* 30, no. 1 (2000): 17–38.

"Yiddish Literary Life in Soviet Moscow, 1918–1924." *Jews in Eastern Europe* no. 2 (2000): 25–55.

"David Bergelson: From Fellow Traveler to Soviet Classic." *Slavic Almanac: The South African Year Book for Slavic, Central, and East European Studies* 7, no. 10 (2001): 191–222.

"Itsik Fefer: A Yiddish *Wunderkind* of the Bolshevik Revolution." *Shofar* 20, no. 3 (2002): 14–31.

"The Kharkiv Yiddish Literary World, 1920s–Mid-1930s." *East European Jewish Affairs* 32, no. 2 (2002): 70–88.

All the illustrations used in the book are reproduced courtesy of the New York–based Yiddish newspaper *Forverts* (Forward).

In Harness

Prologue

IN 1898, LEO WIENER, an instructor in the Slavic languages at Harvard University, was invited to write a book on the history of Yiddish literature, including an overview of contemporary writers and their works. It would have been difficult to find a better candidate to prepare such a study. One of the first significant American academics of East European Jewish extraction, Wiener was a polyglot, speaking many languages indifferently and apparently having no linguistic problems with Yiddish. As we learn from the memoirs of his son, the prominent mathematician Norbert Wiener, Leo's father had been a journalist with the Yiddish press in Bialystok—if an unlucky one. According to family legend, his great enthusiasm for literary German one day prompted Leo's father to change the language of his periodical from Yiddish to German, with the result that he lost almost all his subscribers.[1] As for Leo's own attitude to Yiddish, it may be characterized as that of a skeptical, if impressionable, observer. An important aspect of Leo Wiener's project—heavier in facts than in analysis—was his European trip, which gave him a chance to meet in situ the luminaries of Yiddish letters.

In fact, not all the luminaries lived in Eastern Europe. Abraham Goldfaden, known as the "father of Yiddish theater," lived at that time in Paris. Morris Winchevsky, the leading proletarian poet and journalist, lived in New York, where in April 1897 he took part in creating, and briefly editing, the city's biggest Yiddish newspaper, *Forverts*. Leo Wiener had himself discovered for the English reader another Yiddish proletarian poet, Morris Rosenfeld; Wiener's translations of Rosenfeld's poems, *Songs from the Ghetto,* came out in 1898 in Boston. But despite all this growth, Yiddish literary circles in Western Europe and America were still considered to be colonial outposts of the East European "metropole."

Indeed, by that time a large group of professional Yiddish writers had established itself firmly on the proscenium of the East European theater of

1

Jewish culture and ideology. In Warsaw, Leo Wiener met the popular prose writers Yakov Dinezon and Mordekhai Spector, but he was most enraptured by Yitzkhok Leibush Peretz. Wiener argued that Peretz should be counted among the greatest writers not only of Yiddish literature but of contemporary literature in general. In his hometown of Bialystok, Wiener called on the ailing venerable poet Abraham Baer Gottlober. He did not find any literary heavyweights in Vilna, which had been deserted after the death in 1893 of the popular story writer Ayzik Meyer Dik. But in Kiev he had a long conversation with Sholem Aleichem, whom he praised both as a talented writer of consummate skill and as the publisher of two volumes (1888 and 1889) of the *Yidishe folksbibliotek* (Yiddish people's library). According to Wiener, this annual showed that, had the publisher been more fortunate (the third volume could not leave the press because Sholem Aleichem had gone bankrupt), he would soon have brought Yiddish letters "to a height where they would have taken place by the side of the best in Europe." In the Black Sea port of Odessa, Wiener "learned many important facts" from conversations with the doyens of Yiddish letters, Mendele Moykher Sforim and Yitzkhok Yoel Linetzky. Wiener concluded that Yiddish was "certainly not inferior to many of the literary languages which had been fortunate enough to attract the attention of the linguist and student of comparative literature. In its belles-lettres it compared favorably with those of countries like Bulgaria, which had their regeneration at about the same time. It might appear to the unbiased observer that it even surpassed them in that respect." [2]

By the end of the nineteenth century, the Yiddish world of letters had already become one of the most active literary arenas in imperial Russia. The rapid development of Yiddish literary activities was hardly fortuitous. Modern Yiddish literature had one of the most promising cultural surroundings. "Humanization" of Jews through general education—the missionary idea that seized influential Russian decision-makers—was vigorously, if dysfunctionally, implemented during most of the nineteenth century. This fact, coupled with the modernization of Russia, corroded the traditional Jewish society. As a result, a stratum of Jewish youth emerged educated outside the usual channels. Some of them, inevitably, had the desire to write. Typically, they would first try writing in Hebrew or Russian, but they often ended up writing in Yiddish. Apart from being the native language of the vast majority of Russian Jews, Yiddish had an iconoclastic flavor that naturally attracted some rebellious Talmudic students turned freethinkers. Defiantly calling themselves "Jargonists," they stressed the folkist character of their writing while being apologetic about the "triviality" of their literary medium.

Significantly, these Yiddish culture-bearers were at an advantage over, for example, their Ukrainian and Belorussian counterparts, whose languages were officially regarded—and suppressed—as dialects of Russian, the only legitimate language of the Orthodox religion, education, and literature. In addition, the incidence of literacy among Jews was much higher than among the predominantly underdeveloped, rural Slavic groups. Education had a long-standing importance in Jewish society, which expected males to possess at least the rudimentary skills needed to read holy texts in Hebrew.[3] Because Yiddish literacy was basically an extension of Hebrew literacy, native speakers of Yiddish—male and female—represented a potential market of many millions of readers, both in Russia and around the world. An itinerant *moykher-sforim* (bookseller) had in his stock both religious and secular volumes, offering them for either purchase or loan. Legal and illegal Jewish libraries, which emerged during the last decades of the nineteenth century, also attracted numerous readers.[4]

A Yiddish literary milieu developed mostly around periodicals, beginning with the pioneer Yiddish newspaper in Russia, *Kol mevaser* (Voice of the herald), the first issue of which appeared in October 1862 in Odessa. Spector's Warsaw-based annual, *Der hoyzfraynd* (The family friend), published 1888–89, and, especially, Sholom Aleichem's contemporaneous *Yidishe folksbibliotek* became important landmarks in the history of modern Yiddish literature. Almost all 3,200 copies of the first issue of *Yidishe folksbibliotek* were quickly sold, half of them in the five Jewish centers of Kiev (517 copies), Warsaw (317), Odessa (277), Vilna (221), and Berdichev (186). Characteristically, Demievka, then a settlement near Kiev (into which it was absorbed after 1917), had 14 buyers of the new periodical, more than such cities as Moscow (8) and Kharkov (5).[5]

The late 1880s also saw Sholem Aleichem's construction of a framework for modern Yiddish literature. According to Dan Miron, "until the mid-1880s it is with difficulty that we trace any consciousness of the existence of a Yiddish 'literature.' There seems to have been no sense of accumulation of literary experience."[6] It was Sholem Aleichem who started the ball rolling, allowing Yiddish literature to emerge from the shadow of Hebrew letters as a detached edifice, provided with all three essential dimensions of a full-fledged modern literature. Of these, the first was history. Sholem Aleichem stimulated his fellow townsman Eleazar Shulman to write a pioneer history of Yiddish literature, the first part of which was published in the 1889 volume of the *Yidishe folksbibliotek*. Thus, the literature acquired the past-tense axis. It was also thanks to Sholem Aleichem that Yiddish literature acquired the second dimension—the pecking orders or hierarchies that provide a perspective for the present tense. Through Sholem Aleichem, Yiddish literature acquired the "grandfather" figure of Mendele (Moykher Sforim) and the cream of contemporary literature, namely the hand-picked team of the *Yidishe folksbibliotek* contributors.

The third and last dimension plotted by Sholem Aleichem was literary scandal, which he created in 1888 when he decided (in his own words) to "dismember, cut, dissect into tiny bits, missing no smallest bone, intestine, or vein" [7] the popular Yiddish writer Shomer. The phenomenally prolific belletrist Shomer (Nokhum Meir Shaikevich) wrote formulaic works marketed as "highly interesting novels," which were read voraciously by hundreds of thousands of Russian Jews; earlier in 1888, before Sholem Aleichem's attack, a score of Shomer's novels had come out in Russia with print runs of between one thousand and six thousand copies, and two of his new novels, *A kale af prokat* (A bride for hire) and *A khosn af a vayle* (A bridegroom for a short time), had each been published with a print run of nine thousand copies.[8] However, Sholem Aleichem's attack on Shomer, which appeared in the satirical pamphlet *Shomers mishpet* (Shomer's trial), devastated the latter's reputation. Interestingly, Shomer believed that the real author of *Shomers mishpet* was the Hebrew and Yiddish writer David Frishman, and that Sholem Aleichem had only ordered and sponsored that literary denouncement.[9] Indeed, the attack looked like an all-out assault, launched in 1887 by Shimen Dubnov, then the leading literary critic of the Petersburg-based Russian-Jewish journal *Voskhod*.[10]

In his pamphlet, Sholem Aleichem presented himself as the stenographer of the "trial" and juxtaposed "the primitive Shomer, a Jew not really old but also not very young, not really black-haired but not very gray, not very ugly but also not handsome," with four giants of the "new Jargon" literature: Mendele Moykher Sforim, Yitzkhok Yoel Linetzky, Ayzik Meyer Dik, and Abraham Goldfaden.[11] Ironically, in 1893, five years after Sholem Aleichem's belittling "trial" of Shomer and a few months after Ayzik Meyer Dik's death, a Vilna press reprinted a romance by Dik but marketed it under a new title as "translated by Shomer." [12]

Although Sholem Aleichem was disdainful of the kind of "highly interesting" literature penned by Shomer—and often opprobriously called by the German word for "trash," *Schund,* or the Yiddish equivalent, *shund* (a word also applied, ironically enough, to some of Sholem Aleichem's own stories)[13]—good things had come from the light, entertaining writings of Shomer and his brother writers and imitators. Most significantly, writers of Shomer's school were instrumental in creating the *fin-de-siècle* Yiddish book mass market in Eastern Europe. Thanks to them, reading secular books became a favorite pastime for many of the common people. It was "a dream about literature rather than literature proper," written for a "hidebound reader who strain[ed] to poetry, to poetic values and revelations."[14] Even some highbrow intellectuals—who mostly treated the *shund* writers harshly—had to acknowledge the educational role of Shomerian literature: "A young Jewish shtetl-dweller, who used to think that behind his Kasrilovke the sky dropped down on the earth and the 'mountains of darkness' rose, found out in Shomer's book that somewhere in the world there was Paris, London, love and lords—and his eyes opened. It was the young man's first step towards a new, wider, outlook."[15]

It is characteristic that, in the preceeding quote, Shmuel Niger (Charney), the master Yiddish literary critic, used one of Sholem Aleichem's coinages, *Kasrilovke,* which became synonymous with a remote, parochial East European Jewish community. Sholem Aleichem's laughing interpretations of life required a system of comic renaming, including his own nom de plume.[16] Another of Sholem Aleichem's comic names, Yehupets, stereotyped a Russian city, usually Kiev, with a significant Jewish population.

CHAPTER ONE

Kiev

The Sages and the Literary Youth

AN UNSYMPATHETIC BRITISH COMMENTATOR on East European Jewish life at the end of the nineteenth century reports, "Kieff is chiefly notable, so far as Jews go for its un-Jewish character. For while the Jews monopolise some of the few trades of the town which they are still allowed to pursue, they do not monopolise one's attention, as in almost all the other places to which I went . . . The hatred which the Russians and everybody else you met in Kieff have for the Jews is intense." [1] Sholem Aleichem echoes this negative description: "The large, beautiful gentile city of Yehupets . . . is certainly not the kind of city that would seek to have even a token Jewish population. Quite the contrary, it is well known that, from time immemorial, Jews have been as welcome to the people in the city as a migraine." [2]

Indeed, Jews traditionally regarded Kiev-Yehupets as a *goyishe shtot,* a gentile city. This reputation was associated only partly with the city's legal status; the city had always been exempt from the Pale of Settlement. Only certain categories of Jews—mainly wealthy merchants, graduates of Russian universities, students, and some craftsmen—might hope to obtain official permission to reside in Kiev. Even the city's Jewish communal organization had a peculiar name: Representation for Jewish Charity at the Kiev City Administration. [3] Apart from its legal status, the *goyishe shtot* Kiev was commonly stigmatized as the most anti-Semitic place in the entire empire—"the only town in Russia where the traditions of the mediaeval ghetto had been fully preserved." [4] In April 1881, Kiev was rocked by anti-Jewish pogroms as the populace responded to the assassination of Czar Alexander II. A pogrom also broke out in October 1905, when the manifesto of Nicholas II introduced a constitutional monarchy. In 1911–13, Kiev was the focus of atten-

tion of the Russian and foreign press owing to Russia's "Dreyfus affair"—
the Mendel Beilis case.[5]

In truth, Kiev, a seething metropolitan cauldron, stood out as a model
anti-Semitic place only against the background of the relative idyll of the
Pale's backwaters, where Jews ostensibly got on tolerably well with their
gentile neighbors. A decade or so later, after the massacres of the civil war,
the Kiev brand of anti-Semitism lost much of its superlative. Also, Kiev epitomized the problems of the Jewish intellectual rather than those of the common man, such as professional competition and the *numerus clausus* (quota
of Jewish students). In 1897 more than 15 percent of Ukraine's intelligentsia
was Jewish, including 15.8 percent of Ukraine's private lawyers; 17 percent
of its doctors and other medical and health workers; 21 percent of its scholars, literati, and artists; and 31.2 percent of its teachers.[6] Many of these Jews
lived in Kiev. In any case, the city's Jewish community rose steadily during
the last decades of the nineteenth century. Kiev boasted sixteen thousand
Jews in 1887 and thirty-two thousand in 1897. Officially, more than fifty
thousand Jews (as well as an unknown, but always significant, number of
illegal Jewish residents) lived in Kiev in 1910. Although the majority of
the Jewish residents were artisans or tradesmen living a hand-to-mouth
existence, about fifty-five hundred were rich and a number of them even
fabulously wealthy. The Brodsky family, for instance, controlled about one-
quarter of the empire's sugar production.[7] The wealthy Jewish families created around themselves a circle of "learned wise men who were otherwise
unemployable"[8] or, still, could serve as teachers, secretaries, accountants,
and cashiers. Yitzkhok Yoel Linetzky, for instance, spent two formative
years, between 1863 and 1865, in Kiev working as a teacher for the employees of Moshe Veynshteyn, one of the Kiev wealthy.

Sholem Aleichem's path to Kiev also lay via a position as a private
teacher, ill-advisedly hired to educate Olga Loyev, the daughter in a wealthy
family, whom he eventually married, against her parents' wishes, in 1883. In
fact, Yiddish literature is much obliged to Olga Loyev's *mésalliance*. Thanks
to a handsome fortune the young couple inherited after the death in 1885 of
Olga's father, Sholem Aleichem had a chance to invest money in the *Yidishe
folksbibliotek*. Furthermore, he decided to pay generous royalties—an unprecedented luxury for Yiddish men of letters. In a letter to Linetzky he
stressed that, although the content of the new almanac was rich, original,
and well-thought-out, the greatest innovation was that all contributors

would be paid, and paid properly, so that a Yiddish writer would "no longer be the editor's slave, writing for a glass of vodka and a slice of bread." By paying high honoraria, Sholem Aleichem upgraded Yiddish creative writing to the level of a professional occupation. He even introduced going rates for Yiddish writers, for instance ten kopecks for a line written by Mendele and "almost the same" for a line by Linetzky.[9] It is amazing how he, a novice in Yiddish letters, managed—thanks to his wealth (even if it was of short duration), talent, persistence, and, of course, self-confidence—to become the central figure, towering over the entire Yiddish literary milieu, which was stuck in a kind of cultural adolescence. Sholem Aleichem had suddenly grown up, and he led the denizens of this milieu to maturity.

Sholem Aleichem lived in Kiev for a quarter of a century (1879–1905), and even five years after his departure he was still called by Peretz "Sholem Aleichem of Kiev."[10] For all that, his local circle of men of letters was rather small. Moreover, these people were usually more committed to Hebrew than to Yiddish. This circle of *khakhme Kiev* (Sholem Aleichem's term meaning "Sages of Kiev") included interesting types of *maskilim,* or products of the Jewish Enlightenment, the *Haskalah.*[11] Some of them, such as the physician Isaak Kaminer and the lawyer Mark Varshavsky, graduated from Russian universities. Kaminer, a talented Hebrew poet, wrote a salutatory text that opened the first volume of the *Yidishe folksbibliotek.* Varshavsky, an amateur Yiddish bard, wrote both the words and music of the songs he sang to his friends; Sholem Aleichem encouraged him to publish these songs.[12] The first edition of his *Yidishe folkslider mit noten* (Yiddish folksongs with notes) was printed in Kiev in 1901. Varshavsky's songs—"Oyfn pripetshek" (On the hearth), for example—soon became popular and were widely regarded as an intrinsic component of East European Jewish folk music.

Some other "sages" paid their way with jobs as private teachers, like Abraham Ber Dubzevitsh, who worked for the Brodskys, and Yakov Veissberg. These Hebrew authors also wrote in Yiddish. One of the most popular writers among them was the publican Moshe Aaron Shatzkes, who, apart from selling drinks and writing in Hebrew, became known as the author of the widely read Yiddish book *Der yidisher farpeysekh* (Passover eve, 1881), a humorous portrait of Jewish life in Russia. Bookkeepers and cashiers were as frequent among the nineteenth-century Jewish writers as physicians were in other European literatures. In Sholem Aleichem's autobiographical novel *Funem yarid* (From the fair) we read about the Hebrew poet Yehuda Leyb Levin, known as Yehalel, whom he went to see in Kiev, where Levin was working as a bookkeeper at Brodsky's mill.[13] The pioneer historian of Yiddish literature, Eleazar Shulman, also earned a living as an employee of the Brodsky family, at first as a private Hebrew teacher, then as a cashier. The "sages of Kiev" were close to Uri Nissan Gnessin, a modernist Hebrew writer, and Lev Shestov (Schvarzman), a Russian religious philosopher. Some of the sages knew Eliazar Zuckerman, a pioneer Jewish socialist in Russia and an advocate of Yiddish.

Kiev, as Russia's fifth-largest city and boasting one of the most literate populations in the entire empire,[14] also played an exceptional role as a Jewish student center. Suffice it to say that Kiev's St. Vladimir University had the largest concentration of Jewish students of all Russian universities. In 1911, for instance, the university had 888 Jewish students, making up 17 percent of all its students.[15] Many others attended the Polytechnical Institute, in whose creation (in 1898) Jewish sponsors, most notably the Brodsky family, had played a very significant role. As a result, its quota for Jewish students had been doubled.[16] Kiev had its share of ubiquitous external students (*eksterns* or *eksterniks*). These products of the *numerus clausus* also were quite active in the city's intellectual life. Jewish students were prominent in various radical organizations. One of the strongest social democratic groups in the country, the Kiev Union of Struggle for Liberation of the Working Class, had a predominantly Jewish membership.[17] The students with chips on their shoulders also widely supported the particularly Jewish parties, a direct result of their quest for a modern, secular Jewish identity and forms of Jewish self-government.

In the anti-Jewish atmosphere of Alexander III's reign, this quest dominated Jewish intellectual life, creating a dissenting subculture of ethnic—rather than religious—Jewishness. Many Jewish intellectuals gained inspiration from the idea of Jewishness as essentially culture expressed in the national language and defined by its literature and arts. Their journey of cultural self-discovery had two main destinations: Hebraism and Yiddishism. The latter, the Yiddish language and cultural movement, appealed to a slew of Kiev Jewish intellectuals, including students. While Hebraists, on the whole, saw their ideal of the Jewish nation and its destiny in a past spanning two millennia and their future in a new Zion, Yiddishists discovered their metaphysical homeland in the Yiddish language and East European Jewish culture. From the moment Yiddishism emerged as a tendency, it became enmeshed in areas of culture that could be considered modernist and socialist. Not only had the Jewish revolutionary movement generated a rich culture and body of literature, but the socialists were the leading spirit in a wide range of enlightenment groups and activities, such as the proto-Bundist Jargon committees (1895–98). Founded in Vilna, these committees were signs of the first stirrings of organized Yiddishism. They played an invaluable role in disseminating Yiddish letters, including politically detached works.[18] A. Litvak (Khaim-Yankev Helfand), an activist of the Jargon committees, argued that "the Bund taught the Jewish masses to read. Hitherto, the Jewish workers read only 'highly interesting novels.' Apart from *maskilim*, nobody read Mendele. Only a few individuals read Peretz's *Yom-tov bletlekh* [a populist periodical published in 1894–95]. The Bund created a large circle of readers who were looking for a good book or newspaper."[19]

It is important to add that, although the Bund was the largest pro-Yiddishist political movement, other Jewish political currents were likewise active in the Yiddish reading revolution, targeting the so-called *bavustzinike arbeter* (conscientious workers)—a concept that echoed the Nietzschean *berechenbare Individuum*.[20] Abraham Reisen, the popular Yiddish writer and editor, was arguably the first to campaign for granting Yiddish the status of the Jewish national language; he raised the topic as early as the beginning of the century, particularly in the Krakow weekly *Dos yidishe vort* (Jewish word), which he edited in 1904–5.[21]

In 1899 a Jewish organization was formed by a group of Kiev students representing a fractious mix of ideological currents. Soon, however, some of them, including two students at the university's law school, Moshe Olgin and David Zaslavsky, were attracted by the Bund program. (The former was to become the leading New York Yiddish communist, while the latter would make an impressive career as a Soviet agitprop journalist.) They formed the group Frayhayt (Freedom), which became the basis for the Kiev Bund organization. However, the Bund did not hold such a dominant position in the Jewish workers' movement in Ukraine as it had in Belorussia, Lithuania, and, in part, Poland.[22] Ukraine, with its smaller proportion of Jewish urban and proletarian population, had a social basis for hybrid currents, more nationalist than Marxist. In Kiev in autumn 1903, a group of Jewish socialists formed the Vozrozhdenie (Renaissance), espousing an ideology combining Marxism with Jewish territorialism and autonomism. It was transitional in nature, prone to fratricidal conflict. A year later in Odessa some of its member founded the Zionist-Socialist Workers' Party, also known as the S.S. Party. In Kiev in April 1906, a faction of the Vozrozhdenie group with a variant view of the future Jewish national autonomy, created another party;

Moshe Olgin

named the Jewish Socialist Workers' Party and also known as Seimists or SERP, it was ideologically closer than the S. S. Party to the Russian Socialist-Revolutionary Party.[23]

Doctrinal differences aside, both the Zionist-Socialist Workers' Party and the Jewish Socialist Workers' Party attached great importance to Yiddish cultural activities. An average Zionist or Jewish Socialist was more preoccupied with Yiddish than were his Bundist or Labor Zionist counterparts, who, though also committed to Yiddish, had more imperative agendas. After all, the Bund was a wing of the Russian proletarian movement, struggling for a classless and, significantly, nationless society. The Labor Zionists' ultimate objective was Zion. For the Vozrozhdenie socialists, however, Yiddish was an all-important pillar of the multinational socialist commonwealth, containing Jewish territorial and cultural oases, that they envisaged; hence their special attachment to Yiddish, its culture, and its literature. Contemporaries even distinguished the ranting Zionist-Socialist style of writing, which contained numerous Hebraisms and other stylistic adornments.[24] Among the activists of the Vozrozhdenie group were many Yiddish literati, such as Shmuel Niger and Moshe Litvakov, as well as the former student of the Kiev Polytechnical Institute Nokhum Shtif, later a prominent Yiddish theoretician and linguist, and another philologist, Zelig Kalmanovitz. Kiev and, to a lesser extent, Vilna became the main hub of the Vozrozhdenie milieu.

At the end of 1906, one of the Vozrozhdenie activists, Josef Leshtshinsky (aka Khmurner), together with Khaim Chemerinsky (aka Reb Mordkhele), a popular Jewish activist in southern Russia and a Yiddish fabulist, edited the first Kiev Yiddish daily, *Dos folk* (People). The paper survived only one month before it was closed down by the authorities. At the same time, Moshe Litvakov edited in Vilna a sister publication, the weekly *Der nayer veg* (New way). A Talmudic student until the age of seventeen years, Litvakov later gained an external gymnasium certificate and was a Sorbonnist in the early 1900s. He returned to Russia with the reputation of a pioneer Labor Zionist who had reinvented himself as a leading Zionist Socialist. *Der nayer veg* was closed down by the authorities at the beginning of 1907. During 1907 there were two more attempts to publish the weekly, under the titles *Dos vort* (Word) and *Undzer veg* (Our way). Both these publication, too, were soon closed down.

Disappointed by the defeat of the 1905 revolution, many radicals abandoned direct political activism. In the aftermath of the constitutional coup of 3 June 1907, when the Russian parliament was dissolved and its socialist deputies persecuted, radical parties either lost the vast majority of their members (like the Zionist Socialist Workers' Party and the Jewish Socialist Workers' Party) or were virtually dissolved. Biding their time, many socialists concentrated their efforts in "organic work"—social, cultural, and educational areas.[25] For instance, Litvakov (M. Lirov) and Zaslavsky (Homunculus) found themselves among the leading journalists of the Russian newspaper *Kievskaia mysl'* (Kiev thought), published 1906–18. This newspaper was an important democratic forum, some of whose authors were prominent social democrats such as Leon Trotski and Anatoly Lunacharsky.[26] This is not to say that Jewish intellectuals had become completely apolitical. The 1910 poll of Jewish students at Kiev university and other local establishments of higher education, including fifteen hundred male and female respondents, showed, among other things, that about 11 percent of them were members of Jewish socialist parties, championing Yiddish culture; one-third of them regarded Yiddish as the Jewish national language.[27]

Kiev attracted such activists as Litvakov partly because it was an important cultural center, where people in the intellectual professions could find a job. It was also significant that the Zionist Socialists' Central Committee and the party's umbrella organization—the Jewish Territorialist Organization (ITO), chaired by the Anglo-Jewish writer Israel Zangwill—had its Russian headquarters in Kiev.[28] Apart from writing for *Kievskaia mysl'*, Litvakov took part in Yiddish publication projects, for instance working as an editor—together with Josef Leshtshinsky and Ben-Adir (Abraham Rosin)—of the short-lived Kiev newspaper *Dos yidishe vort* (Jewish word, 1910).

Litvakov played a pivotal role in the Yiddishization of the Zionist Socialists, whose precursor, Nakhman Syrkin, saw Yiddish literature only as a channel to European culture rather than a national goal.[29] Litvakov was a leading theorist of Jewish national Marxism, whose advocates regarded Jews as a historical nation that would flourish as society progressed toward socialism. This strain of Marxism was irreconcilable with classical Marxism's rejection of nationalism. It was also at odds with strategic Marxists who, more flexibly and opportunistically, cooperated with national movements but saw them only as temporary allies in the struggle for international socialism.[30] The Marxist Yiddishist nationalism represented a fantastic combination of ideas. Thus, Shimen Dobin—who had been a linchpin of the Zionist-Socialist Party but later edited *Folks-shtime* (People's voice, 1907), the Kiev-based organ of the Jewish Socialist Workers' Party—once presented a paper analyzing the Maccabean period from the point of view of historical materialism and class struggle.[31]

In 1911 in Demievka, a Kiev suburb with a large Jewish population, a group of Jewish socialists, including Dobin (by that time already a local Bundist activist), founded the pioneering Yiddish secular school. As Demievka was not then part of the city of Kiev, it was not excluded from the Pale. Still, a secular Jewish school was a punishable venture because it was strictly forbidden to open any Yiddish secular educational institutions. Therefore the Demievka school for girls had been registered as a law-abiding heder. To be sure, the local police superintendent knew about the real character of the school, but a hefty bribe kept him silent. A few years later, this school, which was destined to become a model for Yiddish secular educational institutions, had developed a five-year program and had 150 pupils. The school challenged the generally anti-Yiddish policy of the influential and moneyed Society for the Dissemination of Enlightenment Among the Jews of Russia (OPE) and was supported by the Kiev democratic and socialist circles of Jewish intellectuals. The sharpest conflict was about the status of Hebrew at the school. The Demievka teachers did not introduce Hebrew lesson even in order to win the OPE's financial support.[32] In 1912 the second Yiddish secular school in the country was opened not far from Kiev, in Chernobyl. One of its major founders was Yakov Reznik, whose brother, Lipe Reznik, later became a symbolist Yiddish poet.

The Demievka school, whose teachers also held illegal literary parties, was a centerpiece of Yiddish activities in Kiev, consolidating various small groups of Yiddish enthusiasts. Yeshue Liubomirsky, a teacher at the Dimievka school and later a notable Soviet Yiddish theater critic, remembered a party with David Bergelson, then already a writer with published works, and his two friends—the young actor Mikhail (Moshe-Aron) Rafalsky and the beginner *littérateur* Ezra Korman.[33] In the late 1890s, when Rafalsky was a young prodigy actor, he became Sholem Aleichem's a favorite and spent a great deal of time at the writer's dacha playing with his children. Later he dabbled in Yiddish literature and translated Bergelson's prose into Russian. Perhaps he was involved in the ambitious (aborted) plan to create in Kiev a traveling Yiddish theater, which had hoped to set a model for Yiddish troupes all over the world.[34]

One Kiev group of Yiddish enthusiasts met in the house of Rakhil Isaevna, a woman whose salon attracted a few tyro Yiddish writers. The only more or less distinguished habitué of the salon was David Volkenshtein, later a minor Soviet Yiddish story-writer. At that time, however, he was regarded as a promising literary talent, whose Russian stories had been welcomed by Aleksandr Kuprin, the Russian literary star, and Semen Yushkevich, the popular Russian Jewish writer. Another habitué, Borukh Glazman, had behind him a few confessional schools, including the first modern yeshiva in Eastern Europe, opened in the town of Lida by the rabbi Isaac Jacob Reines, where students combined traditional and secular studies. In Kiev, Glazman studied first at a Russian gymnasium and then at a technical school. At the end of 1911 he emigrated to America, where he became known as a Yiddish novelist. Nokhum Oislender, who left memoirs about this circle of young intellectuals,[35] began his Yiddish literary career as a poet, whose work was not of great consequence, but from the mid-1920s he was known as a leading literary theoretician. An offspring of an assimilated Jewish family, Oislender was attracted to Yiddishism by Mikhail Rafalsky, who taught him Yiddish.

Among Rakhil Isaevna's salonists was the novice poet Osher Shvartsman, later canonized as the founding Soviet Yiddish poet. He was directly influenced by Khaim Nakhman Bialik, who spent much time with the Shvartsmans' neighbors the Averbukhs, the august Jewish poet's in-laws. Aron Vergelis, the preeminent Yiddish man of letters in post-Stalinist Soviet

David Hofshtein

Union, defined Shvartsman as the poet "closest to Bialik," particularly because both Bialik and Shvartsman depicted in their poetry Ukrainian village landscapes.[36] Shvartsman first wrote in Hebrew, Russian, and Ukrainian, but in 1908 he switched to Yiddish. His first cousin, David Hofshtein, also wrote poems, initially mostly in Hebrew, Russian, and Ukrainian. Hofshtein's friend, Aron Kushnirov, another novice poet, then earned his bread as a sales assistant in a grocer's shop. In 1912, Shvartsman, Oislender, and Kushnirov developed a (never realized) plan of publishing a collection of their poems.[37] The young men met both at Rakhil Isaevna's hospitable house and at the library of the OPE (20 Malo-Zhitomirskaia Street), where they could, in particular, read fresh issues of Yiddish periodicals.

A few novice Yiddish writers were scions of the Jewish rich. One of them, Yekhezkel Dobrushin, a former Sorbonne student, found himself stuck in his hometown of Kiev (where his father was a wealthy merchant) when his leg was mutilated by a lingering illness. He combined journalism and creative writing (stories and poems) with literary criticism. Among wealthy fans of Yiddish letters were also two young men, Nakhman Meisel, an activist of the Demievka school, and David Bergelson, a novice prose writer, who became the best-known products of the Kiev circle of modern Yiddish literature enthusiasts. Thanks to some assets left to him by his entrepreneurial father, Bergelson was able to live the life of a rentier, while trying to find recognition as a man of letters. He lived in Kiev with his older brother, Yankel, a timber merchant, whose wife, Leyke, and Nakhman Meisel's mother, Khane, were sisters.[38] Meisel was also related to Shimen Dobin[39] and to the Berdichev-born Pinkhas Kahanovich,[40] better known as Der Nister (Hidden one), who was to become one of the most significant Yiddish writers of the twentieth century.

Although recruits to turn-of-the-century Jewish culture-bearing circles are traditionally categorized either as "intellectuals" (people with systematically acquired general education) or as "semi-intellectuals" (usually apostate yeshiva students), Bergelson and Meisel represented another subgroup, which can be called "home-intellectuals." Products of home education that eclectically combined traditional and general subjects, they were more or less equally fluent in Yiddish, Hebrew, and Russian. Meisel recollected that Bergelson read in Hebrew; was under the influence of Ahad-Haam, Gnessin (whom he met in Kiev), and Micah Yosef Berdyczevski; "but lived mainly . . . in the spiritually rich worlds of great Russian classics." Bergelson concentrated on writing, first in Hebrew and Russian and only later in Yiddish. His interest in Yiddish had little to do with Yiddish literature, which he began to read seriously only after he started writing in Yiddish.[41] Bergelson's and Meisel's first Yiddish mentor was one of Sholem Aleichem's "sages of Kiev," Elhanan Kalmanson, who "combined in himself a *maskil,* a revolutionary, a Russian intellectual, and a Jewish folk-type." Kalmanson worked as a bookkeeper (another of the "sages") at the glass factory owned by Nakhman Meisel's grandfather.[42] Later he wrote that modern Yiddish literature had been born by the young literati's thirst for unity with their people.[43]

Although the city was a center for modernist literature, the young Kiev writers were not very interested in an urban setting. This trait, to digress, distinguishes them from their overseas precursors and models, such as the New York Di Yunge (The young ones) group, who actively explored urban subject matter, particularly in their periodical *Shriftn* (Oeuvres), which first appeared in 1912.[44] As for the Kievans, their urbanism was still rather provincial. In a mid-1930s retrospective piece, Bergelson revealed that lack of a suitable Yiddish vocabulary forced him to stage his early works mostly in shtetl surroundings rather than in Kiev, the city where he actually met the prototypes of his literary characters.[45] Kiev Yiddish prose and poetry was populated by young Jewish shtetl-dwellers, villagers, or recent urbanists, who had searching minds but knocked their heads against a wall of segregation and parochialism. Compared with Di Yunge, the Kiev Yiddish poets to a much less extent broke the tradition. The Kievers based their innovation on the existing poetic culture—Yiddish, Hebrew, Russian, Ukrainian, and West European. They were related to the contemporary modernist schools of Ukrainian writers. Like the Ukrainian symbolists, they rejected the narrow ethnographism of their predecessors and strove for a hybrid of Europeanization with national identity; however, the influence of Russian symbolists, especially of Aleksandr Blok, and of the imaginist Sergei Esenin was perhaps even more significant.[46] One of their achievements, particularly of Shvartsman and Hofshtein, was their landscape lyric, a relatively new domain in Yiddish literature.[47] Innovation and the fear of being derivative were characteristics of the Kiev writers' literary credo. In 1916, Moshe Khashchevatsky, then a novice Russian and Yiddish poet, received a letter from Dobrushin, who was already a central figure among the Kievans. Dobrushin criticized his Yiddish poems: "In the so-called '[Abraham] Reisen period' of our literature your poems would perhaps have been suitable. However, after the rigorous thinker [David] Einhorn, the lyrical [Shmarye] Imber, and especially after the American poets (see *Shriftn* nos. 1 and 2), we have a right to demand from our poetry a more complicated color scale, new cultural achievements, etc."[48]

By that time, the Kievans Dobrushin, Bergelson, and Der Nister (the latter, in fact, lived in Zhitomir) had gained access to printing presses and were regarded as mature Yiddish writers. Khashchevatsky, on the other hand, had so far only one outlet to showcase his poems: a handwritten journal that he produced in Uman, a town near Kiev, together with his friends Leyb Kvitko and Ezra Finninberg.[49] Ironically, although Dobrushin held up as an example the American Di Yunge, the American Yiddish poet Jacob Glatstein would later argue that chronologically David Hofshtein preceded Di Yunge as the creator of modern Yiddish lyric.[50]

The Vilna-Kiev Axis

By analogy with Yiddish literacy, Yiddish printing was an extension of Hebrew printing. Therefore, Warsaw, where Hebrew printing had been developing from the late 1790s, became the main Yiddish publishing center in the Russian Empire. As a result of some semiautonomy enjoyed by Congress

Poland, Warsaw-based printers were not hindered by the restrictions opera-
tive from 1836 until 1862, which allowed Hebrew printing only in two
towns: Vilna and Zhitomir. Although after the czar's decree of 26 April 1862
Jewish printing houses could be opened in all places of the Pale of Settlement,[51] Warsaw, with its established publishing infrastructure and largest
concentration of Yiddish-speaking population, remained the most significant
center of Yiddish publishing. The number of Yiddish periodicals in Warsaw
increased after the czar's 17 October 1905 manifesto significantly liberated
the press, particularly in minority languages. The new legal situation augured
rapid development of Yiddish publishing. In 1906 five Warsaw-based Yiddish daily newspapers had a combined circulation of ninety-six thousand. In
addition, three Yiddish weeklies had a combined circulation of thirty-eight
thousand.[52] For the purpose of comparison, all Ukrainian-language periodicals published in 1908 in the country had a total circulation of fewer than
twenty thousand for a population of 30 million.[53]

By the end of the 1910s, the remarkable development of Yiddish literature significantly improved its traditionally substandard status. More and
more works were translated from Yiddish into other languages, including
Russian. Thus, in 1902 Mendele's *Prikliucheniia Veniamina III* (The Travels
of Benjamin the Third) and Peretz's *Khasidskie rasskazy* (Hassidic stories)
were published in St. Petersburg as part of the Jewish Family Library
(1902–04), edited by the Russian and Yiddish writer Meir (Miron) Rivkin.
In 1908 the collection of Russian translations *Almanakh molodoi evreiskoi
literatury* (Almanac of young Jewish literature) appeared in St. Petersburg. In
the same year another collection, *Evreiskii al'manakh* (Jewish almanac), was
produced by Ivan Samonenko, a Kiev publisher. In the Kiev collection, the
subtitle of which was *Per aspera,* Litvakov-Lirov appeared as Bialik's translator. Also, Yakov Slonim, later a leading Soviet translator from Yiddish into
Russian, made his debut.[54] Beginning in 1910, entire collections of Yiddish
writers' oeuvres began to appear in Russian. This was a project undertaken
by the Moscow publishing house Sovremennye problemy (Contemporary
problems), which published eight volumes of Sholem Aleichem (1910–13),
two of Peretz (1911–12), and two of Mendele (1912).[55]

Around 1910 the term *Yiddish* rather than *Jargon* had become firmly established. (Also around that time Ukrainian was less-often defined as the
"Little Russian" language.[56]) Moreover, the word *Jargon,* hitherto neutral
even if somewhat supercilious, now became opprobrious, particularly
among the younger cadre of Yiddish literati. It is illuminating, for instance,

that the St. Petersburg *Fraynd* (Friend), which had appeared in 1903 as "the first Russian daily in jargon," began, apparently under the influence of the first international Yiddish language conference, to call itself "a Yiddish daily."[57] That conference, held by a group of Jewish intellectuals in August 1908 in the then–Austro-Hungarian town of Czernowitz, signaled that Yiddish had found influential advocates among representatives of various ideological currents professing East European Jewish particularism. The conference also drew a line between the folkist and, basically, philistine Jargonism on the one hand, and the future-oriented Yiddishism on the other hand. This separation was stressed by the fact that the Jargonists Sholem Aleichem and Mendele virtually ignored the Czernowitz gathering, whereas Peretz, a working model of a twentieth-century Yiddish writer, was one of its central figures.[58]

Meanwhile, Yiddish readership was growing. Significantly, around this time the combined membership of Jewish socialist parties amounted to many tens of thousands,[59] and the socialists' following certainly did not exhaust the number of Yiddish readers. Russian Jews formed a highly literate society, in which people exchanged millions of letters and read newspapers, pamphlets, and books. Small wonder that Eastern Europe emerged as a lucrative market for Yiddish publishers. Apart from numerous small-time publishers, a few big firms emerged as the main producers of Yiddish books and periodicals. Thus, in 1912 Brothers Levin-Epshtein, established Hebrew publishers, reappeared as an active producer of Yiddish books. In the late 1880s, Brothers Levin-Epshtein published plays by Abraham Goldfaden, novels by Shomer, and other Yiddish books. In 1884 the publishers—then called "Levin-Epshtein"—even invited Shomer to live in Kiev, where they were based. The next year, however, the publishing house—and Shomer—moved to Warsaw.[60] In the 1890s, after a conflict with Peretz, Brothers Levin-Epshtein lost interest in Yiddish publishing.

In 1911 four Yiddish publishers decided to create a syndicate called Tsentral (Central). In particular, the Tsentral took over publication of the daily *Fraynd*. By that time, the paper had moved from St. Petersburg and been relaunched in Warsaw as *Dos lebn* (Life). Only one member of the syndication, Shlomo Zanvel Sreberk, was based in Vilna. Sreberk switched to modern Yiddish literature in 1908; between 1902 and 1912, he also published the popular literary and scientific monthly *Lebn un visnshaft* (Life and science). The other three partners ran their businesses in Warsaw, although all of them were *litvaks* (Lithuanian-Belorussian Jews) who dominated in the field of Jewish publishing. The oldest among them, Abraham Leyb Shalkovitsh, best known as the Hebrew publicist and publisher Ben Avigdor, was also an active Yiddish publisher. Thus he published the first four-volume collection of Sholem Aleichem's oeuvres as well as a number of periodicals, including the weekly paper *Yidishe folks-tsaytung* (Jewish people's paper, 1902–03). Benjamin Shimin, the third partner, in 1907 undertook the publication of the first collection of works by Sholem Asch, then a rising literary star. In 1909–11 Shimin produced the popular *Shimins groyse velt-bibliotek* (Shimin's big world library) of sixty-six original and translated titles, although the waspish Sholem Aleichem dubbed some of them "Berdichev fiords," or poor imitations of te popular Norwegian writers Henrik Ibsen and Knut Hamsun.[61]

The fourth partner, Yakov Lidsky, the son of a Moscow scribe and bookseller, played a remarkable role in modern Yiddish literature. In the early 1890s, Lidsky was involved in book printing in Chicago, but in 1899 he returned to Russia and settled in Warsaw as a representative of American publishers. Around 1900 he established his own publishing house, Progress, whose first editor was Abraham Reisen. A decade later, Reisen edited the Progress's weekly *Eyropeishe literarur* (European literature), which specialized in translations of quality literature from various languages. Lidsky and Reisen certainly knew about the success of Yiddish translations in America, heralded by the best-selling 1890 translation of Leo Tolstoy's *Kreutzer Sonata*.[62] Their highbrow *Eyropeishe literatur,* however, was phased out after thirty-nine issues. While the publication was on the decline, Reisen tried to combine translations with original Yiddish works of modern authors. However, the readers preferred either cheap novels or . . . Sholem Aleichem, the most famous author in the Yiddish-speaking world. According to a 1912 bibliography,[63] about one-third of Yiddish titles in belles lettres published that year in Russia (predominantly in Warsaw) were books by Sholem Aleichem, whose inexhaustible comic talent captured for generations to come the squalor, the vigor, and the injustices of his time. The same bibliography shows decline of Shomer's popularity. Therefore, Shomer's preface (to a posthumous reprint of his novel), in which he wrote with *Schadenfreude* about the dearth of Yiddish novels in Russia's book market after his departure to America,[64] seems outdated. The bibliography also shows the appearance of new best-selling authors, such as Zalman Wendroff, whose fourteen titles, many of them from the cycle *Pravozhitelstvo* (Right of residence), came out in Warsaw and Vilna. At the same time, modernist writers had trouble finding outlets for their experimental works.

Bergelson was one of the tyro writers who could not find a publisher for his prose. Thus, he was rejected by the editors of the Vilna-based *Literarishe monatsshriftn* (Literary monthly, 1908), one of the first significant forums for modernist Yiddish writing. Der Nister, who read his works to Vilna literati as early as 1905,[65] was luckier—his first book, even if a very small one, came out in Vilna in 1907 and the *Literarishe monatsshriftn* editors were glad to find a writer who continued Peretz's tradition of uniting refined modernism with the Jewish cultural legacy. True, Der Nister had a rather cold critical reception. One of the reviewers, Shmuel Rosenfeld, a leading Yiddish journalist, dismissed him a few years later as an "absurd, hazy, and pitch-dark writer" (*umgelumperter farvolknter un shtok-fintsterer shrift-shteler*).[66]

In 1909, when Bergelson had already experienced several failures with publishers, Meisel decided to intervene on behalf of his friend, whose manuscripts did not look like surefire titles. He went to Warsaw and arranged with Lydsky's Progress publishing house a subsidized publication of Bergelson's short novel *Arum vokzal* (At the depot), the embryo of which had been formed as early as 1906 in the unpublished Hebrew story "Emptiness," also set at the railway station Monastyrshchino, not far from the town of Uman.[67] The next year, the same Progress publishing house produced a small book by Der Nister, *Hekher fun der erd* (Higher than the earth). This experience gave Meisel the idea to create his own publishing basis for young Yiddish writers. Around 1910, he appeared as a Yiddish publisher in Kiev, the head of the Kunst farlag (Arts publication house).

Bergelson also partly paid for his next publications, the stories "Der toyber" (The deaf man) and "Tsvey vegn" (Two ways) in the Kunst-farlag's *Der yidisher almanakh* (Yiddish almanac, 1910). These essentially vanity publications brought him some fame, mainly among a select group of sophisticated readers and critics who praised Bergelson's prose as a new voice in Yiddish literature. The publication of *Arum vokzal* was welcomed by A. Weiter, a talented Yiddish writer and political activist, who together with Shmuel Niger and Shmaryahu Gorelik edited *Literarishe monatsshriftn*.[68] In their reviews of *Arum vokzal*, A. Weiter and later Niger, then contributors to the St. Petersburg *Fraynd*,[69] highlighted the influence of Kurt Hamsun, who was immensely popular at that time, particularly in Russia. It is illuminating that for the first issue (February 1908) of *Literarishe monatsshriftn,* Gorelik wrote an article about Hamsun, and for the second issue (March), A. Weiter translated one of Hamsun's stories.

*   *   *

Despite the efforts of Meisel and other activists, pre–World War I Kiev did not become a significant center of Yiddish publishing. Between 1911 and 1914 only forty-seven Yiddish books were published there.[70] In 1912, for instance, only three books were produced by Josef Shenfeld, the main Jewish printer in the city. The name of one of the Kiev publications, the Kunst farlag's two literary collections *Fun tsayt tsu tsayt* (From time to time, published in 1911 and 1912), characterizes the rhythm of the Kiev-based Yiddish publishing center, particularly of Meisel's elitist production. The Kunst farlag was, in fact, a very small enterprise of ten enthusiasts who had pooled the starting capital of 150 rubles.[71] One of them, Ezra Korman, worked at the publishing house as technical editor and proofreader.

In addition to the collections *Fun tsayt tsu tsayt,* the Kunst farlag produced a handful of small publications such as Der Nister's *Gezang un gebot* (Song and commandment, 1912), Meisel's *Vegn Bergelsons Nokh alemen* (On Bergelson's *When all is said and done,* 1913), Bergelson's *Der toyber* (The deaf man, 1914), and Dobrushin's *Esterke* (1914). For all that, this modest set of publications can be regarded as the first collective output of the Kiev Group of Yiddish Writers—the name under which they became known in Yiddish literary history. The imprint of the Kunst farlag books featured the address of the publisher (in Russian), "Kiev, 36 Mariinsko-Blagoveshchenskaia Street, N. Meisel," and the name of the main distributor (in Yiddish), "Boris Kletzkin's Vilner farlag." [72]

Starting in 1905, Vilna had been the most important East European center of Jewish socialist publishing, particularly in Yiddish. The Bund, whose Vilna organization boasted three thousand members in 1905, was the leading socialist publisher in the town.[73] Other Jewish socialist parties, too, launched their periodicals in Vilna. As for literary publications, however, the modern phase in the town's publishing history is associated with Boris Kletzkin, the active Bundist and patron of Yiddish literature. Around 1910, books with the imprint of Kletzkin's publishing house began to appear.[74] (Again, it is hardly a coincidence that both Meisel's and Kletzkin's publishing houses appeared in 1910, a turning point in modern Yiddish cultural history. Interestingly, the modern literary period in America also can be counted from 1910.[75]) Kletzkin appointed his close friend A. Weiter as the first editor of the publishing house. A. Weiter also proposed a strictly not-for-profit character of the publishing house and its aspiration to maximize the author's royalties. Moreover, Kletzkin would from time to time invite writers (including Peretz, Asch, and Bergelson) to live in Vilna; he provided them with board and lodgings.[76] A. Weiter, however, headed the publishing house only briefly because he was arrested and exiled to Siberia.[77] In the meantime, three recent activists of the Vozrozhdenie group, Niger, Shtif, and Kalmanovitz, were recruited as new editors.

Ideologically, the Kiev circle of Yiddish literati was an outpost of the Vilna Yiddishists who challenged the literary mass production, or the "Warsaw trend," in Yiddish literature. The "Vilna trend" represented publications of various political currents, notably the Bund and Zionist Socialists. Four factors determined Vilna's role of the main center for Yiddish political publishing in Russia: Vilna had a long-standing tradition of Yiddish publishing; the local Jewish Teachers' Seminar and yeshivas were reservoirs of dissentient men of letters, recruited by Jewish socialists exiled to Vilna; Vilna was an important point for smugglers of illegal literature; and the town boasted a considerable mass of Jewish workers.[78] In general, "[e]very Jew is connected with Vilna. If he was not born in Vilna, he perhaps lived there, or he at least once used a prayerbook published in Vilna, glanced at a Talmud with a Vilna imprint, read a book and a newspaper produced in Vilna." [79]

The fact of a relatively small divide between local Jewish intellectuals and common people was an important feature of Vilna Jewish life.[80] This fact explains the place of honor that Vilna intellectuals occupied in Yiddishist circles. Ber Borokhov (best known as a founding father of Labor Zionism) formulated basic principles of modern Yiddish language planning, choosing the vernacular of Vilna intellectuals as the model for standard Yiddish pronunciation.[81] Granted, the high reputation of Vilna intellectuals was, perhaps, only one of the reasons that determined his choice. Borokhov, who turned to Yiddish in his late teens, might also like their "received pronunciation" as well as their tendency to carefully approximate the German grammar and avoid vulgar-sounding Slavicisms. Many of them were, like Borokhov, Yiddishist neophytes and either learned to speak Yiddish or returned to it after long years of speaking Russian, Polish, or German. As a result, the Vilna intellectuals' "high" Yiddish usually did not sound like any of the dialects, including the "low" Warsaw Yiddish.[82]

The editors of the Vilna-based party's publications did not expect from belletrists any ideological prose and poetry. Rather, the belletristic departments were seen by the editors as an adornment of their publications.[83] Thus, the party organs became important forums of modernist literature. As a result, they also became sponsors of writers whose popularity often lagged far behind the aesthetic importance of their work. Hence another important trait of the Vilna (and Kiev) trend: sponsorship. Actually, dependence on sponsorship—private, organizational, or governmental—can explain many events in the life of Yiddish writers throughout the twentieth century. Initially, the modernist literature was, to a considerable extent, kept by Boris Kletzkin, who did not limit his sponsorship to the Vilna-based writers, especially because Vilna boasted numerous Yiddish activists, theorists, and educators, but lacked literary talent.

There are many examples of cooperation between the Vilna and Kiev literati. Shmaryahu Gorelik, who in 1908 edited, together with Niger and A. Weiter, the Vilna-based *Literarishe monatsshriftn*, in 1910 edited, this time together with Meisel and Bergelson, an analogous publication in Kiev, *Der yidisher almanakh* (Yiddish almanac). On the other hand, when the Vilner farlag took over the journal *Di yidishe velt* (Jewish world), founded in 1912 in St. Petersburg, and relaunched it in Vilna in January 1913, it was first edited by Bergelson. Importantly, works published in *Di yidishe velt* reached also the American reader thanks to its New York sister publication, *Literatur un lebn* (Literature and life), edited by the prominent journalist Karl Fornberg. Unfortunately, this cooperation, started in 1914, was soon interrupted by World War I. In Kiev, the journal was distributed by Meisel and Leyb Brovarnik. In Brovarnik's apartment Yiddish writers had their literary parties. He was a cofounder of the Demievka school and wrote, together with another educator, Mikhl Levitan, one of the first Yiddish books of arithmetical problems, *Arifmetishe ufgabn*, published in 1914 by Kletzkin.[84]

As editor, Bergelson got Osher Shvartsman into print; his first poem was published in *Di yidishe velt*.[85] Yudel Yoffe, later a prolific Soviet Yiddish writer, lived in Kiev and worked as a tailor; his first significant story, too, was published in 1915 in *Di yidishe velt*. Works by a few Kiev authors, like Bergelson, Der Nister, and Dobrushin, appeared both in Vilna and Kiev. For instance, Dobrushin's first book, *Benkende neshomes* (Homesick souls), a collection of vignettes, one-act plays, and poems, was published in 1912 by Kletzkin. In 1914 his story *Esterke* appeared in Meisel's Kunst farlag. From 1911, Kletzkin and Meisel developed analogous publication programs for children. In Kiev this was the series *Mayselekh far kinder* (Fairy stories for children), remarkable for the artistic design of the books.[86]

Still, all these activities were marginal. Arkady Gornfeld, a literary commentator of the Russian Jewish press, argued that Yiddish literature did not have an intelligentsia. Rather, "there are a few intellectuals who write and sometimes speak in Yiddish, there are people who are sure that Yiddish is viable . . . But Yiddish does not have real intellectuals as a definite group, towering culturally above the populace."[87] Indeed, although the modernist Yiddish literature had secured a niche audience among sophisticated, ideological readers, it was widely ignored by Jewish laypeople. For instance, *Di yidishe velt* published in its June 1913 issue a geographical breakdown of the magazine's rather meager readership—1,853 subscribers and 1,455 regular buyers, including 115 subscribers and buyers in Kiev—the greatest concentration of highbrow Yiddish readers in the territories that would become the Soviet Union. Indeed, although "[c]ompared to Warsaw and Vilna before World War I, Kiev was a provincial backwater in Yiddish letters," it certainly "struggled to become a center of secular Yiddish culture."[88]

In the period between the 1905 Russian revolution and World War I, the Vilna and Kiev Jewish intellectual milieus complemented each other in their endeavors to create a highbrow Yiddish literature and readership. Publishing activities in Vilna and Kiev before World War I can be regarded as a turning point in the Jewish intellectuals' attempt to force-feed Yiddish elitist literature to the East European Jewish masses. The Kletzkin-Meisel publishing axis established the first solvent outlet for modernist Yiddish writers, many of whom lived on a shoestring budget and could not afford to subsidize their own publications. Vilna contributed with its established publishing tradition and cadre, particularly editors. Kiev, on the other hand, was rich with young literary talent. This fact was hardly coincidental. Despite its reputation as the Jerusalem of Lithuania, Vilna was, in modern terms, a backwater. From the 1830s, when the Russian government closed down its university, it was deprived of the fermenting student surroundings, whereas Kiev, whose St. Vladimir University replaced the Vilna University, boasted of thousands of Jewish students.[89] The Kiev Jewish community was much wealthier and certainly included more educated people than did the Vilna community. No doubt Kiev Yiddish writers were influenced by the contemporaneous rapid growth of Ukrainian literature. Also, the impact of Sholem Aleichem and his "sages," some of whom lived in Kiev as late as the 1920s, cannot be underestimated.

But the Vilna-Kiev symbiosis did not last long. During World War I, publications in Yiddish were forbidden by the Russian censorship, which was particularly fierce in Kiev, where all Yiddish outlets were closed down in March and April 1915. As a result, in 1915 no Yiddish books were published in Kiev, although they continued to appear in other places, most notably in Vilna, Odessa, and Warsaw. On the whole, Yiddish literary activity became dormant. Kletzkin, for example, moved his publishing house to Petrograd, but the authorities did not allow local printers to use Jewish letters.[90]

Extraterritoriality and Autonomy

In 1917 the literary collection *Untervegs* (On the way) came out in Odessa, where the ban of Yiddish publications was not as strict as in other parts of the empire. At the end of 1916, Saul Hokhberg, a well-connected journalist, renewed the publication of his newspaper *Undzer lebn* (Our life), which boasted such contributors as Mendele Moykher Sforim, Khaim Nakhman Bialik, Yitzkhok Yoel Linetzky, and Shimen Frug. Moshe Kleinman, a Jewish publicist from Bialik's circle, published in the Odessa collection his essay "The Future Jew." Kleinman argued that World War I had catalyzed the destruction of the traditional East European Jewish life. The war had also discredited internationalism and reinforced nationalism. He stressed that it was imperative to build new forms of Jewish national survival. The success of such an effort would justify the enormous suffering that fell to the Jews.[91] The same year, Shmuel Niger wrote about the responsibility felt by the Jewish intellectuals: "now, after the revolution, it became harder than before. It is harder . . . because there is no more consolation of blaming the *external* factors, which don't let the people to realize its will, its dreams, and so on."[92]

Need for a radical reconstruction of Jewish life was also felt outside Russia. "The life of the Jewish people represents now a big chaos, a terrible disorganization, a complete anarchy," lamented Morris Myer, a prolific man of letters and editor-cum-publisher of the London Yiddish daily *Tsayt* (Time), in the introduction to his 1918 treatise *A Jewish Utopia: A Plan of Reconstructing the Jewish People*. He explained the timing of his blueprint: "I don't need to find an excuse why I undertake such a work as to write the *Jewish Utopia*. All the peoples think now about reconstruction, about renewing a normal life after the World War. . . . Then why can't the Jewish people deal with the same problem?"[93]

Three kinds of dreams divided the politicized, nationalist part of Jewish society: Zionism, or a dream about a nation-state in Palestine; territorialism, or a dream about a nation-state anywhere apart from Palestine; and Diasporism, or a dream about exterritorial national survival. Diasporic dreams were based on the idea of personal (or extraterritorial) autonomy, a concept ascribed to the Austrian Marxists Rudolf Springer and Otto Bauer and much in vogue from the end of the nineteenth century, when it was championed also by the influential Russian Jewish theoreticians Khaim Zhitlovsky and Shimen Dubnov.[94] In its various forms, autonomism suffused all Jewish socialist currents. Khaim-Dov Hurvits, editor of the Petrograd Yiddish newspaper *Togblat* (Daily newspaper), argued in 1918 that national-personal autonomy was "the only possible way to avoid the contradiction between class conscience and national feeling."[95] Myer's utopia, too, envisages a Diasporic, autonomist form of Jewish survival. Even if the Palestinian project succeeded, still the bulk of the Jewish population would, according to Myer, continue to live outside the Jewish state, in autonomous communities with thick institutional infrastructures. The revived Israel, therefore, appears in his blueprint as a linguistically peculiar—Hebrew-speaking—province of the dispersed modern Jewish civilization, glued together by common, predominantly Yiddish, culture.

Jewish intellectuals living in various countries and associated with different ideological movements would agree with Shmaryahu Gorelik's apothegm that "national culture equals national self-preservation."[96] Nathan Birnbaum, an influential Jewish thinker and a founder of Yiddishism, also stressed the exceptional role of Jewish culture. According to Birnbaum, the vast majority of the peoples had "common-to-all-mankind (*klal-mentshlekhe*) cultures," which differed one from another in form rather than content. Only a minority of the peoples had "content [*inhaltlekhe*] cultures." Echoing Shimen Dubnov's postulate that the Jewish people embody the highest type of a cultural-historic or spiritual nation, Birnbaum regarded Jewish culture as more than a "content culture;" it was a faith-based "absolute culture," realizing the "absolute idea" of the Jewish nation's preservation. Such a culture had to have its own linguistic medium, such as Yiddish.[97] Although secular intellectuals did not regard Jews as the chosen people anymore, they insisted on the Jews' uniqueness. The essayist Abraham Koralnik, once a student of the Kiev university, wrote, "Language, national culture! But for us, for Jews, it's not enough. That is sufficient for Letts, Poles, or Ukrainians. . . . Jews need a chimera."[98]

Utopias was a part of the zeitgeist of the late 1910s. In the same year that

Myer, a Romanian-born Jew, wrote his *Utopia* in London, another visionary, Kalman Zingman, a *litvak* brought by the war to Kharkov, penned his short novel, *In the Future City of Edenia*. Hiding himself under the nom de plume "Ben-Yakov," Zingman dreamt about a society where Jews would peacefully live together with Ukrainians, Russians, and Poles.[99] In Zingman's *Edenia* (from the Hebrew *eden*, "paradise"), each of the equal ethnic groups has its own governing body, responsible for all cultural and educational affairs. Yiddish is the language of high culture, with state-sponsored publishing, theater, and schools of all levels, including universities. Religion does not play any role in the future society. In other words, the "linguistic-cultural Jewishness"[100] rather than the traditional religiously defined Jewishness dominates in *Edenia*. Also in 1918, in Kiev, Ben-Adir, formerly a central figure in the Vozrozhdenie group, dreamt—in his brochure *Our Language Problem*—about a world brotherhood of nations, including Jews living as a national collective with a highly developed Yiddish culture.[101] The same idea, although with more details of the envisaged Jewish autonomy, is found in Nokhum Shtif's 1919 propagandist treatise, *Jews and Yiddish*.[102]

In postreligious society, culture was to become the main ingredient of secular attachment to Jewish peoplehood, filling the enormous niche hitherto occupied by religion. Yiddish literature was seen as the most important component of secular, modern culture.[103] Such a worship of literature was hardly surprising "[i]n a country where literature takes the place of life."[104] (In fact, similar importance of texts is emphasized in some modern cultural theories.)[105] Hence the religious terminology employed by such Yiddish literary theorists as Moshe Litvakov: "The creation of genuine modern Yiddish literature was the collective endeavor of the three classical writers, the process which Litvakov calls the construction of the Mount Sinai of Yiddish literature. 'Mendele Moykher Sforim received the first tablets and passed them over to Sholem Aleichem, with Y. L. Peretz creating his poetry nearby,' writes the Marxist critic, paraphrasing the beginning of the talmudic tractate Pirkei Avot."[106]

Dobrushin, Litvakov's fellow-Kievan, wrote in 1918 that "the treatment of literature as a 'holy thing' we had inherited from the Haskalah period, with its reverent celebrating of culture." He also depicted a ceremony of opening a library in a shtetl. Young shtetl-dwellers, foot soldiers of secular Yiddish culture, put in a basement of a *kloyz* (a house of religious study) a bookcase with Peretz's and Sholem Aleichem's volumes and announced that the new bookcase would be their new Holy Ark, "the Divine Presence will come down from the upstairs, because the new Jewish Torah is situated here." [107] Selected elements of traditional Jewish life were to be incorporated in the newly created secular culture. In 1919, Dobrushin theorized—apparently under the influence of Oswald Spengler's "prime symbols of a Culture"—about essential "primitive" components of Yiddish art. [108]

After the language proper, or the main prime symbol of Jewish culture, indigenous literature was envisaged as the most important pit prop of the autonomous, extraterritorial Jewish nation. The "problem of national authenticity" of young Yiddish literature was the most serious one. [109] Bal-Makhshoves (Isidor Elyashev), generally regarded as the founder of modern Yiddish criticism, represented those who sought recipes for indigenous literature. A 1916 article written by him includes an explanation of this stand: "Extraterritoriality [of Jews] is also a kind of territory. For [Jewish] national literature, it would be very sad if the influence of other literatures resulted in overt imitation." [110] Bal-Makhshoves echoed Peretz, who preached in 1910, "should we remain imitators of European literature, creators of entertaining books, ladies' entertainers, we'll work for assimilation, against which we struggle, because Yiddishkayt does not depend on country and language, Yiddishkayt means belief, Weltanschauung." [111] In the same vein of rejecting "imitation," the London-based critic Leo Kenig ridiculed in 1916 the "sickly-melancholic intellectual" Bergelson, whom he advised to write in Russian or any other European language rather than to spoil Yiddish with his Hamsunesque prose. [112] On the eve of World War II, Borukh Rivkin, an American Yiddish literary critic, explicated the ideas formulated before and during World War I: "literature's mission is to organize and consolidate the nation's conscience. For a nation that has no territory, the artificially created territory supplants the actual one. Literature has to provide the alliance among people, classes, and events, as if the nation lives inside the borders of a defined territory and conducts an absolutely independent life in all its societal aspects." [113]

Literature, or culture in general, was seen as a surrogate Jewish territory by many political and cultural pundits, who were annoyed with Marx's rejection of Jewish nationhood. Even the Ukrainian nationalist journal *Literaturno-naukovyi vistnyk* (Literary and scientific herald) maintained that "Jews were and is a nation." [114] Opponents of Marx's disqualification saw Jews as a world nation, whose extraterritoriality represented one of its distinguishing characteristics. Thus, in 1907, Moshe Litvakov amended Marxism, arguing that the Jews had been a proper historic, even if suppressed, nation, with its own cultural values.[115] At the same time, advocates of Jewish nationhood had to admit that extraterritoriality endangered the Jews' survival as a nation, therefore it should be reinforced by cultural and personal autonomy in the countries with a compact Jewish population. A similar vision formed the agenda of the Jewish delegation to the 1919 Paris Peace Conference, which charted the postwar future of the world. That conference was the first occasion when the notions of Jews as a nation and Yiddish as its language received recognition of an international body.[116] The Jewish delegates had a precedent to which they could refer—as early as 1917, Ukraine, particularly its capital, Kiev, became the first testing ground for a state-recognized Diasporic Yiddishism.

∗   ∗   ∗

Between 1917 and 1920, Kiev changed hands many times. After the February 1917 revolution, there began to be formed the Ukrainian national parliament, Central Rada, which in autumn 1917 promised national autonomy to Russians, Jews, and Poles. In January 1918, national-personal autonomy was officially declared. As a result, Ukraine began to look like a promising place for the realization of political and cultural programs of Jewish socialist and democratic parties.

The main players in the Ukrainian Jewish roulette, which combined an unprecedented level of Jewish representation in the government with incessant pogroms, were four parties: the United Jewish Socialist Labor Party (or Fareynikte), the Bund, the Folkspartey, and the Labor Zionists, whose leaders were represented in the succession of short-lived coalitions and governments.[117] The Fareynikte was the strongest of all autonomist parties active in Ukraine. In May 1917 it amalgamated two outgrowths of the Vozrozhdenie group: the Zionist-Socialist territorialists, who advocated Jewish colonization in any autonomous Jewish territory outside Palestine, and the Jewish Socialist Workers' party. The latter originally favored Jewish national autonomy, based on an elected Jewish national assembly, rather than any territorial solutions. For members of the Fareynikte, Jewish personal autonomy in Ukraine was much more appealing than it was for Bundists, who feared the Ukrainian separatism, or for Labor Zionists, who regarded all autonomist projects as temporary—transshipping points on the way to Palestine.

In Ukraine, the Fareynikte launched a few Yiddish newspapers, including the Kiev daily *Naye tsayt* (New time, September 1917–May 1919). Litvakov was one of its editors, and Bergelson briefly edited its literary department. It is characteristic that the daily also appeared on Saturday—a fact that stressed its antireligious stand. On Saturday, 9 September 1917, the newspaper urged the readers to claim Yiddish as their mother tongue during the forthcoming census of the Kiev population. The editors had nothing to worry about—the vast majority of the eighty-seven thousand Kiev Jewish respondents were Yiddish-claimants.[118]

Representatives of the four Jewish parties constituted the Central Committee of the Kultur Lige (Culture League) which was created in Kiev in January 1918.[119] The league was conceived as a supraparty organization whose aim was to construct and promote a new Jewish culture, based on Yiddish and secular democratic values.[120] Among the founders of the Culture League were the Kiev Yiddish activists Litvakov, Dobrushin, Meisel, and Bergelson. The Culture League epitomized the idea of Jewish national-cum-cultural survival as an extraterritorial, autonomous Yiddish-speaking nation. Significantly, it never limited its activities to Ukraine; the Culture League's chapters and replicas were formed in such places as Moscow, Warsaw, Berlin, Amsterdam, and Paris. Ukraine's cultural surroundings lent boldness to the Yiddishists. It was particularly inspiring to see how Ukrainian became a state language after centuries of being treated as a "barbarian jargon" of Russian.[121]

Literary activities played an important role in the league's programs. Although the two issues of the almanac *Eygns*, sponsored and distributed by the Culture League, went little noticed at the time of their publication in Kiev in 1918 and 1920, they occupy a remarkable place in Yiddish literary history as the forum of the trendsetting Kiev Group of Yiddish Writers, which was also known as the Eygns Group. Seth Wolitz explains the symbolically loaded meaning of the almanac's title: "The title of *Eygns* was not accidental. As a noun, *dos eygns* means possession. It can also function as an adverb, *eygns*, meaning *expressly*, or as a neuter adjective in the predicate, meaning *own*. This polyvalent title defined the conscious wish and will of the editors to create a secular Yiddish, indeed, Jewish, culture with all its implications for national cultural autonomy."[122] In fact, the well-read *Eygns* editors could conceivably allude to the left-wing German psychoanalyst Otto Gross, who tied in any new culture-building with liberation of the *Eigenen*.[123]

Ideologically, *Eygns* continued in the tradition of the Vilna-Kiev literary axis before World War I, particularly the Vilna erudite journal *Literarishe monatsshriftn,* which declared in its manifesto a break with the hoi polloi— no concessions to ease of understanding. The Vilna-Kiev elitists argued that literature could not exist and develop freely if it leaned upon an uneducated reader or if it limited itself to satisfying the spiritual and aesthetic requirements of those who had no access to the culture of other peoples.[124] Israel Joshua Singer, who was in Kiev at that time, later recalled:

> [There] was some kind of mystical intimacy among the [people of the Kiev] group, as if they were members of a secret order. They would address each other by their first names, even in their absence. They conversed in confidential tones, always discussing some secret. They believed with all their hearts, as convinced of their rightness as a provincial girl-student [kursistke], that literature was sacred, the holy of holies, that the "Kievers" were the only high priests conducting the divine service, and that Kiev was Jerusalem. . . .
>
> I don't quite remember the poems in *Eygns,* but I do remember the prose published in it. The only stories of artistic value were written by David Bergelson. The rest of the works were "mystical," graphomaniac outpourings, the well-known prose in poems or poems in prose, which the *Eygns* theorists saw as the last word not only in Yiddish literature, but— generally—in world literature. The place of honor was occupied by Der Nister, a writer of pretentious tales about demons, ghosts, daredevils, and hobgoblins. Dobrushin, the "theoretician" of the group, announced openly during one meeting that, had the writers of the whole world been given a chance to read Der Nister's works, they would have broken their pens.[125]

The writers and artists of the Culture League indeed represented a close-knit group, with some even related. Apart from Dobrushin's family connection with the Bergelsons, his sister married the Kiev artist Joseph Tchaikov, while Nakhman Meisel's wife was sister of Boris Aronson, another leading artist of the group.[126] Cross-party spirit was a characteristic feature of the post-1917 Kiev Yiddish heyday. Representatives of various Jewish parties collaborated relatively peacefully in cultural institutions united under the umbrella of the Culture League. Such an abnormality of political concord can be attributed to two factors. First, permanent threat to Ukraine's Jews (hundreds of thousands became victims of pogroms and devastation) forced the adversaries to coalesce, at least temporarily, into a Yiddish united front. Second, the Yiddishist cadre that concentrated in Kiev represented a unique group of activists, whose pan-Yiddishist aspirations were often stronger than their party loyalty.

Apart from *Eygns,* the titles and design of *Oyfgang* (Sunrise) and *Baginen* (Dawn)—both literary publications launched and discontinued in 1919—celebrated the beginning of a new era, the belief in a better world to come. The cover of *Baginen,* for instance, designed by Tchaikov, showed a naked young man, symbolizing the liberation of Jews from the fetters of the past.[127] Kiev almanacs, newspapers, and journals became forums for numerous debuts, such as Leyb Kvitko's, who moved to Kiev after the revolution. Around 1916, Bergelson encouraged Kvitko to continue writing poems, particularly children's poems, and even brought some of them to Kiev, where they were passed from hand to hand. Kvitko—who arrived in Kiev donning a coat, hat, and boots that he had made himself of a thick fleecy, light stuff—was welcomed by the urban literati as a folk talent.[128] Kiev Yiddish publications also resuscitated those literati who did not write during the war. One of them was Lipe Reznik, who resumed his literary career after five years of silence after the publication of his 1914 children's book, *Der alter seyfer* (The old book) in the Kunst-farlag.

David Hofshtein occupied a prominent position in Kiev literary circles. Although his first book came out as late as 1918, and his first poem was published in 1917, Hofshtein was already regarded as a classic of a kind and had a following among aspiring poets. He was not a card-carrying member of the party until 1940, but he sympathized with the Bolsheviks. His sympathies became even stronger after the death of his cousin, Osher Shvartsman, a Red Army volunteer. Shvartsman's elder brother, David, was a Bolshevik, who before World War I was briefly a member of the party's Central Committee. In a slim 1921 literary collection called *Trep* (Steps) and published by the Ekaterinoslav branch of the Culture League, Peretz Markish, himself a meteorically risen poet, compared "the leap forward"—from the sentimental poet David Einhorn to the modernist David Hofshtein—with the Red Army's rapid maneuver from the Caspian Sea to the Vistula river.[129] Interestingly, the Russian poet Sergei Esenin wrote in 1923, in his American travel log, that his American translator into Yiddish, Mani Leyb, promoted "young Jargonists with rather beautiful talents from the period of Hofshtein till Markish."[130] In other words, Hofshtein was perceived as Markish's precursor, although in reality both got into print at more or less the same time. Moreover, a syndrome of early maturing was characteristic of Markish. In his 1922 poetic collection, *Night Prey,* he presented himself as an eminent poet, already tired of the hurly-burly of his life on the literary Olympus:

Ikh zits shoyn tsu lang afn boym . . .
Ikh vil aheym . . .

Ikh bin mit yedn vintele shoyn opgegangen a tants,
un oysgezoygn kh'hob di shayn fun yedn shtral.
Kh'hob shoyn farzukht dem zisn sam fun a tseblitn krants
un af mayn kop
tseshpreyte zalbndike hent . . . [131]

(I've been sitting too long on the tree . . .
I am homesick . . .

I've already danced with every breath of wind
and sucked the shine of every ray of sunlight.
I've already tasted the sweet poison of a blossomed garland
and over my head
I felt anointing hands . . .)

Markish is usually associated with the Kiev Group of Yiddish Writers, although, in fact, he had little to do with the Kiev literary circle, trying to form his own base in Ekaterinoslav. In general, it is difficult to pigeonhole this maverick as a member of any group led by other writers. His poetry to a much lesser extent developed under the influence of Russian and Ukrainian symbolism, which was characteristic of the Kiev poets. Rather, Markish was more influenced by Émile Verhaeren and Walt Whitman.[132] The collection *Trep* was opened with a story by his friend I. J. Singer, whose prose had been rejected by the Kiev pundits, most notably by Bergelson. In general, Markish and Singer always disliked Bergelson, while Bergelson and his friends paid back in their own coin.[133] Thus, Nokhum Shtif, an admirer of Bergelson's writing, later ridiculed Markish's poetry, arguing that the young poet still needed "a teacher, an editor who could [have] stopped him from jabbering and [demonstrating] lack of taste."[134]

The Yiddish Olympus that was built in postrevolutionary Kiev turned out to be of shaky construction. Euphoria soon gave way to pessimism. Political instability was only one of the reasons for the change of mood. Lack of mass consumers of Yiddish cultural production was another reason. Bergelson was among those who expected that the revolution would bring Yiddish writers a wider audience of awakened, sophisticated readers, most notably the "conscientious workers." However, his experience with *Eygns* brought

Peretz Markish

him to the conclusion that Yiddish modernist literature did not have a sufficient number of readers. Bergelson's article "Literature and Society," published in 1919 in issues 4–5 of the Kiev-based *Bikher-velt* (World of books) as an answer to Litvakov's criticism of *Eygns*,[135] was one of his first serious pieces of journalism, an endeavor to sum up his experience as a Yiddish man of letters. According to Bergelson, the *Sturm und Drang* demands of the immediate postrevolution years resembled the ideological climate during the early years of Christianity, when all previous forms of culture had been replaced by such "naked forms" as the cross. Hence, he argued, the vexing popularity of the "naked forms" of Markish's poetry, which eclipsed the much more complicated lyrics of Kvitko and Hofshtein. He predicted that "cheap Futurism" would dominate Yiddish literature in Russia for some time.

> Solitude of Yiddish literature is terrible, even against the backdrop of the general strong solitude of the contemporary poetry. . . . Our middle class is not interested in Yiddish creativity. As a result, Yiddish poetry is left, on the one hand, with the uneducated common man, who has not grown to the civil tradition and understands only pictures containing primitive lines, or the *lubok* (cheap popular print); on the other hand, Yiddish poetry has the intellectual reader, but he has been educated on foreign poetry and comes to us having finished his meal at somebody else's tables.

Still, Bergelson was confident that, in the long run, society could not be satisfied with the current intellectual fad of cheap popular literature and would eventually return to tradition, as had happened once established Christianity was no longer under threat. Bergelson did not attack Litvakov, even though Litvakov's friendly criticism had hurt him, despite the fact that Litvakov had also presented Bergelson as "the creator of the real artistic Yiddish novel, the originator of artistic modernism in Yiddish literature." In effect, their respective positions were quite close, although Bergelson was always milder than the political animal Litvakov. For instance, while Litvakov dreamt about an antireligious and universal literature, Bergelson stood for a nonreligious universalism that did not suppress individuality.[136]

The year 1919 was the busiest in the Culture League's activities.[137] In 1920, however, Kiev finally went communist, but did not become a Soviet capital. As a punishment for being the hub of Ukraine's independence movement, Kiev was relegated to a secondary status. The capital of Ukraine was moved to Kharkov. Yiddish organizations either stopped functioning or had to transform into Soviet institutions. On 16 September 1920, the Kiev Yiddish daily *Komunistishe fon* (Communist banner) reported a meeting of Jewish communist culture activists. The newspaper welcomed the decision to Bolshevize the Culture League, stressing that, under the specific conditions of Ukraine, the independent league became a refuge for all kinds of former socialists as well as for the nationalist bourgeois intelligentsia.[138] On 17 December 1920, the Central Committee of the Culture League was liquidated by a decree of the Kiev Province Revolutionary Committee. Instead, there was appointed an Executive Committee dominated by communists. Under the new conditions, the league's varied educational and cultural functions were gradually reduced to activities of a publishing house, which existed until 1931.[139]

The party was over. Both the guests and hosts were leaving Kiev. Many of them moved to Moscow.

CHAPTER TWO

Moscow

The Moscow Circle of Yiddish Writers and Artists (MCYWA)

AT THE TIME of the Bolshevik Revolution and the ensuing civil war, Kiev—rather than Moscow or, for that matter, any other place in Russia, Ukraine, and Belorussia—set the tone in Yiddish literature. As a Yiddish publishing center, for instance, Moscow was far behind Kiev and could not keep step with Odessa and Petrograd. In Moscow, 110 Yiddish titles were published in 1917–21, making up only 13 percent of all Yiddish titles printed in Russia, Ukraine, and Belorussia. At the same time, Kiev boasted 39.9 percent, Odessa, 15.3 percent, and Petrograd, 13.5 percent.[1] In view of such statistics, it is easy to overlook the numerous and more important trendsetting group of Yiddish men of letters active in Moscow after 1917. This is especially the case because there has been hardly any scholarly research on Jewish literary life in the early Soviet metropolis. True, much useful information can be drawn from such sources as Abraham Abchuk's quasi-academic chronicle[2] and the memoirs of Daniel Charney and Menashe Halpern.[3] A wealth of relevant particulars is also scattered in the biographical entries of various encyclopedias, particularly Zalman Reisen's multivolume *Leksikon fun der yidisher literatur, prese un filologye* (Biographical dictionary of Yiddish literature).[4] In addition, some facts have been gleaned from Israel Serebriani's "Chronicle of Soviet Yiddish Literature."[5]

Before the 1917 revolution Moscow was by no means a Jewish cultural center. After thirty thousand Jews were expelled from Moscow in 1891, only about five thousand privileged Jews remained in the city.[6] Nonetheless, in 1917, Moscow Jews already numbered sixty thousand (3 percent of the city's population), mainly recent migrants brought into the city by the vortexes of the war and revolution.[7] The in-migration increased the number of Yiddish-speakers hitherto represented in Moscow mainly by the former Jewish soldiers, known as *nikolaevske soldatn,* or "czar Nicholas soldiers."[8] Statistics of the Moscow Labor exchange give some notion of the Jewish migrants' language competence in 1914–16. Out of about three thousand Jewish males and females who gave language-related information in their registration forms, more than 80 percent were literate in "a Jewish language."[9] Some of the migrants were dedicated Yiddish culture-bearers. Significantly, during the First World War, when Jewish publishing was severely impaired by the military censorship, Moscow appeared as a relatively liberal place, attracting Jewish journalists and printers who created in the city an infrastructure for publishing Jewish periodicals and books in Russian, Hebrew, and Yiddish.[10] For instance, Boris Kletzkin's publishing house for modern Yiddish literature had been evacuated from Vilna to Petrograd, but it remained dormant there until the beginning of 1917, when it found the possibility of producing books in a Moscow printing shop.[11]

In postrevolutionary Moscow, which became the Soviet capital in March 1918, Yiddish cultural life continued in the shadow of the central Bolshevik authorities, particularly the machinery set up for the Jews: the Jewish Commissariat in the government and the Jewish Sections (or Evsektsiia) in the party. By the time of the revolution, there were few Yiddish literati among the Bolsheviks; therefore, Soviet Jewish institutions had to start working, by and large, through recent political opponents. Even among the handful of people who, on 18 January 1918 in Petrograd, inaugurated the Jewish Commissariat, only its head, Shimen Dimanshtein, was a veteran Bolshevik.[12] In March 1918, when the Commissariat moved to Moscow along with the other Soviet governmental agencies, it numbered only three functionaries: Dimanshtein and his two deputies—the Left Social-Revolutionary Eliahu Dobkovski, who was sacked in May 1918 on the (unconfirmed) suspicion of collaboration with the czarist secret police,[13] and the Anarchist turned Bolshevik Shmuel (Sam) Agurski. The latter, an ambitious propagandist, was dispatched to Vitebsk, then the most populous Jewish center in Soviet Russia proper. As a result, Dimanshtein was left in the office with the former Bundist Simkha Tomsinski (Simkha, or Semen Tomsinskii), who later became a well-known Soviet historian of the workers' movement in Russia. To help produce the Commissariat's Yiddish publications—most notably the daily *Der emes* (Truth) and the journal *Di komunistishe velt* (Communist world)—Dimanshtein employed "for a few pounds of millet and *vobla*"[14] a few noncommunist literati, including Daniel Charney, an experienced Yiddish writer, who in 1915 evacuated from Vilna and, with a few intervals, had since been living in Moscow. Charney effectively edited *Der emes* from July 1918 to February 1919, while Dimanshtein, the titular editor in chief, wrote ideological articles. At the close of 1918, Dimanshtein moved to Vilna, where he served as a commissar in the short-lived Lithuanian-Belorussian Republic. As a result, *Der emes* lost its ideological head and was phased out.

Charney was the Moscow representative of the liberal Folkspartey, inspired by the Jewish historian and social theoretician Shimon Dubnov. The Folkspartey attracted many Jewish intellectuals, including such Yiddish writers as A. Weiter and Moshe Taitsh. As the Moscow party boss, Charney had at his disposal a four-room apartment, where he hosted a literary salon and operated a kind of transshipping point for Jewish politicians, writers, and artists. Some of them were Charney's personal friends while the others were friends of his brothers, known by their pseudonyms: Shmuel Niger, whom we already met in the previous chapter, and Borukh Vladeck, an influential American labor leader and the manager of the New York Yiddish daily *Forverts*. Niger spent some part of 1918 in Moscow, contributing while there to the periodicals of the Jewish Commissariat. Charney also was the Moscow representative—pompously called "general secretary"—of the Yiddish cultural network Culture League, whose headquarters were in Kiev. His influence became even stronger when Joseph Rosen, the head of the relief mission of the American Joint Distribution Committee, came to Moscow in 1921. A note from Charney to Rosen, a friend of Vladeck, often served as a coupon entitling an undernourished Jewish intellectual to a lifesaving food parcel. The vast majority of Charney's beneficiaries were members of the Moscow Circle of Yiddish Writers and Artists (MCYWA).

The MCYWA was created in the summer of 1918 as an organization for mutual professional and material help. Thirty-five writers and artists took part in the first meeting of the group. Charney and a few other European-educated Jewish intellectuals formed the circle's nucleus. Among the founders were the poets Moshe Broderzon and Menashe Halpern (or Heilperin) and the artist El (Lazar) Lissitzky. Charney and Halpern became the first chairmen of the MCYWA. Broderzon was a scion of a Moscow Jewish merchant family that had to move to Lodz after the 1891 expulsion of the Jews; he returned to Moscow during World War I. Halpern, also a scion of a rich family, spent the second half of 1917 and the beginning of 1918 in Petrograd, writing for the Yiddish newspaper *Togblat*. Lissitzky, an avant-garde architect, painter, and illustrator, represented the artistic wing of the circle.

Literary and artistic cross-fertilization among Yiddish associations was

Moshe Taitsh

an ordinary phenomenon of that time. It is sufficient to mention such literary-cum-artistic groups as Di Yunge in New York, the Culture League in Kiev, and the Yung Yidish (Young Yiddish) in Lodz. At that time a "generation of young Jewish artists, organically associated with the reformed Yiddish literature," [15] was active. The creation of the MCYWA also mirrored the general tendency, characteristic of bohemian life in post-1917 Russia: in the face of limited patronage, they were forced to form benevolent associations.[16] In fact, to survive professionally and physically during the tempestuous years of War Communism (1918–21) a Yiddish bohemian usually had to rely upon two sources of support: on the one hand, the MCYWA, and on the other, the Jewish Commissariat and its party twin, the Evsektsiia. In his 1943 memoirs Charney recalled,

> In the years 1918–22, Bolshevized Moscow also became the capital of Soviet Yiddish literature. There was not a single Yiddish writer in Russia in those days who did not pass through Moscow, as if it provided a quarantine from the raging plague. Some Yiddish writers came to the Moscow "quarantine" because they wanted to leave the country secretly and emigrate to Kovno, Warsaw, Berlin, New York, or even further away. Other Yiddish writers came to Moscow to imbibe the impetus of the October Revolution and find a place in the emerging Yiddish proletarian literature. Procommunist Yiddish writers would first visit the Evsektsiia and then come to the office of the Moscow Circle of Yiddish Writers and Artists. As for the emigrating and ready-to-emigrate writers, they would first come to the chairman of the Moscow Circle and only afterwards go to the Evsektsiia.[17]

Apparently, it was not very difficult to combine a noncommunist out-look with Soviet employment. In the early days of the Soviet regime, Diman-shtein and his scanty team were rather tolerant of different trends of thought. For example, in January 1918, Dimanshtein stood up for the Petrograd non-communist *Togblat* and its staff.[18] In Moscow he and the Commissariat's staff briefly shared premises with Zionist institutions and even ate at their kosher canteen. (It should be noted that in early postrevolutionary years the Bolsheviks did not regard Zionism as a totally counterrevolutionary move-ment.)[19] Bolshevik and non-Bolshevik Yiddish activists shared more or less the same views concerning Jewish culture. In essence, all Yiddishists shared the same dream: to synthesize the universal (mutatis mutandis, European, and proletarian, for example) and Yiddish cultures. It is, therefore, no coin-cidence that the Soviet authorities enthusiastically supported the Yiddish State Theater, particularly when Marc Chagall helped its founding director, Aleksandr Granovskii, combine Jewish folk motifs with desirable revolu-tionary messages.[20] Yiddishists of various denominations often esteemed the same cultural icons, such as Mendele Moykher Sforim, who was regarded as the founder of the modern, progressive Yiddish literature and literary lan-guage. Thus, one of the first Dimanshtein projects was a reissue of thirty thousand copies of *The Nag,* Mendele's allegory on the anti-Jewish persecu-tion in Russia,; in contrast, the Yiddish translation of Lenin's *State and Rev-olution* had a print run of only three thousand.[21]

The founders of the MCYWA could take pride in successes achieved even before the institutionalization of their group. Many of them partici-pated in one of the most popular Yiddish cultural projects, that of writing, il-lustrating, and printing children's books. For instance, among the eighty-two Yiddish titles published in 1915 (the year when Yiddish and Hebrew publi-cations were almost fully suppressed by military censorship), twenty-five were children's books.[22] Also, about one-quarter of all Yiddish books pub-lished in 1917–21 in newly revolutionary Russia, Ukraine, and Belorussia were children's books.[23] For the artists, illustrations for Yiddish books repre-sented one of only a few domains (including Yiddish theater) where the Jew-ishness of their art was indisputable. One of the most splendid Yiddish picture books was Broderzon's story in verse *Talk on Ordinary Matters, or a Legend of Prague,* illustrated by Lissitzky. In spring 1917 it was published in Moscow as a boxed scroll resembling the traditional Scroll of Esther. Al-though its print run was minimal, its publication was an event in the history of book printing.[24] In 1918, Halpern, a man of means, bought a printing house and the small Yiddish press imprint Khover (Friend), which were set up in 1917 by Herts Aktsin, a translator of European literature into Yiddish. The Illustrated Children's Library published by Khover included Halpern's *Tales,* Broderzon's *Little Tamar,* Herts's adaptations of Leo Tolstoy's *Fables* and Mark Twain's *The Prince and the Pauper,* and Charney's tale *The Gold-thirsty King.* Soon, however, the Jewish Commissariat purchased this printing house.

In addition to children's books, Broderzon, Charney, Halpern, and Gershon Broida published *Zalbefert* (Four together), a thirty-two-page collection of poems. The book appeared in 1918 with the imprint of Lebn (Life), another Moscow Yiddish publisher. Topically, the poems included in *Zalbefert* had nothing to do with the revolution. Rather, it was a collection of love lyrics, such as Charney's erotic poem "Between" about his lyrical hero's affair with two sisters, one blonde and one brunette girl. Halpern and Broida—the latter settled in Moscow after years of studies in Germany and Switzerland and earned his living from commerce—combined the roles of sponsors and aspiring poets. In fact, without sponsors it would have been difficult to publish Yiddish books in Moscow—more so because in the years of War Communism books had to be mostly distributed rather than sold.[25] Nonetheless, the most important Moscow-based outlets for poetry, prose, and criticism were Communist and other—usually short-lived—periodicals. For instance, Broderzon's translation of Aleksandr Blok's celebrated poem "Twelve" was published in the first issue of the Poalei-Zionist journal *Dos naye vort* (New word), published 1918–20. Interestingly, another Yiddish translation of Blok's poem came out in Warsaw in 1920. The translator, Alter Katsizne, made his literary debut in the 1918 volume of *Eygns* and later became a prolific Yiddish writer.

In August 1918, the MCYWA sponsored an exhibition of forty Jewish painters and sculptors.[26] The exhibition was combined with literary parties. On 25 August, which was the last day of the exhibition, Niger lectured on psychological problems of Jewish artists who had to overcome religious restrictions concerning the representation of human beings. The key speaker, however, was S. An-sky, an acclaimed writer (most notably of *The Dybbuk*), ethnographer, and political activist who lived in Moscow until the aggravation of the Bolshevik regime's terror.[27] The exhibition culminated the early period of the MCYWA activities. By the end of the year the circle became largely inactive, most importantly because a large number of its members left Moscow. Thus Broderzon traveled to Lodz in 1918, where he joined the

Yung Yidish group.[28] The same year Niger went to Vilna.[29] In 1919, Lissitzky left Moscow; he was invited by his old friend, Chagall (both were former students of the famous Vitebsk art school opened in 1897 by Yehuda Pen), to return to Vitebsk to become professor of architecture and head of the applied arts department at the local art school. Chagall, whom Anatoly Lunacharsky, people's commissar for enlightenment in Lenin's government, appointed to be responsible for the artistic affairs of the province of Vitebsk, was the organizer and principal of the new school.[30]

Those who remained in Moscow were trying to survive the privation of War Communism, when, in Leon Trotski's words, "80 percent of people's energy were spent on procuring food."[31] By 1920 Moscow's population had fallen below the 1897 level; it decreased by 40 percent during the civil war alone, when the shortage of food was one of the major factors driving people from the city.[32] Der Nister recalled later: "The city [was] half dead, a kind of Pompeii. . . . Few [Yiddish] literati were in Moscow [in 1920]. Prose was silent. Poetry was shouting . . . Seven nonentities and untalented people were always at each real talent's side, and seven rogues and drones made a living from them. The best writers overstrained their voices, but nobody could hear them outside Moscow."[33]

Nonetheless, the MCYWA renewed its activities in 1920. Its increased membership became even more heterogeneous than it had been. Some Yiddish literati already had experience as Soviet employees, including the translator Yekhezkel Bleikher, the pedagogue David Hokhberg, and the linguist Ayzik Zaretski. A few of the members, notably Khaim Gildin and Moshe Taitsh (the latter having already jumped off the Folkspartey bandwagon), came to Moscow obsessed with opposition to the past and radical ideas concerning the further development of culture. Chagall was a member of this circle. In 1920 he returned from Vitebsk to Moscow and began his fruitful collaboration with Granovskii's Yiddish theater. A significant number of Yiddish writers came from Kiev. The publishing department of the Evsektsiia employed Bergelson as editor of Yiddish and Russian literature, Hofshtein as editor of foreign literature, Der Nister as editor of children's literature, Dobrushin and Volkenshtein as translators, and Markish as a proofreader.[34] All of them suffered from a hangover after the intoxicating, surrealistic Jewish autonomy in the pogrom-ridden Ukraine. In 1920 the managing committee of the MCYWA included the Communist faithfuls Shakhne Epshtein, the new chairman of the MCYWA, and Ber Orshanski, who was previously active in Vilna as a playwright and editor. The Kievans were represented by Dobrushin, Hofshtein, and the artist Yissachar-Ber Rybak. Charney was the sole holdover from the founding group.

Epshtein was one of the numerous ex-Bundists who converted to Communism during the civil war. In 1916, Ber Borokhov had called him "a good Bundist," or a Bundist who could not forget about his party affiliation even while writing literary criticism.[35] Such "good Bundists" presented good material for good Communists. Indeed, Epshtein joined the Bolsheviks soon after his return to Russia from America in 1917. In summer 1920 in Vitebsk he edited the newspaper *Der shtern* (Star), an organ of Belorussia's Communists published 1918–21. In April 1921, Epshtein moved to Moscow, where in November 1920 he was appointed editor in chief of the daily *Der emes*. The newspaper was relaunched as the central organ of the Evsektsiia rather than of the Jewish Commissariat, the publisher of the original *Der emes*. Thus in 1920 the MCYWA was already headed by a seasoned party functionary.

Small wonder then that in 1920 the MCYWA acquired a more militant hue. For example, its leadership did not want to renew the membership of Zalman Wendroff, a prolific author of Yiddish belles lettres. At the beginning of the century he traveled the world trying different jobs. His peripatetic youth included a stint in England, a brief spell in Moscow in 1905 as a teacher of English, and a job in Yiddish journalism in America. In 1908 he came back to Russia as a reporter for the *Morgn-zhurnal* (Morning journal), the second-largest New York Yiddish daily. In 1918 he joined Charney and Niger in their journalistic and editorial work for the Jewish Commissariat.[36] The following year the Lebn publishing house issued his collection of stories, *Arbet un noyt* (Work and need). Nevertheless, in 1920 during MCYWA reregistration Wendroff was accused of counterrevolutionary and Zionist activities, including collaboration with the Moscow Hebrew theater Habima, where he briefly worked as administrator. Epshtein and many other Yiddish monoculturists were annoyed that the "Zionist Habima" was able to survive and obtain generous state subsidies. No doubt, the Evsektsiia functionaries could not forgive Wendroff his anti-Evsektsiia and pro-Habima speech during the public discussion, which took place on 13 March 1920.[37] They wanted him to know that he was playing with fire.

Regardless of their ideology, Yiddishists placed all Hebrew cultural activities in the enemy camp. Even the Labor Zionists came out, during their April 1920 party conference in Moscow, against any state support for the

Habima troupe or other Hebrew institutions.[38] In conformity with a resolution of the first All-Russian Congress of Jewish Educators and Activists of Socialist Culture (July 1920), any "moral or financial support of such an institution as the Habima was 'criminal.' "[39] A few months earlier, Dimanshtein called the Habima "a caprice of the Jewish bourgeoisie," which played a negative role by catalyzing chauvinism among Jews. He argued that Hebrew—a dead language—"stank like an unburied corpse."[40]

In January 1921, Wendroff wrote a sharp letter arguing that he had never belonged to any party. Moreover, he added, he hated all parties, from Zionists to Communists. As a proof of his non-Zionism, he adduced his ten articles written from Palestine, none of which contained a line about Jews. The Habima, according to him, was also far from Zionism, although the theater performed in a language that was incomprehensible even to some of the actors. Of course, a few years later such an apolitical credo would not be acceptable, but in the relatively liberal 1921 it produced the desired effect: Wendroff's membership was renewed.

Yiddish literati kept coming to and leaving the capital. David Bergelson, for example, who hoped to launch in Moscow a literary journal, fled the cold, hungry city in March 1921.[41] Der Nister and Kvitko also left the city. All three of them decided to try their luck outside Russia. The same year Yudel Yoffe, who would a decade later become a writer of popular stories, moved to Moscow; Shmuel Rosin, already an author of two poetic collections, published in Ekaterinoslav (1918) and Kharkov (1919), made the same move. In September 1921 a new managing committee of the MCYWA was elected. Rosin was among its members, together with the experienced writers Moshe Taitsh, Abraham Wieviorka, and Yehudye Margulis. Both Wieviorka and Margulis were 1917 returnees. The former, editor of a few periodicals in Berlin and London, came from England; the latter came from America, where he had been one of the founders of Di Yunge group.

Shtrom and *Yungvald*

As time went on, polarization of the MCYWA intensified. Yiddish literary life was influenced strongly by the concurrent controversies in the Russian and, to a certain extent, Ukrainian and Belorussian literary milieus. Nonetheless, the number of competing Yiddish groupings was much smaller, first of all because the Yiddish literary world per se was relatively small. By 1922

David Bergelson

the MCYWA, with more than forty members, contained only two significant factions: the writers of the literary journal *Shtrom* (Stream) and the proletarian writers.

The first issue of *Shtrom,* with a cover designed by Chagall, appeared in February 1922. As the journal's motto the editors had chosen two lines from one of Osher Shvartsman's poems: nor unter feldz her ikh / rint un rinzlt frish a shtrom (but I [can] hear [that] under the cliff / a stream is running and flowing). Shvartsman had written a few versions of the quoted poem. Thus, the preceding line was either af feldzn-shtegn kh'blondzhe blind (I am roving blindly on rocky paths) or un kh'veys mayn veg nit, ikh bin blind (And I do not know my way, I am blind).[42] In any case, the motto mirrored the perplexity of the writers, who were overwhelmed by, on the one hand, enthusiasm about the revolution and, on the other hand, horror over the unprecedented slaughter of the Jewish population, particularly in Ukraine. *Shtrom* was, in essence, a new forum of the Kiev Yiddish literary and artistic group. All three *Shtrom* founding editors, Yekhezkel Dobrushin, Nokhum Oislender, and Aron Kushnirov, came from Kiev. Many Shtromists were fellow travelers, or intellectuals who welcomed the revolution but had doubts about specific aspects of the Soviet regime. At the same time, some of the Shtromists were staunch Bolsheviks, like Oislender and Kushnirov, who had only recently been demobilized from the Red Army. All in all, *Shtrom* was, undoubtedly, a Soviet journal, marked externally by the iconoclastic phonetic spelling style of all Hebrew words. The new spelling code was introduced by the Evsektsiia in 1920 and became, symbolically at least, associated with the phonetic spelling of the word *emes* in the Moscow Yiddish newspaper's title.[43]

Apparently, Dobrushin was the main figure in the editorial triumvirate because he dealt with the nitty-gritty of compiling and producing the journal. He also was the principal literary critic of this forum. In his programmatic article, "Our Literature" (published in the first issue of the *Shtrom*), Dobrushin formulated his requirements for literature and writers:

> For Yiddish literature, "the national" has to become object rather than subject. As a result, the problem, the objective world-problem will become the essence of Yiddish literature, because Yiddish literature will become part of the wide range of general world-problems, and—with the accumulated means of expression in the form of new Yiddish lexical material—literature will create the book of the age. . . . Instead of the writer who introspectively presents the tangle of his hollow emotional "heard-seen-experienced," there has to come the writer who works with objective things, the writer who unites his verified knowledge of the world with his poetic vision, thus synthesizing his intellect with his emotions, or—in other words—his sober erudition with his imaginative intuition.

However, while striving for a "sober" (meaning "partisan") literature, Dobrushin and his kind apparently were not ready to become a poetry and prose department of the Bolshevik Party. For some of them, the process of complete "sobering" would last for another decade or so.

The Shtromists' indisputably Soviet counterparts were enthusiasts of the Organization of Representatives of Proletarian Culture (Proletkult), which emerged in Russia in 1917 as a mass movement, with about four hundred thousand members by 1920, including eighty thousand workers taking part in various forms of creative activities. The Yiddish "proletarians" were vociferous, even if small in numbers. As early as October 1920, during the First All-Russian Congress of Proletarian Writers (a spin-off of the Proletkult organization), Khaim Gildin, a card-carrying Communist with considerable demagogic energy, spoke as the representative of the Yiddish proletarian writers. In particular, he argued that poetry of political agitation had to supplant aesthetic literature. In fact, it is not clear whom Gildin actually represented during the congress. A contemporary Yiddish article on proletarian culture cites only Russian poets.[44] Gildin's own poem, "In the factory," published in *Di komunistishe velt* in 1919,[45] was a rare sample of Yiddish industrial poetry, written in the style of the Russian poet Aleksei Gastev, whose themes were the chorus of factory machines and the amalgamation of man with machine.[46]

Ba shtitser, ba tigl, ba rizn-mashinen,
antbloyzn di brust un di arbl farshartst,
es yogn zikh aylik geshtaltn, geshtaltn,
fun shtoyb un fun sazhe farkhoyshekht, farshvartst.

Tseshvidlt es fayfn di ayzerne valn,
es vign zikh kerpers, es flatern hent.
Es kenigt der impet af muskul un hamer,
un fibert di shoybn, un fibert di vent.

Af shkivn getsoygn di lederne strunes
in takt fun motorn—a groylike lid,
tseklungen, tsezungen es tantsn di hamers
un regenen funken fun ayzn-geshmid.

Es zingen mashinen, di hamer, di shtitser,
es hoylt un es zumt monoton der motor.
Fun khaos gegosn, geshafn fun shtraytn,
es shaln harmonish in ginen fun tsaytn,
triumfn-gezang fun a mekhtikn khor.

At the tongs, crucible, and giant machines,
With bared chests and rolled-up sleeves,
Numerous figures are rushing,
Darkened and blackened by dust and soot.

The iron shafts gather momentum and whistle,
The bodies swing, the hands flutter.
The impetus reigns over the muscle and hammer
And makes feverish the dusts and the walls.

The leather springs are taut on the pulleys,
In time with the engines—a gruesome song,
The hammers sing and ring away, they dance
And rain sparks from the hot iron.

The machines, hammers, and tongs sing,
The engine growls and buzzes.
Molded from chaos, created from strokes,
It sounds in harmony with the time—
The triumph song of a powerful chorus.

In 1921, a small collection of proletarian poems by Gildin, Monye Gure-vitsh, Elishe Rodin, and Hirsh Riklin appeared in Gomel. Belorussia, partic-ularly Vitebsk (although after the revolution Vitebsk was officially part of Russia), was the cradle of Yiddish proletarian literature in the Soviet Union.[47] In Moscow, the first meeting of a Yiddish proletarian group took place much later—on 5 January 1922. On that day, four people—Taitsh, Gurevitsh, Shmuel Persov, and a certain Bukshorn—gathered in Gildin's flat. Later a few other young literati such as Josef Rabin and David Utkes joined the group. The former came to Moscow in 1921 from Vilna, where he was the head of the illegal Komsomol organization. The latter imitated the Russ-ian propagandist poet Demian Bednyi and even signed his poems as "Dovidl Kaptsn" (both the Russian *bednyi* and the Yiddish *kaptsn* mean "poor"). The following is a sample of Utkes' poetry written during the civil war:

Ven es faln itst di keytn
fun der shklavn-tsayt—
helf di parazitn teytn,
shtey nit fun der zayt![48]

When there are falling the chains
of the slavery era
help to kill the parasites,
don't remain aloof!

In January 1922, the general meeting of the MCYWA decided that the organization should be renamed Moscow Association (*fareyn*) of Yiddish Writers and Artists (MAYWA). The new name was to express the existence of the two competing factions, the Shtromists and the proletarians. Because the Shtromists were stronger, Gildin announced that the proletarian writers would regard themselves as an opposition. In 1923 the group led by Gildin and Taitsh failed to launch its journal *Royte heftn* (Red writing-books), although *Shtrom* had already announced (in its third issue) the start of the new magazine, directed by "Comrades Gildin, Taitsh, Persov, and others." Given the policy of postwar Communist economic rationality, the "comrades" apparently did not manage to win the confidence of the State Publishing House. Another hard blow fell on the group in October 1923, when Utkes and Gurevitsh published letters in *Der emes* announcing their decision to leave the Gildin-Taitsh group. Utkes and Gurevitsh explained that originally they had joined the group due to its proletarian stand and their detestation of the Kievers "individualistic, petty-bourgeois writing." Later, however, they were disappointed by the bombastic, combative tone of the group's leaders and their lack of real understanding of proletarian literature. Eventually, Utkes and Gurevitsh abandoned Yiddish literary activities.

Shtrom, too, experienced sharp conflicts. In 1923, Kushnirov, Shmuel Godiner, Wieviorka, Persov, Abraham Shoikhet, and a few other writers decided to publish another journal. In a letter to his friend the Kiev poet Moshe Khashchevatsky, Kushnirov complained about the difficult atmosphere around *Shtrom,* particularly reflected in the endless compromises of the editors, who were repeatedly attacked from all sides. He stressed that "not a single issue had come out without intrigues and conflicts."[49] On 18 October 1923, *Der emes* announced that the new journal, *Ekran* (Screen), edited by Wieviorka, Kushnirov, and Shoikhet, was to appear by 15 November. It was stressed that its authors based their literary work upon the ideas of the October Revolution. The name itself of the new journal apparently stemmed from Kushnirov's poem with the same name, which opened his 1921 collection *Vent* (Walls) and was a poetic manifesto rejecting the "velvet ribbons and gilt frames" and hailing mass culture, targeting the "multi-thousand glance of the crowd."[50] Many Bolsheviks, including Lenin, regarded cinema as an important mass culture medium; therefore "screen" was a byword for "popular."

The group counted on support of such writers as Izi Kharik, Zelig Akselrod, and Taitsh. (Taitsh by that time had lost some of his postrevolutionary radicalism and was even purged from the Communist Party.)[51] The *Ekran* project, however, came to naught. Apparently, a temporary compromise was found between the breakaway group and *Shtrom.* As a result, the last double issue of *Shtrom* (numbers 5 and 6) published works by the young poets Izi Kharik and Itsik Fefer, whom the editors previously did not regard as acceptable contributors. The last issue also contained a letter, signed by Wieviorka and Kushnirov: "With this [letter] we announce that—because the publication of *Shtrom* is now becoming more secure, and from issue 7 it will be possible to use *Shtrom* also as a forum for current problems of literature and art—we find it unnecessary at this moment to split our strength into two organs, and thus we are giving up [the idea] of publishing *Ekran*."

It is not clear what kind of financial security it had been promised, but *Shtrom* itself indicated that the magazine was struggling for its survival. Although the first issue appeared in three thousand copies, imprints of the following issues showed a print run of only two thousand. The last two issues contained a number of advertisements, including (in issue 4) ads for the Petrograd State Shipbuilding Trust and the All-Russian State Syndicate of Agricultural Machine-building Factories. These advertisements can hardly be regarded as free publicity for state enterprises. Most likely, they were attempts to sponsor the beleaguered magazine.

In the meantime, the number of proletarian writers was continually augmented by a steady influx of young literati coming to Moscow in search of both a solid general education and an opportunity to write in Yiddish. This fact was especially true as Moscow became a much more satisfying place when, in the spring of 1921, the barrack-style War Communism was replaced by the much more liberal New Economic Policy (NEP). Significantly, in 1921 the Evsektsiia was reinforced by numerous former Jewish socialists, most notably Bundists, who either sincerely or opportunistically accepted Bolshevism. With the civil war over and Moscow no longer isolated from other Jewish centers, capital-based publications and institutions were becoming central not in name only but in fact as well.[52] In particular, Moscow emerged as a Yiddish theatrical center. Granovskii's theater was not the only Yiddish troupe in the city. In the early 1920s, Moscow boasted at least three other Yiddish theater groups *(studyes)*: the Culture League group, founded by Ephraim Loiter in Kiev in 1919 and brought to Moscow in 1922 in search of aesthetic guidance; the Belorussian Yiddish theater group, headed by Mikhail Rafalsky; and the Sholem Aleichem *studye* (chaired first by the Russian Jewish writer Andrei Sobol and later by David Hofshtein), which was designed to contrast Granovskii's avant-gardism with a realist Yiddish theater.[53]

In 1921 the Central Jewish Party School opened in Moscow with 100 students. The school in January 1922 became the Jewish Section of the Com-

Shmuel Godiner

munist University for National Minorities of the West, known in Yiddish as "Mayrevke." [54] The same year, Itshe-Meir Shpilrein became the first Yiddish lecturer at Moscow University.[55] Chairs for Yiddish language, literature, and history were also established at the Second Moscow University. The Moscow School for Yiddish Printers, opened in 1922, produced all issues of *Shtrom* after the first one. The school also published its own journal, *Mir geyen* (We are going), with an epigraph from a poem by Hofshtein: mir geyen in dayne forntike reyen, shpanendike mentshhayt (we are going in your marching mankind, front columns).[56] In all, Moscow appeared to be arguably the largest center of Yiddish higher and vocational learning. In addition, aspiring Yiddish literati came to study at other Moscow educational institutions. Thus, the talented young writers Izi Kharik, Zelig Akselrod, and Shmuel Godiner were students at the Briusov Institute for Literature and Art. Abraham Shoikhet, a Kiev poet, and Yasha Bronshtein, later the leading literary critic in Belorussia, came to study at the prestigious Institute of Red Professors.

*   *   *

Communist, the Moscow Jewish workers' club that opened in 1922, became the hub of Yiddish cultural activities. Few of its members were from Moscow or even from Soviet Russia as a whole—the vast majority of them were

Yasha Bronshtein

either political emigrants from Poland and Lithuania or returnees from the United States and England.[57] Such a disproportionate representation of emigrants and returnees among the club members was not coincidental; this very cohort played a significant part among Soviet Yiddish apparatchiks, literati, students, and activists in general, including in the Moscow Yiddish literary milieu.

In 1924 the first issue of the central Yiddish pedagogical journal *Af di vegn tsu der nayer shul* (On the way to the new school), published 1924–28, came out in Moscow. This change was part of the outflow of Yiddish cultural institutions from Kiev to Moscow: the Moscow pedagogical journal replaced the Kiev-based *Pedagogisher buleten* (Pedagogical bulletin), published 1922–23). The next year the Moscow children's monthly *Pioner* (Pioneer), published 1925–28, replaced the Kiev magazine *Freyd* (Joy), published 1922–25. Moscow periodicals welcomed young writers. For example, Kharik made his literary debut in *Di komunistishe velt,* where in 1920 he published a poem under the pseudonym of A. Zembin.[58] In 1921 an attempt was made to reregister the Culture League as an organization with headquarters in Moscow and "chief committees" in Kiev and Minsk. The new application was signed on 15 December 1921 by Moshe Litvakov, Maria Frumkin (alias "Esther"), Mikhl Levitan, Aleksei Granovskii, and Josef Bregman.[59] But it was a stillborn project.

The Komsomol journal *Yungvald* (New growth), published 1923–28, which was first issued in April 1923, became the main forum for young Yiddish writers. *Yungvald* put in the forefront of Soviet Yiddish literature sev-

eral professional writers, including the novelist Josef Rabin, then a student at
the Moscow Yiddish Printing School. In a sense, *Yungvald* continued an earlier initiative, the Kharkov 1923 journal *Libknekhts dor* ([Karl] Liebknecht's
generation), whose editor, David Monin, from 1925 edited the *Yungvald*.
Another initiator of that short-lived Kharkov periodical, Sonya Fray, was
likewise a member of *Yungvald*'s editorial staff. The first *Yungvald* editor
was Khaim (Kheml) Dobin, son of the Kiev Yiddish activist and cofounder of
the Culture League Shimen Dobin. Khaim Dobin later switched over to
Russian journalism and criticism, where he was known as Efim Semenovich
Dobin. A gifted translator from Russian, he translated for *Yungvald* stories
by such Russian writers as Andrei Platonov and Ilya Ehrenburg.

The magazine had two ideological supervisors: Muni Zorki and Maria
Frumkin. Zorki was a legendary Komsomol leader and the head of the Press
Department at the Komsomol Central Committee. Frumkin, a former leading Bundist, headed the Communist University for National Minorities of
the West and was a member of the Evsektsiia's Central Bureau. Another
leader of the Evsektsiia, Moshe Litvakov, was one of the advisers of the
young literati grouped around the magazine.

The Soviet Literary Cadre

Although Shakhne Epshtein was the first editor of *Der emes* when it was revived on 7 November 1920, the new period of the central Yiddish daily is de-
servedly associated with the name of Moshe Litvakov. In summer 1921,
Epshtein was sent back to the United States, where he was instrumental in
organizing the Yiddish Communist press, and Litvakov filled his editorial
post. By that time Litvakov was one of the most experienced Yiddish editors
in Russia: in 1906–19 he edited a few newspapers in Vilna and Kiev, including the Kiev *Naye tsayt*, arguably the best Yiddish daily in postrevolutionary
Russia. In his new role of the Moscow daily's editor he almost immediately
became the main watchdog of the Soviet Yiddish cultural world. Apparently,
he saw himself as a paternal figure, arguing that it would have been "wrong
to leave artists alone during such an important epoch; they should be vigi-
lantly controlled with love and attention." [60] Suggesting that Soviet literature
was being built according to a plan, he apparently regarded himself as the
Yiddish literary site's work superintendent. An admirer of the Marxist literary theories of Georgii Plekhanov,[61] Litvakov echoed the latter's words that a
critic had to recognize the class struggle. He was rather skeptical about the

fellow travelers, arguing that literature was a sector of the ideological front and as such it had to rely on communist cadres. Ironically, he still did not support the Gildin-Taitsh Communist group. This former Sorbonne student of literature and highbrow Russian literary critic saw Gildin's and Taitsh's proletarian poetry as trivial and worthless. Gildin would later comment that Litvakov was dreaming about a proletarian Yiddish Goethe, but did nothing in order to find and educate such a genius.[62]

When Litvakov was appointed editor in chief of *Der emes*, he became fully aware of the acute shortage of professional Yiddish writers. The majority of experienced Yiddish journalists had fled the country. A few Communists with some experience in Yiddish journalism had switched to "general Soviet work." In a fit of temper, on 9 January 1922, Litvakov attacked the "Yiddish literary emigration in Moscow." In particular, he accused them of boycotting his Communist daily. It is no coincidence that Litvakov's attack fell at the time when cost-accounting had been introduced as part of the NEP and *Der emes* had to begin operating on a profit basis.

On 13 January five representatives of the Moscow "emigration"— Oislender, Godiner, Dobrushin, Hofshtein, and Wieviorka—published a letter defending their position. They argued that their small group simply wanted to concentrate all its efforts on literary activities, such as the books appearing with the Lirik (Lyric) imprint—launched in autumn 1921 at the Kiev publishing house of the Culture League—and the forthcoming journal *Shtrom*. However, they stated that they did not oppose *Der emes*, which they hailed as "the only politically creative and actively inspiring journal for Jewish workers of the whole world."

In his second article, published on 15 January, Litvakov let mercy season justice. True, he did not approve of the Lirik-Shtrom writers' ivory tower, where—as in Yavneh—hidden from the revolutionary storms, they "were creating a new *Masorah*."[63] He suggested that their writing had ceased to be pioneering or advanced. Rather, it was "crowning," or concluding the pre-revolutionary literary process. Litvakov expressed the opinion that the Moscow writers were more advanced ideologically than aesthetically. Therefore, he urged them to publish in *Der emes* at least their ideological *hirhurim* (reflections), which would help them to overcome their "Yavneh period." In addition, he advised that publication in *Der emes* might be useful for the writers' public relations: workers would be more likely to buy a book written by an author whom they already knew than one written by an unknown.

Litvakov did not expect Yiddish writers to become primitive singers of

the revolution. Apparently, his position was close to the position of Lunacharsky, who was against caging real talents: "A talent who has adjusted
to life in a cage turns from a nightingale into a siskin, from an eagle into a
hen. This does not mean, of course, that only siskins and hens can be revolutionary poets and artists. On the contrary, a free artist, a free poet may be
revolutionary to the bottom of his heart, but only because his creativity co-
incides with his free aspiration." [64]

In his quest for revolutionary nightingales and eagles, Litvakov was disappointed with *Shtrom,* especially with its prose works. According to Litvakov, neither Mendele Moykher Sforim, with his "careless language," nor
Sholem Aleichem, "choked with anthropological material," could be models
for contemporary writers. Sholem Aleichem was a genius, but ideologically
he represented "a blind alley" rather than a "program." Thus, Litvakov de-
rided Wendroff as taking the line of least resistance and becoming a pure im-
itator of Sholem Aleichem. This view predated Litvakov's Bolshevik
acculturation. As early as 1916, he described Sholem Aleichem as "a great
temptation for the young Yiddish literature." Notice the "cold neutrality" of
Litvakov and his kind toward the favorite of Yiddish mass readers. [65]

In Litvakov's opinion, Yitzkhok Leibush Peretz was the first pioneer of
Yiddish literary style, whose successor, the symbolist Der Nister, he crowned
as the first master Yiddish prose writer. (Because he associated David Bergelson, "the Yiddish Hamsun," with the realistic tradition of Mendele and
Sholem Aleichem,[66] Litvakov ranked him lower than Der Nister.) Hence, Litvakov's quest for a further development of Der Nister's achievements. In general, he saw Der Nister as the only existing model for a revolutionary Yiddish
writer. Der Nister, according to Litvakov, was the only established Yiddish
writer who never went through a crisis and always wanted to write for a
mass reader.[67] Shmuel Godiner, Der Nister's disciple, seemed to be the most
promising among the handful of Soviet Yiddish prose writers, although according to Litvakov Godiner remained ideologically a protorevolutionary
writer. To all appearances, Litvakov rejected realism because any realist
work mirrored the world he simply did not want to see. Rather, he preferred
to dream about a socialist Yiddish-speaking Jewish society, populated by sophisticated proletarians and genius culture-bearers. Dobrushin made explicit
this concept of antirealism, which provoked fury in the camp of proletarian
watchdogs. He wrote, "In the periods of stormy horror one has to register
the palpitating thought in invented and fictitious images, or in personages of

extreme antiquity, moving thus far away off the too sharp light of the blinding today." [68]

In poetry, Litvakov crowned Hofshtein as "the first Yiddish classic," who—together with a few other poets of the Kiev Group—had found a *kfitses-haderekh* (shortcut) to modern creativity. This leap, however, had exhausted their energy; therefore, the revolution was greeted, according to the critical editor, by Hofshtein's artificial rhetoric and Peretz Markish's placard verses. Nor was Litvakov happy with Hofshtein's and Kushnirov's passion for Sergei Esenin's Imaginism. All in all, Litvakov divided contemporary Soviet Yiddish poetry into three types: (1) political poetry *(politishe tsayt-ferzn)* written in the toastmaster *(badkhonishn)* style of the Yiddish bard-minstrel Eliakum Zunser; (2) placard poetry, introduced into Yiddish literature by Markish, which later degenerated into pompous, bombastic verses; and (3) "industrial rhetoric," borrowed by Gildin from some Russian poets. Even the motto chosen by the *Shtrom* editors did not suit Litvakov, because he saw it as an allusion to the motto of Ahad-Haam's Hebrew journal *Hashiloah*: "Like the [river] Hashiloah that flows quietly." It was more important, however, to find out the direction toward which *Shtrom* was streaming. Litvakov diagnosed blindness in its writers, who, like the singers in Lipe Reznik's poem (published in issue 1 of *Shtrom*), were singing in "quiet corners" of NEP:

> un gasn,
> oysgenikhterte fun duln umgeyn,
> kumen opruen a regele
> af shtiln rog
> un blaybn dort
> mit . . . blinde zinger.

> and streets,
> sober after mad wandering,
> come to rest for an instant
> at a quiet corner
> and remain there
> with . . . blind singers.

Nevertheless, to judge from Litvakov's October 1923 review article, Moscow's *Shtrom* was far better than the petit bourgeois magazine *Milgroym* (Pomegranate), published in Berlin. Although Litvakov still did not know where *Shtrom* was streaming, he was sure that it was not flowing backward. At the end of 1923, *Shtrom* had not become an organ of the Evsektsiia, but the gap between it and *Der emes* was diminishing: now *Shtrom* was "a good neighbor of the proletarian revolution." Hofshtein, Kushnirov, Godiner, and a number of other Shtromists began to write also for *Der emes*. As for *Milgroym*, Litvakov did not like any of its materials, including new works by Der Nister, David Bergelson, and Leyb Kvitko, who then lived as emigrants in Germany.

The following quote from an undated letter sheds light on the relations between the Shtromists and Litvakov. The letter was written by Dobrushin to Oislender, who was in Kiev, at the time when issue 4 of *Shtrom* was ready to be sent to print.

> I wish I had known before how difficult it would be [to publish] a journal in our miserable situation. Very often I feel regret and want to get rid of the whole business. I am not ashamed anymore. People will think that the reason is intellectual impotence, but in reality it is simply physical impossibility. It's too much work and thinking for one man, let alone [the fact] that I am torn between various jobs, lectures, the university and visits of beginning writers. . . . Today, Litvakov fixed me up in Minsk for two weeks. . . .
>
> The other day we had our usual scandal with Litvakov. Afterwards, he came to our [literary] Tuesday [i.e., regular literary evenings at the club Communist—G.E.] and, as usual, surrendered all his positions, until the next time.[69]

Litvakov was not a popular person. His colleagues in *Der emes*, however, respected him and knew that this small, bald, choleric workaholic could tell funny stories about himself. One such story was how he, then a young man, came to visit his fiancée, whose maid announced him with the words "*Something* came." Another story was about a young poet, whom Litvakov had criticized. The poet came to Litvakov's flat, swore at him, and then shut the door on his hand.[70]

Lenin's death in January 1924 gave impetus to his cult, which resulted in voluminous Leniniana. Thus, Josef Rabin's first publication (in *Der emes*) was his poem "Lenin," written under the influence of Vladimir Maiakovky's "Vladimir Ilyich Lenin."[71] Among the first works of Yiddish Leniniana was the 1924 collection of poems, stories, and articles published by the MAYWA.[72] Hofshtein was among the contributors. Soon, however, he was dethroned as "the first Yiddish classic." Moreover, he became a nonperson, an object of ostracism, having been one of the signatories of a memorandum backing Hebrew teaching. The "Hofshtein affair" was discussed during two meetings of the MAYWA, on 17 January and 3 February. In January, Hofshtein expressed his regret for signing the memorandum, but in February he "regretted his regret." The wordy, highly charged resolution of the February 1924 general meeting demonstrates the writers' fluency in the bombastic denunciatory style of Soviet Newspeak. For example,

> By creating for the bourgeoisie the possibility to accumulate material wealth, the NEP has also revived among the bourgeoisie the hope of restoring its political influence in various domains of life. Offensive actions—sometimes open, sometimes camouflaged—are undertaken against numerous achievements of the working class, both on the all-Union scale and among the Jews.
>
> Regarding the Jewish sector as the weakest one of the Soviet and [general] Communist front, the Jewish bourgeoisie persistently tries to organize an ideological and cultural breakthrough in this sector. [If it succeeds,] a tidal-wave of ideology will be released which is alien to the Jewish and non-Jewish working class and to Soviet rule. The Jewish bourgeoisie determinedly and systematically besieges Soviet institutions, capriciously arguing for abolition of the revolutionary achievements of Jewish workers. . . . Although defeated, the bourgeoisie does not halt its NEP-offensive. Moreover, new attacks are directed against the very basis of Communist education of Jewish workers, that is the principles of using their mother-tongue and of separation of religion from the school.

The resolution stipulated that Jewish writers or artists associated with such pronouncements had automatically excluded themselves from the milieu of both toilers and creative workers. In other words, Hofshtein had committed the ultimate sin of supporting Hebrew and, therefore, forfeited the right to be a member of the MAYWA. It is characteristic that this resolution was signed by people representing diverse cliques of Moscow Yiddish bohemians: the veteran of the circle, Charney; proletarian writers; editors of *Shtrom*; representatives of the Yiddish theater; and even the talented Yiddish and Hebrew poet Elishe Rodin fell into line.[73] By the end of February, Hofshtein had been disowned by all Soviet Yiddish dailies.[74]

Hofshtein claimed that the whole affair was based on distorted facts, that it was a direct result of the general atmosphere of intolerance and cruelty to anybody who had simply made an error.[75] In despair, he finally left the country. He stayed a short time in Berlin, then moved to Palestine. However, in 1926 he repented of his action and returned to the Soviet Union.

The "Hofshtein affair" signaled the final transformation of the MCYWA to MAYWA: from a circle of Jewish idealists seeking mutual professional and financial assistance to an organization demanding obedience to strict ideological rules. In its new form the association apparently became obsolete. In December 1924 it dissolved itself, with many of its members proceeding to form the Yiddish section of the Moscow Association of Proletarian Writers (MAPP). Symbolically, Charney, the most active member of the MCYWA/MAYWA, left the Soviet Union in May 1924. Apart from him, the last board of the MAYWA included Wieviorka, Dobrushin, Kharik, Godiner, and Kushnirov.[76] The "Hofshtein affair" exemplifies a distinct feature of Soviet Yiddish literary—as well as nonliterary—circles: their initiative in self-policing, which could seriously damage a Yiddish activist's career but which little affected the non-Yiddish circles. Characteristically, the other signatories of the memorandum backing Hebrew teaching were never seriously criticized outside the Yiddish circles. Also, in spite of the Jewish communists' anti-Hebrew rancor, the Habima was able to survive and obtain generous state subsidies because it was supported by influential individuals, such as Stanislavsky, Lunacharsky, Shalyapin, and Stalin.[77]

At the end of 1924 the last issue of *Shtrom* (numbers 5–6) was published. The journal desperately tried to obtain a state sponsorship. However, some of its antagonists, most probably Gildin, managed to ruin its chances of receiving a subsidy. The compromise with the *Ekran* group also turned out to be a short-lived truce. On 14 December, MAPP's Yiddish section organized a public "literary trial" of *Shtrom*. Public "literary trials" were popular in the early 1920s. The Moscow club Communist was a venue for many trials. On 11 October 1924, for instance, the journal *Yungvald* was on trial for four hours. The critic Isaac Nusinov acted as one of the "prosecutors," Kushnirov appeared as a "prosecution witness," and Litvakov was one of the "defendants." *Yungvald* was "accused" of such offenses as ineffective distribution of the journal, heavy style and superficiality of its material, and lack of young contributors. In fact, *Yungvald*'s circulation was relatively high—thirty-three hundred—but the "trial" demanded five thousand copies, as well as an increase in the number of realistic works.[78]

While the "trial" of *Yungvald* aimed at stimulating the further development of the periodical, the "trial" of *Shtrom* was more a funeral service. *Shtrom*, the only Yiddish literary journal in Russia in the early 1920s, was phased out in 1924, marking the end of the romantic period in Soviet Yiddish literature. This appeared to have been a result of centrifugal forces tearing apart the Shtromists. It would be a mistake, however, to see the situation as a conflict between the Soviet Yiddish establishment and a dissident group of writers. Rather, it was mainly a conflict of various aesthetic currents rather than a purely ideological disagreement. It would also be incorrect to create a "scale of Sovietism," arguing, say, that Gildin was more Soviet than Litvakov, or that Litvakov was more Soviet than Dobrushin. Essentially, they were equally Soviet, even if they saw their Sovietism rather differently: Gildin aimed for propaganda mass literature, Dobrushin for highbrow revolutionary literature, Litvakov for an impossible hybrid of both.

During the "trial" of *Shtrom,* Wieviorka, by that time the author of the first Soviet Yiddish play, *Honenkrey* (Cockcrow), published 1922, was the chairman and Taitsh the secretary of the "court," which also included three proletarian readers. The "prosecutors" were Kushnirov and Gildin, Shoikhet was the "counsel for the defense." The "defendants" were Dobrushin and Oislender, while the "witnesses" were Godiner, Kharik, Persov, Rosin, Daniel-Meierovich, and Shmuel Halkin. This cast reveals that Kushnirov had broken with the other editors and joined the militant group. He, indeed, became—together with Gildin, Wieviorka, Shoikhet, and Rabin—a member of the executive of MAPP's Yiddish section.

Everything seems to indicate that for Kushnirov and some other Shtromists the change was not an easy decision. Abchuk's 1934 chronicle includes minutes and some other documents of MAPP's Yiddish section. They show that, on 3 November, the organizing group of the section—Gildin, Shoikhet, Rabin, Taitsh, and Persov—decided to invite Kushnirov and a few other Shtromists to join the section. On 8 November the invitation still had not been accepted. A letter to Gildin, written on 24 November by Daniel-Meierovich and Godiner, explains their position: "We inform you that, in our opinion, the overwhelming majority of the Yiddish section's writers have failed to prove that they are able to create revolutionary works whose artistic level can match the achievements of the post-revolutionary Yiddish literature . . . therefore, we are not joining the Yiddish section of MAPP."

Nonetheless, Godiner and Kushnirov soon became members of the section. This happened, probably, as a result of Gildin's diminishing role in the section. It is illuminating to note that Gildin did not figure in the 1925 publication of the section, *Oktyabr* (October). He left Moscow soon after, spending the rest of his life in Ukraine. Apart from Gildin's departure, the situation generally became quieter and, significantly, more productive—especially compared with the first years after the Bolshevik Revolution when little artistic literature was written in Yiddish. In November 1924, Oislender complained to the American Yiddish poet H. Leivick, "We have very few writers here, still less writing, and extremely few published works. . . . Our writers are mainly young men of letters. Dobrushin, I, and Hofshtein . . . are already regarded as the older generation. Kushnirov, who began to write not long ago, is also not considered a young Moscow writer."[79]

In 1926, the critic Isaac Nusinov categorically argued that until 1924 there had been virtually no Yiddish literature written in the Soviet Union. More importantly, there were few readers. According to Nusinov, "nobody" was reading either *Shtrom* or *Der emes*—simply because the potential readers were busy with their physical survival. As a result, the authors of works, mostly poems, written during that time could not expect a mass readership. Hence, there were basically two types of contemporary Yiddish writing: the "industrial abstractions" by the proletarian writers and the "sound-and-color abstractions" by the "intellectual-formalist" Shtromists.[80] Charney echoed Nusinov's opinion. He accused the "Kievers" of bringing to Moscow lofty ideas about literary work and creating a "wall of China between the contemporary Yiddish writer and the emerging mass reader."[81] A Moscow Yiddish typesetter accused writers of having "civil war" with their readers. Yiddish printers joked that a Yiddish book usually had only three readers: the author, the censor, and the typesetter.[82] (In fact, the early 1920s saw a sharp crisis in Yiddish book printing all over the world;[83] this situation was later overcome mainly as a result of the development of secular Yiddish schooling.) In November 1924, during the First All-Soviet Congress of Jewish Cultural Activists, Lunacharsky criticized Soviet Yiddish culture for being constructed "downward" rather than "upward"; that is, for failing to maintain contact with the masses.

Instead of literary authors, the early postrevolutionary period produced a cadre of writers acculturated to Bolshevism and taught them to be dependant upon the support of state institutions. As a result, Yiddish authors of "elite literature," who never had and could not seriously expect any sizable readership, saw a real chance to become established, state-sponsored writers. The centralized system of publishers regulated the market. To be a successful writer meant to be recognized by the literature-planning authorities and critics rather than by mass readers. It is significant that dependence upon a committee's decision was part of the utopia created by a noncommunist writer, Kalman Zingman, in his 1918 sci-fi novel, *In the Future City of Edenya*.[84] By the mid-1920s, the majority of Soviet Yiddish writers were ready to move forward an Eden(ya) (Paradise), that is, to further institutionalize their literary life, especially since institutionalization implied generous sponsorship, albeit with strings attached. In reality, many modernist Yiddish writers were already dependent on Maecenas, such as the Vilna publisher Boris Kletzkin.

By the mid-1920s, Moscow was touting itself as the nucleus of the Soviet Yiddish literary world. However, some of the writers and journalists who had ripened in the Moscow environment began to feel cramped in the capital. In Moscow their works were subordinated to the immediate demands of the regime; elsewhere, however—notably in Ukraine and Belorussia— they were in high demand. As a result, the Moscow "Yavneh period" was over, and Kiev, Minsk, and Kharkov emerged as booming centers of Yiddish literature in the Soviet Union.

The emergence of the Yiddish section of MAPP had dramatically changed the atmosphere in Soviet Yiddish literary life. It was not a benevolent organization along the lines of the MCYWA or a salon literary group similar to the circle around the Demievka school. Instead, it was a militant, expansionist organization, fighting for its full hegemony in Soviet literature. At this juncture it was the *principle of organization* that divided those who joined MAPP and those who did not want to become minions in MAPP's propaganda factory. Shoikhet, Kushnirov, Gildin, Wieviorka, and Rabin complained, in a memorandum addressed to the Press Department of the Party's Central Committee, that the vast majority of Yiddish writers still preferred to group themselves according to their "creative" differences and did all they could to prevent an ideological division. This memorandum, written on 20 November 1924 and supported by the secretary of MAPP, Dmitrii Furmanov, was, in fact, an application for a party-sponsored Yiddish literary periodical.[85]

In 1925 two new Moscow Yiddish literary periodicals published their first issues: MAPP's *Oktyabr* and the more Kiev-Group–derived *Nayerd* (New land). The differences between them reflected the general Soviet literary controversies of the mid-1920s, most notably between dogmatic proletarian writers and their opponents, led by the Russian critic and editor Aleksandr Voronskii.[86] The *Nayerd* group gravitated toward Voronskii and his fellows. Yet the differences were apparently less intransigent than between the Russian counterparts, because Kharik, for instance, could combine his membership on the editorial board of *Nayerd* with the position as *Oktyabr*'s secretary.[87] In any case, both Yiddish writers' groups failed to continue their Moscow publications. New literary forums were launched outside Moscow: *Di royte velt* (Red world), published 1924–33 in Kharkov, and *Shtern* (Star), published 1925–41 in Minsk. To a considerable degree, *Di royte velt* was a continuation of *Nayerd,* whereas *Shtern* was a continuation of *Oktyabr.* Only a decade later were Moscow Yiddish writers allowed to produce their own periodical, *Sovetish* (Soviet), published 1934–41.

CHAPTER THREE

Offshore Soviet Literature

Comintern Writers

IN THE 1920S AND 1930S, hundreds of thousands of Jews outside Russia revered Moscow as the capital of the future just and democratic civilization. Such sympathetic sectors of the Jewish population were successfully targeted by local representatives of the Communist International, or Comintern, whose Moscow headquarters directed and coordinated pro-Soviet activities all over the world. Jewish sections, modeling the Evsektsiia, mushroomed at the Communist Parties formed under the influence of the Bolshevik Revolution. Those sections (often called by such names as bureaus) launched Yiddish periodicals, which became centers of gravitation for pro-Soviet literati.

In contrast to the predominantly anti-Soviet Russian émigré literary circles, pro-Soviet Yiddish writers represented a sizable part of the international world of Yiddish letters.[1] It is hardly an overstatement to define Yiddish literature of the 1920s as the most pro-Soviet literature in the world. The Ukrainian literature, which boasted an American and a Canadian branch of the proletarian literary organization Hart,[2] had, nevertheless, a much smaller number of pro-communist writers living outside the Soviet Union. One of the strongholds of Yiddish communist literati emerged in Argentina, where as early as 1919 a group of Jewish left-wingers, led by Menakhem Rosen, accepted the Comintern program. On 7 November 1923, or the fifth anniversary of the Bolshevik Revolution, Argentine Jewish communists launched their newspaper *Der royter shtern* (Red star). Later the communists began to publish a few journals, one of which, *Der yidisher poyer* (Jewish peasant), was dedicated to Jewish agricultural projects in the Soviet Union. PROCOR, the organization which agitated and raised money for Soviet projects, welcomed in Argentina the high-ranking Soviet Jewish functionary Yankel Levin and helped a couple hundred local enthusiasts to emigrate to the Soviet Union.[3] In 1931–32 two Yiddish writers, exiled from Argentina for their communist activities, settled in the Soviet Union: Hirsh Bloshtein and Moshe Goldshtein. In 1930 the proletarian writer Salvador Borzhes (Bezaleel Borodin) emigrated from Brazil to the Soviet Union and settled in Birobidzhan. Communist literati were active also in other Latin American countries. Thus, in Uruguay they grouped around the newspaper *Undzer fraynd* (Our friend), sponsored by the Soviet embassy and edited by Ber Halpern, later a Soviet writer (and a prisoner of the gulag).[4] A group of pro-Soviet Yiddishists was active in South Africa, where they controlled a few organizations, including the Yidisher Literarisher Fareyn (Yiddish literary union).[5]

Poland attracted many writers and journalists who were active in postrevolutionary Russia. Nakhman Meisel, for example, settled in Warsaw, where in 1924 he, together with Peretz Markish, I. J. Singer, and Melekh Ravitsh, founded the weekly *Literarishe bleter* (Literary papers), one of the most significant Yiddish literary and cultural periodicals of the 1920s and 1930s; Meisel was its editor until 1937. While Meisel also tried to replant in Warsaw the Culture League traditions—and the league proper[6]—Markish, reputedly the most good-looking man in the history of Yiddish letters, embodied the iconoclasm of Russia's Jewish literary world. Importantly, he did not leave Russia as a counterrevolutionary. Rather, he was not happy that the revolution had brought freedom only to selected strata of society. As a contributor to the Warsaw "journal for the new poetic and artistic expression," *Albatross,* edited by the neoprophetic poet Uri Zvi Greenberg, Markish helped create the group's manifesto, which inter alia stated, that Markish and his fellow poets only temporarily ran away from the revolution, hoping that it would ultimately bring freedom to the whole population.[7] In the meantime, Markish certainly influenced the pro-Soviet writers of the Linke shrayber-grupe (Left writers' group), who later published their periodical *Literarishe tribune* (Literary tribune).

On 20 April 1934, a pro-Soviet newspaper, *Fraynd* (Friend), was launched in Warsaw under the management of Boris Kletzkin, one of the best-known and most respected members of the Yiddish publishing world. This publication was the most successful attempt to issue a legal Yiddish newspaper sponsored by the underground Polish Communist Party. Edited by Alter Katsizne, the newspaper had among its active contributors such significant writers as Kadie Molodowsky and David Mitsmakher. Khaim Grade and Elkhonen Vogler from the literary group Yung Vilne (Young Vilna), uniting either members of the illegal Communist Party or its sympathizers, published some of their first works in *Fraynd*. David Sfard, the leader of the Linke shrayber-grupe, was the party's representative, given power to prescribe what the paper could or could not publish. *Fraynd* began to form a network of worker correspondents, but in eleven months' time the police banned the paper after revealing its communist links.[8]

In the early 1920s, Berlin emerged as a major address on the map of Yiddish culture, "a throbbing Yiddish cultural microcosmos which soon radiated to and influenced most of the Yiddish-speaking world."[9] During 1922–24, Germany, most notably Berlin, was second only to Poland as a Yiddish publishing center. The German-based publishing houses usually played the role of offshore enterprises, exporting their production all over the Yiddish-speaking world.[10]

In May 1921, a small Yiddish-Hebrew publishing house, Klal-farlag (Public publishing house), opened in Berlin at 73 Markgrafenstrasse. Its founder was the seasoned Yiddishist activist Zev-Wolf Latzki-Bertoldi, who played a prominent role in post-1917 Jewish life in Kiev, where for a short time he took on the Jewish Minister portfolio. He also co-owned the Yidish folks-farlag (Yiddish people's publishing house). In 1920, Latzki-Bertoldi decided to move his publishing enterprise to Berlin; before leaving Ukraine he invited Bergelson to follow him, especially because Bergelson had received an advance from the Yidish folks-farlag.[11] Kvitko and Der Nister were also invited to come to Berlin. In a sense, the latter followed the advice, once given to him by Peretz, to leave the provincial Kiev for St. Petersburg, Warsaw, or Berlin.[12] No doubt, desire to see the world outside Russia strongly motivated the Kiev writers' decision to move to Germany or Poland.

In the spring of 1921, Bergelson made his way to Berlin, where he found many of his friends and colleagues. The Romanisches Café, also known as the Rakhmonishes Kafe (Café of pity), became the hub of the Berlin Yiddishist circles with Bergelson acting as the café's central figure.[13] According to poet Abraham-Nokhum Stencl, a habitué of the café, it was "swamping with prominent Jewish cultural and communal activists, with well-known Jewish lawyers from Moscow and St. Petersburg, with famous Jewish writers from Kiev and Odessa, with flying about party leaders—from the extreme left to the most right currents; it was swamping like in a beehive." The writers who lived in poverty were supported by the American Joint Distribution Committee; Sholem Asch came to Berlin as the committee's representative. Still, some of the writers, such as the poet Moshe Kulbak, lived from hand to mouth. He came to Germany in 1920 to "breath in Europe"; he wanted to study at a university but ended up living for three years from casual earnings before returning to Vilna.[14]

To all appearances, once in Germany Bergelson had to find other outlets for his publications. Thus, his collected works appeared in 1922 under the imprint of the Wostok (East) publishing house rather than that of the Klal-farlag. According to Beti Kvitko, Leyb Kvitko's widow, all the promises given by Latzki-Bertoldi turned out to be nothing more than soap bubbles. In order to survive, one had to contribute to the "reactionary press," but Kvitko did not want to do this. As a result, Kvitko and Der Nister moved to Hamburg, where they labored for Soviet foreign trade enterprises.[15] Der Nister characterized Berlin as the city where "the Jewish intellectuals are left without roots, [and] rot one by one and collectively."[16] Yet Bergelson lived there quite comfortably, although he continued to write melancholic prose, including his stories set in Berlin.[17] Two years after arriving in Germany, the Bergelsons occupied a small garden house given to them by their well-off relatives. David Bergelson's son, Lev, remembers his father's routine of writing in the mornings and spending afternoons with his family or friends.[18] According to Nakhman Meisel, Bergelson loved Berlin and wanted to write a novel dedicated to the city.[19]

Bergelson published stories and essays in the "reactionary" New York daily *Forverts,* whose honoraria, paid in dollars, handsomely provided for writers based in inflation-ridden Germany. More pertinent than the *Forverts*'s ideological bias was the fact that Bergelson was much more popular than the newcomer Kvitko and even Der Nister, whose "élitist, uncompromising, and utopian art" was mostly ignored by contemporary critics outside the Kievers' camp.[20] Therefore Abraham Cahan, the dictatorial editor of the *Forverts,* was happy to employ Bergelson but did not need the other Kievers. Characteristically, in a 1922 *Forverts* advertisement, marking the quatercentenary of the newspaper, Bergelson's name, printed boldface, appeared among the names of such leading contributors as Sholem Asch, Yona Rosenfeld, David Einhorn, Edouard Bernstein, Karl Kautski, and Vladimir Medem.[21] In general, *Forverts* presented Bergelson as one of the best Yiddish writers.[22]

In 1922, Bergelson and Der Nister edited the literary section of the first issue of *Milgroym.* It was an unashamedly highbrow, excellently illustrated journal, which had Yiddish and Hebrew versions of each volume. After its first issue, however, the names of Bergelson and Der Nister disappeared from its editorial board, and in the third issue of the Moscow Yiddish journal

Shtrom they published a joint letter announcing their resignation from *Milgroym*. To all appearances, to continue editing the Berlin journal would mean spoiling relations with those of their friends who had regrouped around *Shtrom*. It is illuminating that in the same issue of *Shtrom* the artist Joseph Tchaikov characterized *Milgroym* as "a gravestone inscription," a "dead [publication,] created for dead people." Bergelson's only article published in *Milgroym* was a tribute to his Russian antecedents: he praised young Russian Yiddish poets and expressed his regret that non-Soviet criticism, "as if deliberately," ignored their literary achievements.

In 1924, Bergelson went to Bukovina and Bessarabia. It was a mission sponsored by the ORT Union.[23] Organized in 1880 in Russia as an organization for promoting vocational education among Jews, ORT was relaunched in post–World War I Berlin as a world organization with a multifaceted program of supporting Jewish workers, artisans, and peasants, most notably in Eastern Europe. Leading positions in ORT's Berlin headquarters were occupied by such committed Yiddishists—former activists of the Zionist-Socialist Party in Russia—as Nokhum Gergel and Aron Singalowsky. A remarkable person, who combined in himself a Russian Jewish intellectual and a Western-educated professional, Singalowsky, the secretary general of ORT, was close to Bergelson. In December 1924 both of them took part in founding in Berlin the Sholem Aleichem Club for Yiddishist intellectuals.[24] A former Territorialist, Singalowsky was carried away by projects of Soviet Jewish colonization. In general, by the mid-1920s many people in Bergelson's surroundings became enthusiasts of Soviet policy toward Jews, although their enthusiasm did not necessarily change their anti-Bolshevik stance.

We know about some of Bergelson's antipathies of that time. First, he ridiculed Yiddish writers from Poland and argued that Ukraine was the cradle of real talent. This particularist theory was jointly formulated by Bal-Makhshoves, Nokhum Shtif, and Bergelson, and was committed to paper by Bal-Makhshoves, who had been inspired by the impressive achievements of young Kiev writers.[25] Second, Bergelson disliked the Bund. True, he initially did not favor the Communists, either. One of his opponents in Berlin was the historian Moshe Lurye, a Communist and "the eyes of Moscow" in the local student union.[26] In 1926, however, Bergelson presented himself as a pro-Soviet writer. He became the central figure in the pro-Soviet journal *In shpan* (In harness), published by Boris Kletzkin. Apart from Bergelson, we find in the editorial group of *In shpan* the recent émigré from Moscow, Daniel

Charney, who settled in Berlin after he was rejected by the Ellis Island doctors. Singalowsky also participated in the group, but did not make public his involvement because he did not want to compromise his position at ORT.[27]

On 2 March, the Moscow Yiddish daily *Der emes* published Bergelson's penitential letter he had written on 24 February. Bergelson apologized for having sniped at Soviet Jewish Communists and expressed his desire to be a Soviet writer. He maintained, however, that he did not yet deserve to return to the Soviet Union and had to "suffer exile" for his anti-Soviet stance. In April he moved his literary allegiance from what was, in the Communist prism, the "yellow" *Forverts* to the "red" New York Communist daily *Frayhayt*.[28] On 29 May, *Der emes* began to serialize Bergelson's story "Hirsh Toker" (in later versions "Hershl Toker"); two other installments appeared on 30 May and 1 June. A footnote, published with the first installment, quoted Bergelson's letter to the editors of *Der emes* relating the causes of the rupture of his relations with the *Forverts*.

All these publications created the high-profile image of an émigré Yiddish fellow traveler, especially as Bergelson was the only Kiev Group writer who had established himself as an internationally renowned literary figure. The congenital recluse Der Nister, for instance, was not material for high-profile status. He always remained an outlandish writer, respected by aesthetes but little read by laymen.[29] Bergelson's case also cannot be compared with those of Markish and Kvitko, who always remained pro-Soviet although they lived abroad. Kvitko was a member of the German Communist Party, while Markish lived in Poland and toured there and in other countries as a revolutionary firebrand, a Yiddish answer to the Russian poet Vladimir Maiakovsky. As early as 1923, Kvitko, Der Nister, and the poet Moshe Lifshits published in Berlin a small anthology titled *Geyendik* (Going) with an imprint of the Moscow-based Jewish Section at the Soviet Commissariat (Ministry) of Education. By 1926, Bergelson too found himself in the gravitational field of Moscow.

✳   ✳   ✳

The strongest and largest phalanx of pro-Soviet Yiddish writers emerged in the United States. Functionaries at the Moscow headquarters of the World Revolution did not forget about the importance of the American Jewish Left and dispatched to them a few Comintern agents, recruited among the post-1917 returnees from the United States. The first of them, Sam Agursky, came in 1919, forcing his way through the Soviet-Polish front and working his passage to New York as a stoker at an English ship. Agursky could share his firsthand experience of building Jewish sections at the Bolshevik party, which later would be modeled by American communists.

Another Soviet envoy, the former Bundist Shakhne Epshtein (who had played a visible role in American Jewish social and literary life between 1909 and 1917), came to New York in the summer of 1921 to set up and edit the newspaper *Der emes*. It was the precursor of the longest-running Yiddish communist newspaper, *Frayhayt* (later *Morgn-frayhayt*), launched in April 1922.[30] Interestingly, this was the second American mission for Epshtein (who after his return to Russia in 1917 edited the Kiev Bundist daily *Folks-tsaytung*); he had earlier been sent to America as a representative of the Ukrainian Rada, but he had failed to go further than Odessa, being over-taken by the news that Symon Petliura had become Ukraine's new leader. In New York, Epshtein edited *Frayhayt* together with Moshe Olgin, who turned from Bundism to Communism after his 1920 trip to Moscow.[31] Epshtein and Olgin were reputable Marxist literary critics and envisaged their paper as a forum for the most trenchant writing of their time, thereby continuing the tradition of earlier Jewish socialist organs with strong bel-letristic departments.[32] In his 1900s and 1910s publications, Olgin, himself a minor prose writer, categorically rejected the notion of proletarian literature containing "only battle songs, military marches and popularization of eco-nomic and social issues." He argued that a proletarian, as a *homo sum,* needed "the whole literature."[33] With his Ph.D. in Russian literature de-fended at Columbia University, Olgin was unique for the Yiddish critical guild, which was dominated by people who lacked systematic schooling in the humanities.

Morris Winchevsky, the legendary Yiddish journalist and sweatshop poet, was also one of the founders of *Frayhayt*. His contribution to the inter-national labor movement was marked by a Soviet state pension and red car-pet receptions during his May 1925 visit to the Soviet Union. Earlier, in July 1924, a Winchevsky Week was organized in Moscow, with numerous cul-tural events dedicated to the veteran man of letters.[34] In the left-wing mythol-ogy he was regarded as the "grandfather" of Yiddish and Hebrew worker poetry, similar to Mendele's general grandfatherly position in modern Yid-dish and Hebrew literature.[35] *Frayhayt* also recruited such popular writers as Abraham Reisen, H. Leivick, Isaac Raboy, Lamed Shapiro, Menakhem Bor-eisha, Moshe-Leyb Halpern, Moshe Nadir, and David Bergelson.

Nadir later recalled his and Halpern's descent into Communism: "The

New York Yiddish daily press already was our—my and Moshe-Leyb's—debtor; it did not give us bread or wine, and we paid back . . . as we could pay. 'Look,' tried we to convince each other, 'a new newspaper, a poor one, with no money. It will perhaps attract the most original writers. In that case,' we decided, 'it is our duty to join the paper.' M. L. Halpern hesitated a while. I immediately became a *Frayhayt* staff member."[36] Some of "the most original writers" joined *Frayhayt* a few years later. Abraham Reisen, for instance, became a *Frayhayt* writer as late as 1926, after the newspaper had celebrated Reisen's fiftieth birthday and sorted out financial issues of his cooperation.[37]

Apart from the fellow travelers, there was a group of Yiddish literati outside the communist orbit who liked some aspects of Soviet Jewish life. The New York folkist-liberal daily *Der tog* (Day) had among its writers a few critical supporters of the Soviet Union. One of them, the popular novelist Joseph Opatoshu, visited the Soviet Union, where his works were published in Yiddish, Russian, and Ukrainian. The following fragment from the minutes (written in English) of the editors' meeting on 12 January 1927 illuminates his friendly relations with the *Frayhayt* editors: "Apotashau [Opatoshu] received a letter from [I. J.] Singer, who informed him that he would be willing to write for the Freiheit. M[elech] Epstein asked Apotashau to inform Singer, that he will take up this question at the meeting of the Editorial Committee and he [Singer] will be informed about it. M. Epstein recommends that Singer shall be employed as the Polish correspondent and also write stories for the Freiheit. The conditions shall be the same as with Bergelson."[38] Ultimately, Singer remained a *Forverts* writer.

Having a galaxy of literary lions, the *Frayhayt* editors did not pay much attention to young aspirants, mainly recent immigrants, who combined their toiling at sweatshops with literary efforts. Desperate to find an outlet for their works, these young writers eventually founded their own publication called *Yung kuznye* (Young smithy). Alexander (Yehushe) Pomerantz, Shlome Davidman, and Khaim Pet were the initiators of the new journal. They had much in common: *litvaks,* who arrived to America in the early 1920s, they had already published their first works and chosen for themselves a Yiddish teaching career—all three of them studied at the Workmen's Circle Teachers Seminar. In general, Yiddish teaching was the main refuge for poets and prose writers who could not, or did not want to, work as newspaper hacks.

The first number of the literary collection *Yung kuznye* came out in August 1924. Pomerantz was its editor, and Davidman and Pet were the members of the editorial board. The trio also led the Yung arbeter shrayber fareyn

(Young worker writers' association), which sponsored the publication. In his programmatic introduction Pomerantz presented the new publication as an attempt to overcome the crisis of the Yiddish book market, which he put down to the estrangement between the writer and the reader:

> Our publication, we think, will be *different*: it will mirror and present the milieu in which the American worker lives; it will mirror and present the experience brought from another side of the ocean, from the war, revolution, pogroms, etc., which form the context, the psychological background of the American Jewish youth's feeling and perception.
>
> Our writers will not be professional literati, producing literature by rote. Rather, they will be young workers, part of the young worker collective, its flesh and blood, who during the day work together in shops and in the evening slake their creative thirst by writing.

This program paraphrased ideas of the Russian Proletkult. In 1920, the Bolshevik leadership transformed the Proletkult into a governmental agency, and those who did not want to lose their independence formed a new association called Kuznitsa (Smithy).[39] It would be, however, wrong, to interpret the name of the New York publication as a sign of its allegiance to the splinter group. In reality, the Yiddish "young smiths" simply had got everything all mixed up. For them anything emanated from Soviet Russia was revolutionary and worthy of imitation.

Pomerantz's "New York," a fragment from his poetic circle of the same name, opens the collection. He sees the city as a sad place, with subway trains as catafalques, delivering live corpses to the factories and later bringing them back to their tenement graveyards. (New York as a cemetery was hardly a fresh image. For instance, in A. Liessin's "A Morning in New York" the city-dwellers stream "from their tenements to the shops" like "from their graves to the hells."[40]) While Pomerantz depicts the misery of working-class life, Kalman Hayzler concentrates on its positive aspects. Hayzler's poetic hero ("In Shop") loves his machines and the shop girl ("To a Shop Girl"), who is "a quiet adornment of my working world." Yosl Cohen (Kahn) ("Gypsy love"), however, is more interested in a whore called Josephine, whose life ended in a knife fight with Pedro.

Pomerantz was happy to announce that all 1,500 copies of issue 1 had been sold out. The other four issues were published in October 1924 (number 2), January (number 3), June (number 4), and December (number 5) 1925. In fact, *Yung kuznye* appeared also in October 1925, although in the form of the Yiddish department in the trilingual—Russian, English, and Yiddish—collection *Spartakus,* published by the American-based Russian proletarian literary group Rezets (Chisel). Beginning with issue 3 the editors naturalized the spelling of *Yung kuznye,* applying to the Hebrew lexical items the same phonetic and morphological rules as to any other words. This spelling, emancipating Yiddish from Hebrew, had been earlier introduced by a group of American avant-garde poets known as introspectivists, and by Soviet Yiddish reformers. The introspectivists' respelling was, essentially, a poetic Fronde, whereas the Soviet reform pursued ideological and practical ends. The "young smiths" were apparently motivated by ideological reasons, similar to the perception of Yekhiel Shraibman, a young Rumanian-based left-wing writer who debuted in the 1930s in the New York journal *Signal,* a successor of *Yung kuznye*: "the word *khaver* (comrade/friend) written with a 'khof,' an 'alef' and a doubled 'vov' [i.e., phonetically] stirred up the flight of my fancy. . . . From this erroneous unusual *khaver* came the breath of unlikeness and renewal. . . . In a sense, this new *khaver* epitomized both justice and romantic visions." [41] In America, however, naturalized spelling would never be implemented in the large-circulation *Frayhayt*; rather, it remained a trademark of Yiddish proletarian publications, which targeted a specific, well-defined audience.

Issue 3 of *Yung kuznye* opened with "An Appeal to the Proletarian and Revolutionary Writers," signed by the members of the International Bureau of Proletarian Literature (IBPL), which had been formed in Moscow in July 1924, during the Fifth Congress of the Comintern. It was the first attempt to create a literary phalanx of the international communist movement. The Russian department of *Spartacus* informed its readers about the IBPL and some efforts to form its American chapter. In particular, the IBPL saw its mission as popularizing the approved Soviet proletarian writers, such as Demian Bednyi, Andrei Bezymensky, and Aleksandr Fadeev. Characteristically, the loud-voiced poet of the revolution, Vladimir Maiakovsky, did not appear in this list of kosher authors, because his futurist Left Front of Arts (LEF) group was in opposition to the Soviet organizations of proletarian writers.

The New York proletarian writers, as Pomerantz would admit later, knew very little about the Soviet literary landscape.[42] In their vocabulary "proletarian" meant generically Soviet. Nonetheless, in 1925, in issue 5, Pomerantz wrote more specifically that *Yung kuznye* was moving in the direction of the LEF. Again, this choice had nothing to do with analyzing various literary manifestos and programs. To put it simply, in 1925, Maiakovsky

Jewish colonists in the Crimea, 1926–27

disembarked in New York hoping to win the American readers' hearts. In effect, he found a relatively limited number of admirers, mainly among young Russian Jews. (In America, Maiakovsky had become so closely linked with Jewish circles, in particular with communist supporters of the Jewish colonization in the Soviet Union, that after returning home he took part in making a documentary on Jewish settlements in the Crimea.)[43] *Frayhayt* published a few Yiddish translations of his poems, including one by Pomerantz. A link with futurism emerged in *Yung kuznye* earlier, in issue 2, when it reproduced two pictures by Miakovsky's teacher, David Burliuk, regarded as the father of Russian futurism. Presumably the editors met this Russian iconoclast, who had settled in New York in 1922.

Only a few rhymed poems appear in the *Yung kuznye* collections, which were otherwise dominated by vers libre. The "young smiths" did not introduce vers libre in Yiddish poetry. Rather, they discovered it, mainly through other, older American Yiddish poets. Introduction of free verse in Yiddish literature is usually associated with the introspectivists, led by Aron Glantz-Leyeles, Jacob Glatshtein, and N. B. Minkov, who published in 1919 an anthology *In zikh* (In oneself),[44] although a few free-verse poems occur also in M. Basin's 1917 anthology, *Five Hundred Years of Yiddish Poetry*. It is doubtful that all the *Yung kuznye* poets were directly influenced by American free-rhythm poetry, although the general atmosphere of the American poetic world certainly played an important role.[45] Ironically, Meir Grinshpan, the translator of Walt Whitman's poem published in issue 2 of *Yung kuznye,* lived in Kovno rather than in New York. Granted, it was not the first Yiddish translation of Whitman's poetry. Among his early Yiddish translators was the sweatshop poet Joseph Bovshover. L. Miler (Eliezer Meler), then a member of Di Yunge literary group, appeared as a Whitman translator in 1919 in the group's periodical *Shriftn*. In his 1921 book *Groyse neshomes* (Great souls), published in Dresden, Shmarayhu Gorelik, the pioneer of modern Yiddish literature (already discussed in relation to pre–World War I Vilna and Kiev), wrote about Whitman and translated excepts from his poems. "Young smiths" could read Whitman in Russian, too. In the 1900s, Whitman's poetry, hitherto forbidden in Russia, found its way to the Russian reader.[46]

Communist poets and critics regarded Whitman as a significant precursor of proletarian poetry.[47] Whitman was an important component in the "mixing bowl" of ideas, inspiring Mike Gold, one of the first American proletarian critics and writers, to write in 1921 the essay "Towards Proletarian Art."[48] Small wonder, then, that proletarian poets played the central role as Whitman's Yiddish translators. The translator of English poetry Abraham Asen published his translation of a poem by Whitman in issue 4 of *Yung kuznye*; a decade later, in 1934, his collection *25 lider fun Volt Vhitman* (Twenty-five poems of Walt Whitman) would come out in New York. L. Miler, a communist-affiliated poet from 1928, published in 1940 *Lider fun bukh bletlekh groz* (Poems from the book *Leaves of Grass*).

Among the "young smiths," Yosl Cohen was arguably the most Whitmanian poet. Characteristically, he was not a *greener*—he arrived to America in 1909 and even experienced local schooling. Cohen apparently was regarded as a rising literary star. In any case, his 1926 book *Shtot* (City) was the only poetic collection brought out under the Yung kuznye imprint. In his poetic introduction, "My Poems," Cohen explained his credo, which echoed the credo of *proste reyd* (simple speech) formulated in 1922 by Itsik Fefer, the leading proletarian poet in the Soviet Union:

> boyg ikh nit mayn kop in troyer
> vos iber mayn vort
> veln mentshn babrilnte zikh nit griblen

un di shtern kneytshn,
un di eybikayt loz ikh iber
tsu di, vos viln az zeyer vort
zol af farshtoybte politses
ayngemarenirt vern

I don't bow my head in sorrow
that over my word
bespectacled people won't sweat
and knit their brow,
and the eternity I leave
to those who want their word
to be on dusty shelves
preserved in marinade

Interestingly, only a small part of his collection contains ideological verses; these include "To Russia" ("Rusland, in mir zidt dos blut / fun dayne zin"—Russia, inside me the blood boils / of your sons); "Our Mud," dedicated to the Soviet Yiddish poet Izi Kharik; and "Not Now," which argues that contemporary life demands a poetic "groan" rather than highbrow poetry. He paints the New York landscape ("Dawn") through an ideological prism, with the Hudson River as "the sister of our Volga" (certainly an ideological simile for an immigrant from a Belorussian shtetl, situated about a thousand miles from "our Volga"). The vast majority of Cohen's poems, however, worship Eros rather than Communism. Granted, he tries to justify this topic in his poem "I am Coming to You" (echoing Whitman's "A Woman Waits for Me," in which the poet proclaimed, "sex contains all"):

durkh mir vet zikh tsien vayterdike energye
in di zin un tekhter, vos veln helfn
a nay lebn oysshmidt.

my energy will last further
in my sons and daughters who will help
forge a new life.

Nonetheless, in his poem "If I were," he admits that the main reason for his strong interest to women is simply that he is not a eunuch. In later times, erotica continued to inspire the proletarian poets. Another sample of erotic Yiddish proletarian poetry, Menke Katz's 1932 *Three Sisters,* was repub-

Itsik Fefer

lished in 1993 in a coffee-table format, with the eccentric imprint of Three Sisters Press, based at a remote Welsh farm.

In Harness

Bergelson's article "Three Centers," published in the first issue of *In shpan,* caused a sensation in literary circles. It is difficult to say who first raised the question of Yiddish literary centers. Oislender, for one, wrote as early as 1924 about decentralization—into Russian, American, and Polish centers—as a significant problem for the postclassical period in Yiddish literature.[49] In his article "Three Centers," Bergelson, however, was apparently alluding to the American Yiddish poet H. Leivick, who, during his 1925 visit to the Soviet Union, had spoken about the three competing centers and particularly emphasized the antagonism of Moscow.[50] Recognition of regional centers undermined the extraterritoriality of Yiddish literature and the cultural homogeneity of the Yiddish-speaking Ashkenazic Diaspora generally. Bergelson, based at the main crossroad between the centers, Berlin, went even further: he denied any future for Yiddish literature in America and Poland. For Bergelson, American Jewish allrightniks formed a pathetic milieu of people who wanted to assimilate but could not. Only those he called, in a collocation from Soviet-speak, "politically conscious workers" represented a link with quality Yiddish literature. In Poland, he argued, Yiddish was in the hands of Jewish orthodoxy and Zionism, while "sentimental Yiddishism" played a marginal role. Bergelson saw Polish Jewry as a gray mass, and in consequence thought it pointless to expect any important achievements from its local literati, including such talents as Sholem Asch and I. M. Weissenberg, because they were obliged to pander to the taste of their readership. All in all, concluded Bergelson, the Soviet Union remained the only place where Yiddish literature had a future.

In the same issue of *In shpan*, Alexander Khashin (Zvi Averbukh) published his article "Inflation in Yiddish Literature." Khashin was a seasoned journalist and political activist (one of the founders of the Labor Zionist movement), who would later return to Russia after years abroad to work as an editor of the Moscow daily *Der emes*. The main antihero of his article was Markish, Bergelson's old bugbear, whom Khashin characterized as a pseudo-revolutionary and an idle shouter. The squabble got ugly after Markish retaliated in Warsaw's *Literarishe bleter*: he compared Bergelson to a former beauty who had exhausted all her charms and was now forced to offer her girlfriends' services as well.[51] Markish pinpointed the Achilles' heel of the journal: Bergelson's failure to attract a representative team of contributors. Indeed, the list of contributors to Markish's own literary enterprise—the avant-garde collections *Khalyastre* (Gang), published 1922 and 1924—outshone *In shpan*.[52]

Of course, Markish was not the only one who attacked Bergelson and his new publication. In the world of Yiddish letters, where people were sharply divided along ideological lines, Bergelson's reorientation ignited sharp confrontation among critics of adverse camps. On 20 June 1926, because of a remarkable concurrence of editorial decisions, two reviews appeared in two dailies separated both geographically and ideologically: Litvakov published an article in Moscow's *Der emes* and Niger published an open letter in New York's *Der tog*. Litvakov characterized *In shpan* as a pointless and even harmful exercise: neither Soviet nor pro-Soviet readerships needed it because they already had their own periodicals. Niger's letter was imbued more with regret than with invective. He appealed to Bergelson not to tie himself down to communist ideology. He preferred to see Yiddish literature as one large coherent body and rejected the very idea of class literature, especially because it hindered efforts to transform Yiddish literature from a folk into a national literature.[53] In other words, Niger remained true to his old principles of Jewish nation-building, whereas Litvakov, previously a like-minded Yiddishist, had already been transmogrified into a constructor of Yiddish proletarian culture.

Bergelson, however, appeared impervious to Niger's criticism. In his tart response,[54] Bergelson drew a line between his past, given over to the "art of tedium and decadence," and his present, dedicated to Jewish life in the Soviet Union. He repeated his conviction that he was a committed realist, in particular his belief that contemporary life was the only breeding ground for literature. One year before, in the autumn of 1925, while lecturing in Riga, he had argued that realism distinguished Yiddish literature from Hebrew literature; as exceptions to the rule he singled out the Yiddish poet Moshe Kulbak and the Hebrew poet Saul Tchernichowsky.[55] One could not write about a life that did not exist. In 1918, he related, he had started to publish in the Kiev *Eygns* his prose work *In fartunklte teg* (During darkened days), conceived by him as the beginning of a vast canvas about the life of the Jewish upper and middle classes in Russia. The revolution, however, had wiped away these classes and he could thus not continue this work. In contemporary life, he insisted, he saw the working masses as the only safeguard for the survival of Yiddish literature. The gulf between the Jewish upper class and the masses was even wider than the gulf between different nations, particularly because the rich usually despised Yiddish. The Yiddish-speaking petite bourgeoisie was satisfied with newspapers and generally did not read quality books, apart from those people who were forced to give up commerce, become productive members of society, and, as such, merge with the working masses—as was happening to artisans, peasants, and poor tradesmen in the Soviet Union. The working class was the only bearer of a new, secular Jewish wholeness, which had replaced that religious wholeness of traditional Jews rejected by Bergelson and his kind. In the West, the Yiddish establishment wanted to ignore this reality. Unity between intellectuals and workers existed only in the Soviet Union, and Bergelson proclaimed his desire to see his works numbered among the works of proletarian Soviet writers.

Bergelson quite clearly understood that he had to revise his vision of realism, because as a pro-Soviet writer he was expected to be an apologist for the new society.

Of course, this deficiency of [Soviet] literature is very palpable, since dithyrambs are not the purpose of belles-lettres. On the contrary, the greatest literary works usually became remarkable because their creators were unhappy, spiritually resistant people who rebelled against the general surrounding contentment. None the less, in the name of the new life that we have to allow to come into bloom, belles-lettres in Russia temporarily fold their fighting arms. So, what is wrong about this? Let the new life grow, become strong and more or less quiet, then there will be possibilities for a new, stronger literature.[56]

In other words, by the beginning of 1926, Bergelson had already subscribed to the idea that truth could be postponed. Some six years later this peculiar kind of realism would be called "socialist realism." [57] Bergelson's pronouncements sound like a paraphrase of Litvakov's programmatic article, "Legacy and Hegemony," in which Litvakov claimed the hegemony of Soviet Yiddish literature. Their respective timing, too, linked Litvakov's publication to that of Bergelson—the former was serialized in Der emes on 14, 16, 21, and 23 February 1926, while the latter appeared in April 1926.

Moscow critics felt that Bergelson did indeed have the potential to become a Soviet writer. As early as 1922, Dobrushin hailed Bergelson as the pioneer of "the constructive way" in Yiddish literature. By literary constructivism, Dobrushin meant rejection of the writer's personality and of all writings based on what the author had "heard-seen-experienced." Instead, the constructive writer was obliged to process objective reality, combining the intellect of a "sober" constructor with the feelings of a "dreamy" artist.[58] Such theories, interpreting art as a constituent of the historically inevitable transformation of society rather than as a representation of life, became part of Russian avant-garde prolegomena to socialist realism.[59]

Both issues of In shpan contained fragments of Bergelson's new novel, Mides-hadin (Severe judgement), which finally appeared in 1929 as a separate book under the imprint of the Vilna Kletzkin publishing house and, in the same year, of the Kiev Culture League. According to Yakov Shternberg, an expert on Bergelson's life and work, the writer had by then "cut his impressionist vein" and "was moving, page by page, to obvious tendentiousness." [60] It seems clear that Mides-hadin was written under the influence of Ilya Ehrenburg's The Life and Downfall of Nikolai Kurbov, which was published in Berlin in 1923.[61] The epigraph to Ehrenburg's novel—$x = -(p/2) \pm \sqrt{[(p^2/4) - q]}$— underlined the idea that the revolution was product of historical forces, predetermined like the roots of the quadratic equation and foreseen in the Marxist theory of dialectical materialism.[62] Like Ehrenburg's Kurbov, Bergelson's protagonist, Filipov, is a Soviet security officer. Both Kurbov and Filipov are unstable personalities. In fact, they are hardly human at all. They represent the merciless power that eliminates enemies of the revolution. Both must perish when they discover some human feelings in themselves. Bergelson could see Kurbov-Filipov's mission as a communist realization of God's redemption: the first messiah, Ben Joseph, was doomed to die after winning the purifying, final war, and only then the second messiah, Ben David, would come to bring the everlasting peace.[63] In *Mides-hadin,* the generation of the Filipovs has replacements: such people as Pinke Vayl, a young Jew from Kiev, whom Bergelson portrays with great warmth. In this succession of generations, when normal people replace the Kurbov-Filipovs, Bergelson apparently found an explanation for, and a justification of, the Bolsheviks' cruelties. All in all, *Mides-hadin* proclaimed Bergelson's acceptance of the Soviet system as the only "satisfactory answer to the desire for order in the universe." [64]

In 1926, Bergelson visited the Soviet Union. On 6 August, *Der emes* tersely announced that Bergelson had arrived the day before and that, after a few days in Moscow, he would go to the Crimea. Indeed, on 16 August (also according to information published in *Der emes*) he left for the Crimea. A month later, on 18 September 1926, he received a mixed reception at the Moscow Yiddish club Communist, the venue of many fierce debates. An audience of eight hundred people gathered to see the literary celebrity. The meeting was chaired by Shmuel Godiner, the leading Yiddish prose writer of the younger Soviet generation. Litvakov was the main speaker. Everybody knew that Litvakov was chronically moody, irate, and often more ready to make enemies than to make friends. The audience was consequently astonished when he finished his introduction without spelling out any direct accusations. Instead, he praised Bergelson's "rising" above being a contributor to *Forverts,* but stressed that there were to be no half-measures in changing political orientation: now Bergelson had to follow the Communist line rather than simply the Soviet line. Litvakov drew a parallel between Bergelson and Aleksei Tolstoy, the Russian prose writer who had returned from abroad. True, he noted that Bergelson continued to write in the genre of "entertaining, light literature." The revolution, however, had changed everything, and one of the results of these changes was that Soviet writers had begun to create literature for future generations rather than writing for entertainment. Soviet writers, who were creating new forms and imageries, could therefore not be as prolific as their foreign counterparts. Litvakov's implied disparagement of the nature of his work apparently hurt Bergelson more than any ideological censure. He reminded Litvakov that he was an established and experienced writer of impressionist prose that was neither entertaining nor light, and that he also labored hard over every one of his writings. He accused Litvakov of creating simplistic theories and of trying to enforce their conformity without regard to writers' individualities.

A few writers and activists took part in the self-purging discussion that followed. Thus, Shmuel Palatnik, a Soviet Jewish educator, explained, "If you take our side, you also have to accept some instructions. We say this seriously and openly." Bergelson was attacked by Khaim Gildin, who ridiculed the émigré's stories about the civil war. Gildin recalled how he had appealed to Bergelson in 1917, when they were both in Odessa, to write for the masses, but at that time Bergelson had followed Khaim Nakhman Bialik's advice to ignore Gildin's appeal. Dobrushin, the former Kiev Yiddishist who had already been assimilated into the Soviet environment, obviously wanted to clear the air. He reassured the audience that Bergelson had no illusions about becoming an apprentice Soviet writer, particularly because Soviet writers had to stand head and shoulders above their European colleagues. In any case, the bottom line of the meeting was "Bergelson is ours!" [65]

It is not surprising that Bergelson did not walk out when the Moscow hosts began to read him a lecture. He was ready to be reprimanded. He even joked that on the eve of the meeting he spent time before a mirror, swearing at himself in order to be ready for the inevitable grilling. He saw himself as a prodigal son who had to be rebuked before being allowed to return to the bosom of the family. Markish later described the ritualistic character of such public "welcomes." [66] The second half of the 1920s was generally marked by a record number of returnees and visitors; some of them settled in the Soviet Union, while others began seriously to consider moving to a country that held out such alluring possibilities for Yiddish culture. Kvitko returned in 1925, and Der Nister and Markish in 1926, when Markish was writing about Russian poets who "steal through the border, from the holy cross towards the hammer and sickle." [67] Hirsh Bloshtein of Buenos Aires, who was to settle in the Soviet Union in 1931, wrote a poem in 1926 about those people who dreamt of becoming Soviet citizens. In Bloshtein's allegory, they were like nomads who, exhausted from roaming in dark capitalist countries, reach out to the ever-sunny Soviet Union.[68] In fact, at that time to be pro-Soviet meant to be almost mainstream. Moshe Nadir, a popular American Yiddish writer, argued during his 1926 visit to Kiev that the Soviet Union rather than the United States was the country of real freedom.[69]

Truth to tell, in the mid-1920s the Soviet Union could indeed look like an exciting place. The NEP had transformed the country. In 1926, Russia had achieved its pre–World War I GNP, and an average worker's salary equaled or even exceeded the prewar level.[70] It is illuminating that in 1926 thousands of Russians living in the United States were contemplating returning to their homeland.[71] The resolution on literature adopted by the Central Committee of the Soviet Communist Party on 18 June 1925 called for tactful treatment of fellow travelers and refused to allow any literary organization, including the militant proletarian coteries, to speak in the name of the party.[72] The Moscow *Pravda* published articles that demonstrated consideration for fellow travelers and condemned the proletarian writers' demand for hegemony in literature; it was explained that the party was not going to delegate its hegemony to any other agencies.[73] Although Litvakov gave the impression of embodying the general line in Yiddish literature, in reality he represented only one of several cliques, and literati in Ukraine and Belorussia often ignored or even ridiculed his judgments.

For Yiddish culture-bearers—and Jewish activists generally—the Soviet Union held a special appeal as the country where the government and various foreign agencies sponsored numerous promising projects, most notably the project of establishing a Jewish territorial unit in the Crimea. This campaign was supported by Mikhail Kalinin, the titular head of the state, who spoke of the Committee for the Rural Placement of Jewish Laborers (KOMZET), founded in August 1924, as some kind of Soviet Jewish government.[74] Moshe Katz, a former editor of the Kiev *Naye tsayt* and now a leading journalist of the New York *Frayhayt* (he would later work in the Soviet Union and again return to America), reported in a memorandum, written in September 1926 for the Soviet Foreign Office, "no other campaign of the Soviet government have made there [in the United States] such an exceptionally good impression as it does the land settlement of Jews."[75] Litvakov wrote about the Crimea as "our Palestine," stressing that the Jordan could not be compared with the Dnieper, nor were the friendly Crimean Moslems (Tartars) like the hostile Palestine Arabs.[76] Indeed, some Jews even emigrated from Palestine to try their luck in the Crimea; in 1925, for instance, twenty-five emigrant families founded a commune called Vojo Nova ("New Way" in Esperanto), situated not far from the town of Evpatoriia.[77] Emigrants from Palestine continued to come during the 1920s. One of them, Shira Gorshman, later a popular Yiddish story-writer, settled in Vojo Nova in 1929.

Interestingly, the Palestinian project proper was treated at that time rather charitably by Soviet leaders. In 1925, Feliks Dzerzhinsky, the formidable head of the Soviet secret police, praised the Zionist program;[78] the same year Petr Smidovich, the chairman of KOMZET, stated that he had nothing against creating a home for Jews in Palestine, provided Zionists did not meddle in Soviet projects.[79] The Halutz (Pioneer) Zionist youth organization was allowed to plod along and from time to time get permissions to emigrate to Palestine. It can hardly be coincidental that in 1925, Boris Pilnyak, then one of the most widely read of Soviet Russian writers, published his *Story about Springs and Clay*, a portrayal of the *aliyah* from the early Soviet Union. It seems that the story was based on a tourist trip, undertaken by Mikhail Koltsov (Friedland), one of the most popular Soviet journalists.[80] Bergelson's felicitous Yiddish translation of this story appeared in the second (and last) issue of *In shpan* and was serialized in the *Frayhayt* (26–30 September 1925).

The establishment of a Jewish territorial unit would bring the Jews into conformity with Stalin's definition of a nation. Soviet Jewish territorialism found a theoretician in the person of Maria Frumkin, alias "Esther," a legendary leader of the Bund turned Communist apparatchik. In her speech to the 1926 All-Soviet Conference of the Jewish Sections of the Communist Party, she presented a strategy of sorts, but hardly a doctrine, for future Soviet Jewish activities. According to her dual program, all-but-certain assimilation was prepared for the proletarians and other productive cohorts of the Jewish population, whereas some part of the nonproductive elements who could not eke out a living in the shtetls should be settled in rural areas, where they would eventually consolidate into a full-blooded socialist Jewish nation.[81] The Soviet president, Mikhail Kalinin, also appealed to Soviet Jews to settle in the Crimea and other colonies in order to preserve the Jewish nation.[82]

Bergelson's first piece from Moscow to be published in the *Frayhayt* was "On the Threshold of 'This World' and the 'Other World' "[83]—sketches about the headquarters of the Organization for the Rural Placement of Jewish Laborers (OZET), an ostensibly nongovernmental twin of the KOMZET. One of Bergelson's characters, a former Zionist activist, had failed to prosper in Palestine, where the land had swallowed his money "like an alms-box," and he had returned to become a peasant in the Soviet Union. Excitement about Moscow spills out from Bergelson's other reports.[84] He is happy to find himself in the vibrant, mercurial Moscow of the NEP, the chief city of the only country in the world that is free of the sadist called CAPITAL. It is a city that lives according to its own time, because "the big invisible world-

Boris Pilnyak

clock, a most modern, reliable and correct one," hangs somewhere above Moscow and "shows the time of tomorrow and the day after tomorrow—the time of the future." Moscow stands in stark contrast to the cities of Europe, where "people walk with injured bodies under smoothed clothes, with fettered movements and with fettered glances; they feel that the evil boss's crooked, sadistic eye follows them at every turn and silently dictates how they have to look and feel." Moscow, Bergelson writes, is a place without a Big Brother: people move about in liberty, they look around freely, they almost fly—because they know that nobody is following them. In general, the Soviet capital emerges as the City of the Sun, where people never grow old. Bergelson quotes a Moscow Communist who argues that he is four times sixteen rather than sixty-four years old.

Granted, Bergelson ends his Panglossian article with a gripe, but he does it only for the sake of "satisfying his colleague Niger," as he puts it: the visiting writer mentions a few shortcomings of Soviet urban life, particularly the difficult housing conditions of Moscow residents. However, he cheekily explains to Niger that Muscovites do not feel cooped up in their overcrowded flats because they spend very little time at home: they are happy to be at their workplaces—the temples of free work. In a sense, Bergelson was right. A whole generation, which experienced the upheavals of the wars and revolutions, had not learned to construct and enjoy a private life, instead seeking public excitements in default of a habit of private fulfillment.

In his account of the Crimean colonies, Bergelson distinguishes three groups of pioneers of the Crimean Jewish colonization: (1) agronomists and physicians, whom he describes as a self-sacrificing group of people, although he finds in them some residual traits of czarist intellectuals, particularly evident in their reluctance to speak the language of common people; (2) local Crimean Jews who—according to Bergelson—are like "regular" Jews save for their bad Yiddish (some of them were, in fact, also resent settlers who had started to establish agricultural settlements even before the centralized campaign and were often unhappy about KOMZET/OZET functionaries meddling in their affairs); and (3) *halutzim,* who have organized a few communes in the Crimea to train young people before dispatching them to the kibbutzim in Palestine. Bergelson visits two of the communes, Tel Hai and Mishmar.

Tel Hai was the largest commune created by Zionist youth in the Crimea. Its name commemorated the founder of the Halutz movement, Joseph Trumpeldor, who met with a tragic death while defending the Galilee settlement of Tel Hai in 1920. Bergelson tried to persuade the young people to take part in the Evsektsiia's Crimea project rather than to stack "ricks that wink[ed] at Zion." [85] Although the *halutzim* have achieved impressive agricultural results, Bergelson's pen is charged with bile when he writes about these "children of bourgeoisie," for whom the Crimea is only a staging post so that they are not interested in helping the new Soviet Jewish colonies. However, he reserves his most venomous lines for the Jewish settlers who had come from shtetls: "The land around is a virgin from the distant past, and the world around too seems to be virgin and ancient. This world is for a wild, hairy man who will come to plough the land. On the other hand, it is perhaps a perfect place for an uprooted Jewish shopkeeper from a ruined shtetl, because nowadays, against the backdrop of the new construction in the Soviet Union, these Jewish shopkeepers look wild, hairy and ancient." [86]

More sober views were penned by other foreigners who visited the Soviet Union in 1926. Thus, the German critic Walter Benjamin wrote about the housing conditions in Moscow: "People can bear to exist in [such accommodation] because they are estranged from it by their way of life; their dwelling place is the office, the club, the street." [87] According to Benjamin, "[m]ore quickly than Moscow itself, one learns to see Berlin through

Moscow."[88] Apparently, Bergelson felt much more at home in the noisy
crowds of dirty Moscow streets than in Berlin's clean quietness. I. J. Singer,
who toured the Soviet Union in 1926, praised the Soviet capital—notwith-
standing its numerous homeless waifs, prostitutes, and drunkards. He did
not find Moscow a place without Big Brother, however; on the contrary,
Singer noted that the secret police's "eyes" were everywhere. Singer's con-
trasting report about the *halutzim* completely contradicted Bergelson's portrayal: Tel Hai, Singer thought, was the best Crimean Jewish agricultural
settlement he had seen. Amusingly, Singer was particularly impressed by the
halutzim's achievements in pig-breeding.[89] (A former member of the commune reminisced later how their pig-breeders had been awarded the first
prize at the all-Crimean agricultural exhibition, where their unusually large
and fecund Yorkshire pigs, presented to them by the Joint, became an object
of general attention.[90]) Interestingly, a certain Shubin from the Soviet Foreign Office's Department of Press and Information reported to Evsektsiia
that the Warsaw-based *Haynt* did not want to publish Singer's articles because they were too favorable toward the Soviet regime.[91]

In 1926, Aron Singalowsky spent time in the Soviet Union and also reported enthusiastically about the unprecedented scale of the Jewish colonization. In particular, he condemned the position of those who were against
supporting Soviet Jewish projects, arguing that "the Soviet government de-
serves to have rickety [Jewish] citizens."[92] In 1927, Abraham Cahan, the editor of *Forverts,* visited the Soviet Union. He also did not see Soviet Jewish
colonization as a viable nation-building project. Rather, he endorsed the foreign Jewish charities' support of the colonies in Ukraine and the Crimea, de-
scribing the colonists as "martyrs" of postrevolutionary social and economic
developments.[93]

Bergelson's visit to the Soviet Union had surprisingly little impact on the
degree of precision informing his portrayal of Soviet life. This deficiency is
particularly striking because Bergelson had hitherto paid close attention to
telling details about people's way of life. His prose set in Soviet surroundings
does not contain a fraction of the detailed recreation of everyday life that is
characteristic of many works by other Soviet writers, for instance Abraham
Abchuk.[94] Perhaps to compensate for his lack of knowledge about real Soviet
surroundings, Bergelson demonstrated a penchant for symbols, or the
"naked forms" he had condemned in 1919: for example, the red flag under
the head of the dying Soviet undercover agent as a symbol of the Bolsheviks'
invincibility ("Hershl Toker"), or two characters each symbolizing one of the

two alternatives open to survivors of the civil war pogroms—either to join the Bolsheviks or to commit suicide ("Birth").[95]

The scandal provoked by Bergelson's political reorientation greatly boosted his name and fame. His popularity grew, especially in the pro-Soviet camp all over the world. His notion of "Three Centers" was taken up by other writers. In October 1926, for instance, Borukh Glazman, a popular American Yiddish prose writer, spoke about "New York–Warsaw–Moscow" during an evening at the New York Central Opera House; the evening, advertised in *Frayhayt*, was dedicated to Glazman's forthcoming visit to the Soviet Union. During 1928–30, Bergelson's collected works were published in eight volumes under the imprint of Vilna's Kletzkin publishing house. His books—in Yiddish, Russian, and Ukrainian—came out in the Soviet Union as well.

Bergelson's name began to appear as a separate entry in other bio-bibliographical handbooks—not only in Zalman Reisen's *Lexicon of Yiddish Literature, Press, and Philology*.[96] A separate entry on Bergelson was included in the German *Encyclopaedia Judaica*.[97] Isaac Nusinov, who occupied leading positions in both general Soviet and particular Yiddish literary history and criticism, wrote the entry on Bergelson for the first *Soviet Encyclopaedia* (1927), highlighting two events associated with Bergelson's name: first, the introduction of impressionism as part of Yiddish literature and, second, the displacement of the Yiddish writers of Poland and Lithuania who lost their leading positions ("hegemony") to Yiddish writers from Ukraine.[98] In 1930, Nusinov extended this assertion in the *Literary Encyclopaedia*, claiming that Bergelson had moved the leadership of Yiddish letters "from Ukraine, and later [to] the USSR." Nusinov also defined Bergelson as a "continuer of Flaubert's traditions."[99] Gustave Flaubert, the founder of literary impressionism, was generally favored by Soviet theorists of proletarian literature and represented a much more respectable lineage than the controversial Hamsun. According to Nusinov, Bergelson served as the interface between two epochs in Yiddish literature—before and after 1917—and his style became dominant, forcing out the style of Sholem Asch.[100] To all appearances, Bergelson's style influenced almost all Soviet Yiddish prose writers.[101]

Bergelson lectured in various countries. In 1929 he spent six months in America as a guest of the *Frayhayt*. The same year he celebrated two decades of literary activity, dating from the first publication of *Arum vokzal*. Nakhman Meisel dedicated a whole issue of *Literarishe bleter* (number 37) to Bergelson. At that time, too, Bergelson began work on a long novel, later

Nakhman Meisel

known as *Bam Dnyeper* (On the Dnieper), about a man of his own generation. The jubilee issue of *Literarishe bleter* published a chapter from its first
volume, *Penek*. However, Meisel failed to attract prominent contributors of
other material for this commemorative issue. In the end, Peretz Hirshbein
was the only contributor with a top name in Yiddish literature.

In 1929, Bergelson emerged as a playwright. He always liked theater and
even worked briefly as the literary director of the Culture League's theater
school. We know also that during his American tour he starred in an amateur
performance of his story "Bam telefon" (At the telephone), which he had
adapted as a play.[102] For his dramatic debut in 1929, he had reworked one of
his first stories, "The Deaf Man," into a play, *Oybn un untn* (On the top and
at the bottom), later known as *Broytmil* (The flour mill). It is hardly a coincidence that Mikhail Rafalsky, Bergelson's old friend from Kiev and now the
director of the Belorussian Yiddish theater, was the first producer of the play.
Rafalsky, who in his youth had dabbled in literature, was the first to translate
"The Deaf Man" into Russian. In the stage version, the plot of this story un-

derwent many changes in order to highlight the class struggle between the "top" and "bottom" characters. Meisel, who heard Bergelson read the play in Berlin, was among the first to recognize one of the symptomatic problems of Bergelson's writing—he was much more successful in portraying characters from the "top" than from the "bottom." [103]

In August of the same year, after the Soviet Union and the Comintern had sided with the Arabs following the Arab riots in Palestine, Bergelson, like any other Jewish left-winger, had to reconsider his stand. Abraham Reisen, H. Leivick, and a few other leading writers resigned from the *Frayhayt*;[104] Bergelson remained among its contributors.

In 1930, Bergelson went to Warsaw. On the eve of his trip, Meisel explained the importance of Bergelson's first visit to Warsaw after twenty years, interpreting it as an indication that Warsaw was no longer regarded merely as the center of cheap book production. Two years earlier, during his visit to Berlin, Meisel also spoke about the striking, positive changes in Polish Jewish cultural life.[105] Now he expressed the hope that Bergelson would like Poland and that, coupled with Bergelson's recent American experience, this visit would reinforce his old friend's position as a writer for the whole Yiddish-speaking world. Meisel stressed how important it was to keep the integrity (in other words the "extraterritoriality") of Yiddish literature.[106]

Bergelson, however, was not prepared to adapt his position to Meisel's carefully worded overture. In his lecture, given on 3 July, he again used a horological allegory, comparing Yiddish literature in America and Poland with beautiful clocks that had no hands; as a result they did not show time. (Markish, according to another Bergelson allegory, was like a clock with a broken striking mechanism—it struck so many times that one never knew the real time.[107]) As the main deficiency of contemporary Yiddish writings in the West, Bergelson singled out its Zionist character. Speaking about the two non-Soviet Yiddish centers, he indulged in generalization and provocative judgments, overemphasizing the role of cheap literary production on their book markets. The understanding of literary creativity he expressed represented a cross between the postulates of Soviet theorists of proletarian literature and Litvakov's theory of the "creative vacuum" (*puster kholel*). According to Litvakov, this vacuum divided contemporary Yiddish writers from Mendele, Sholem Aleichem, and Peretz, who were regarded as Yiddish classics.[108] In Bergelson's words, "the masses create everything—the language, imagery and motifs, whereas the writer, a representative of the masses, embodies all these in a literary work." The three classics were pioneers who had lived side by side with the masses. Unfortunately, the writers who came after this classic triumvirate "did not give a damn" about the masses. Hardly an original literary theoretician, Bergelson apparently based these views also on Oislender's treatise, *Main Features of Yiddish Realism,* written in 1916–18. According to Oislender, Yiddish classic literature emerged as an organic continuation of oral folk literature.[109] Bergelson's overall conclusion remained the same as it had been in 1926: the Soviet Union was the only place where the vacuum between tradition and modernity could be successfully filled.[110] Meisel was obviously disappointed by his old friend's blind pro-Sovietism. His words sounded uncannily prescient when he warned Bergelson not to play with fire because the Soviet Yiddish literary experiment might come to a tragic end.[111]

In the fall of 1931, Bergelson once again went to the Soviet Union, where he spent three months. This time, the Moscow Yiddish club Communist and the Moscow State Yiddish Theater jointly organized a grand reception dedicated to Bergelson. Yet Litvakov could not stop himself from having a sly dig at the guest, recalling Bergelson's sin of not condemning in 1929 the American writers who left *Morgn-frayhayt.* To all appearances, however, this action did not put Bergelson out of humor, especially as it was not a serious sin, because he then remained a *Morgn-frayhayt* writer and now announced his desire to move in the Soviet Union. Markish, by that time already a seasoned returnee, warned Bergelson that it would be hard to get used to a Soviet writer's existence, which implied an "iron discipline" and the "pangs, even if sweet ones, of being reformed into a new man and artist."[112] Nonetheless, when Bergelson came back to Berlin in January 1932, he confirmed his decision to settle in the USSR.[113]

Proletpen

By 1926, Olgin, who once panned proletarian literature, became its advocate. An interesting public discussion between him and Shmuel Niger, chaired by H. Leivick, took place on 17 October 1926 in the New York Central Opera House. Niger argued that he was not against proletarian literature as a literary genre, including such types as children's, village, and urbanist literatures. He was against proclaiming proletarian literature as the alternative to "creative" varieties of literature. Olgin, however, defended the drive for proletarian literature as the only way out of the "deadlock," the "darkness and narrowness" of the contemporary Yiddish literature, which could help writers to stop their soul-searching in the "I" and concentrate on the collectivist "we." He emphasized that proletarian theorists did not negate the nonproletarian Yiddish literature; rather, they looked at it from the class viewpoint, selecting the best works. For instance, 90 percent of Sholem Asch's works had to be rejected as being unpalatable for the worker.

Olgin, who dreamed about a Yiddish work on the level of Sinclair Lewis's *Main Street,* was not ready to mention any positive examples of proletarian writing.[114] As a result, he decided to create a model proletarian prose work. In 1927, his book *Havrila and Yoel* was published with the Frayhayt imprint[115]—hence using the same non-Soviet style of spelling as in the newspaper. The genre of the work is defined by the author as a "story," apparently rejecting "novel" as an outdated kind of writing. In effect, it can be seen as the first significant proletarian prose work in Yiddish, preceding such pioneer Soviet novels as *Der mentsh mit der biks* (The man with a rifle) by Shmuel Godiner (1928) and *Hershl Shamay* by Abraham Abchuk (1929). The scheme of the work is defined in the very first sentence: "This is a story about the *sheygets* (Gentile young man) Havrila and the *bokher* (Jewish young man) Yoel, whom life twice brought together in a very extraordinary way."

The first time they meet during a pogrom, when Yoel, a fragile salon socialist, is easily overpowered by the mighty young peasant Havrila. The collapsed Yoel cannot protect his girlfriend, Rivka, from Havrila's obsessive desire to rape a Jewish girl, an embodiment of the hated Jewish breed. Soon after the pogrom, Havrila is conscripted into the Russian army, where he step by step begins to see clearly that the rich rather than the Jews are his real enemies. By 1917 he has already become a politically conscious soldier and even a member of the Bolshevik party. In the meantime, the police arrests Yoel, and the czarist prison becomes his school of life. It hardens him, educates him as an internationalist (whereas hitherto he sympathized with Zionists), and, predictably, also brings him into the ranks of Bolsheviks. Rivka, now Yoel's wife, is his comrade-in-arms. Olgin brings the two enemies together for a second time when Havrila on his own initiative tries to prevent a pogrom by a group of deserters, while Yoel is appointed to lead a Red Guard detachment to the same place. Yoel recognizes his old enemy and, being sure that Havrila is one of the culprits, shoots him. With all that is left of his strength, the wounded Havrila helps to stop any further bloodshed. He survives and begs Yoel to forgive him. Both understand that they are now different people, committed fighters for communism, and they part forever.

Olgin apparently regarded his work as a yardstick, beside which writings of the American "young smiths" could not qualify for the *Frayhayt* editor's recognition. Feeling that they could not jostle their way through the established writers, the proletarian literary youth continued producing their *samizdat*. By the end of 1926 they began to publish a new journal, *Yugnt* (Youth). At that time the American communists reformed their ranks according to the Comintern directive: all ethnic (English, Jewish, Russian, German, Finnish, etc.) federations were replaced by factory and district cells, numbering fifteen to twenty communists of various nationalities and conducting their activities in English. This restructuring, billed as "Bolshevization of the party," threatened to throw overboard many of the communist-affiliated cultural programs. A way out was found in Workers Clubs, including Yiddish clubs. *Yugnt* represented an attempt to recruit readers among young members of these front institutions, which were "[p]articularly successful in tapping the latent idealism and personal anxieties of immigrant workers." [116] However, after publishing only four issues— dated November–December 1926, January 1927, February 1927, and March 1927—the journal was phased out because of financial problems.

The *Yugnt* proletarian poets dreamed about a revolution in America, and such dreams helped them to endure the burden of their immigrant life. Communism appears as the Most High in Borukh Fenster's "We Sing:"

> Iber undz a harber ol tsert undz tog un nakht,
> mir zaynen lebediker, tsarter royb—
> nor iber alts azoy sheyn zingt horepashne makht—
> zingen mir derfar,
> in veytekdikstn tsar—
> mir zingen [117]

> A heavy yoke reigns over us by day and night,
> we are the live, tender game—
> but the toilers' power sings so beautifully above everything—
> therefore we sing,
> in painful sorrow—
> we sing

A. Prints's "Song of Steel" does not advocate hatred toward America; rather the nation appears as a landscape propitious for proletarian revolution:

Nit monsters zaynen dayne himlkratsers—
libe-lider zaynen zey;
nit shtilkayt-lekhtser zaynen mir:
dayn fun-yam-biz-yam-gedrang iz muzik—
fun undzer freyd un vey.

Zaynen mir oysgevaksn in dayn erd,
tsunoyfgeshmoltsn mit dayn shtol,
iz shtol in undzere shtayfe muskuln un nervn,
shtol in undzer blut un gal,
shtoln mir oys undzer shtoln-lid.

Serp, grob-ayzn, aker, hamer
shmeltsn zikh in shverd.
Shvingen-klingen shverdn in di hamers.
Shmidn mir oys undzer shtoln-lid.[118]

Your skyscrapers are not monsters—
they are love songs;
we don't seek quietness:
your from-one-sea-to-another-sea rush is music—
of our joy and pain.

We have grown in your land,
fused with your steel,
our taut muscles and nerves are of steel,
steel is in our blood and gall,
we smelt our song of steel.

Sickle, spade, plough, hammer
smelt themselves into a sword.
Swords swing-clink in the hammers.
We forge our song of steel.

Pomerantz and his fellow proletarian writers were given a party assignment to organize the worker correspondent movement, but they failed to
achieve any success in replanting the Soviet experience.[119] In May 1928 the
former "young smiths" and contributors to the *Yugnt* formed the core of a
new proletarian writer organization, called Union Square. The name pinned
down the group's political affiliation: Union Square (also known as New

York's "Red Square") was the address of the Communist Party's headquarters and periodicals. The group numbered about thirty members, including such talented poets as Leon Feinberg, Bezaleel Fridman, Joseph Greenspan, Malka Lee, Aron Kurts, Isaac E. Rontch, and Leyb Sobrin. Many of the Union Square writers were either card-carrying Communists or would later become members of the party. Still, the Jewish Section of the party and the *Frayhayt* literary pundits were skeptical about the group, apparently still regarding them as literary second-raters. The aesthete Olgin, for instance, disliked the declarative character of their poetry.[120]

The discussion about the 1928 book *Kinder-lider* (Children's poems) by Fayvl Meltser revealed the tension between the *Frayhayt* editors and the proletarian poets. A New York typesetter, chiropractor, and left-wing poet (but not a member of the Union Square group), Meltser was criticized by the non-communist critic Shmuel Niger. Meltser rebuked him in *Frayhayt*. Olgin, however, was not happy that Meltser overemphasized his proletarian credentials. In a 26 August 1928 article, the communist editor argued that it was generally wrong to hide literary flaws behind a smokescreen of proletarian rhetoric. The Union Square writers rightly decided that Olgin meant also them.

On 15 September, *Frayhayt* published their protest, "Proletarian Critic and Bourgeois Influences," reminding Olgin about their chronic orphanhood, particularly that *Yung kuznye* could not continue its existence because "no one of the local left proletarian activists and writers, including Comrade Olgin, helped us in our first steps, our proletarian-literary pioneer work. In general, the local Jewish Section has not paid any attention to our activities. . . . The proletarian writers recently renewed their collective literary activities and, without any support from the proletarian circles, organized the group Union Square."

Olgin answered with three articles: "An Answer to Our Young Proletarian Writers" (1 December), "The Communist Party and the Proletarian Writers" (9 December), and "Publicity" (16 December). He admitted complicated relations between the young writers and *Frayhayt* and explained that the main problem was the quality of the writers' work. He stressed that so far the young sector, even in the Soviet Union, had not brought forward creators on a par with the *aribergekumene* (those who went over to the communist camp) fellow travelers.

The climate in Yiddish literature had ominously changed in 1929, or the year of the Great Break as it was called in Soviet Newspeak. In the new cli-

mate, Soviet Jewish functionaries made much less penetrable the barriers between Soviet and noncommunist western literary milieus. The same year the
most venerable western Yiddish novelist Sholem Asch, the honorary chairman of the Yiddish PEN Club, who visited the Soviet Union, was torn to
pieces in Soviet critical articles.[121] Relations with the West became even more
confrontational following the Arab riots in Palestine, when a number of
Jewish left-wing culturati reconsidered their stand after the Soviet Union had
sided with the Arabs and blamed the Zionists.

In fact, the party's relations with fellow travelers began to deteriorate
from the outset of that year, when Olgin, carrying out an order of the party's
Jewish Section, called a meeting of hot communist literati without inviting
the fellow travelers. The vast majority of the roughly thirty writers invited
were members of the Union Square group. Olgin told them that the time had
come to form the Frayhayt Writers' Association, because the communist
paper could rely no longer on such petite bourgeois writers as Reisen. *Frayhayt* needed writers who would write "with swords in their hands." Still, at
that juncture *Frayhayt* did not show the "petit bourgeois" writers the door,
although some of their manuscripts were rejected. The communists were
particularly annoyed with the fellow travelers' active membership in the recently founded noncommunist Yiddish Cultural Society, chaired by Khaim
Zhitlovsky. Leivick was the secretary of the society. Thus, Leivick, Reisen,
and others' rupture of relations with *Frayhayt* was a *process* rather than an
overnight decision. After September 1929, Y. L. Peretz Writers' Organization, the Yiddish writers' trade union founded in 1915, expelled those of its
members who had not walked away from the communists, most notably
Moshe Nadir, the only significant American fellow traveler remaining with
Frayhayt.

On 13 September 1929—a month after the Arab riots, ten days after the
fellow travelers' mass departure, and a month before the Wall Street Crash—
the Frayhayt Writers' Association was transformed into Proletpen, which
became the biggest Yiddish communist writers' organization outside the
Soviet Union. Thus, the Yiddish Red Decade began a month earlier than
the general Red Decade (between the Wall Street Crash and the Molotov-
Ribbentrop Pact), and—in literary life—Proletpen foreran John Reed clubs
of American English-language pro-Soviet writers, which first emerged in October 1929. The name of Proletpen was coined as an antonym to the Yiddish
PEN Club, which was inspired by such activists as Nakhman Meisel and Leo
Kenig, who professed exterritoriality and nonpartisanship in Yiddish litera-

ture.[122] Proletpen's spiritual center was in Moscow, at the headquarters of the International Union of Revolutionary Writers (IURW)—the literary arm of the Comintern.[123] The second conference of IURW, which was convened in Kharkov in 1930, adopted a resolution on Yiddish literature. It stressed the importance of Proletpen, although it reproved the American communists for alienating indiscriminately all fellow travelers.[124]

On 14 September 1929, Nadir published his open letter to the "runaways," in which he got under their skin by announcing that he wanted to become a card-carrying member of the party. He also wrote:

> Ikh ken aykh gut, ikh ken aykh oysgebundn,
> ir temne yidish-shrayber fun der shtot Nyu York;
> ir lekt di hant, vos makht undz toyte vundn,
> un nemt umshterblekhkayt baym folk oyf borg. . . .
>
> ikh ken aykh lang. Ikh vil aykh mer nit kenen,
> ir fintstere farreter fun a klas;
> baym fayer fun tsvey veltn, velkhe brenen,
> farroykhert ir zikh shtil a papiros.[125]

> I know you well, I know you unbundled,
> you, shady Yiddish writers from the city of New York;
> you lick the hand which deadly wounds us
> and hire our people's eternity. . . .
>
> I've known you for a long time. I don't want to know you anymore,
> you, dark traitors of the class;
> at the fire of two worlds, which are blazing,
> you calmly get a light for your cigarette.

Some of the "runaways," such as Raboy, Feinberg, and Lee, would come back a few years later, but all in all after 1929 Yiddish communist literature was created by its own cohort of writers, who were kept apart from the non-communist literary circles. It was a strictly compartmentalized world, in which poets were published and praised only in periodicals of their own ideological affiliation. A book of poetry by an American Yiddish proletarian—or, for that matter, by a poet of any denomination—had no commercial value and would appear only thanks to a group of comrades and organizations that formed a sponsoring committee. Pro-Soviet writers could even expect a pilgrimage to the Soviet Union, supplemented by the pilgrim's book publication and generous royalties.

After Winchevsky's visit in 1924, a few other *Frayhayt* contributors came to the Soviet Union. Borukh Glazman, representing the newspaper, remained in the country for almost a year. In 1925 a collection of his stories came out in Moscow; the next year another collection was published in Kiev. In 1925, Leivick spent a few months in the Soviet Union, and during this time his three books—two of his poetry and a travel log—were published in Moscow and Kiev. Abraham Reisen's visit during the end of 1928 and beginning of 1929 was marked with a 1929 publication in Moscow of his *Selected Works* in three volumes.[126] The same year collections of his works were published in Kiev and Minsk. Amazingly, in 1930, or after his departure from the circle of pro-Soviet writers, a collection of his stories came out in Kharkov. Many pro-Soviet writers were represented in two anthologies published in 1932: *The Contemporary Proletarian Yiddish Poetry in America* and *In the Shadow of Gallows: Almanac of Yiddish Proletarian Literature in Capitalist Countries.*[127] Abraham Wieviorka, who edited the latter collection, underlined the affinity of Soviet Yiddish literature with proletarian Yiddish literature outside the Soviet Union, rejecting at the same time any kinship with the literature, which he defined as "petty bourgeois, fascist and nationalist."[128]

Nadir went to the Soviet Union in 1926, and the next year his book *Fun dir un fur mir* (Concerning you and me) came out in Kiev. In 1937 his *Geklibene verk* (Selected works) was likewise published in Kiev. This publication was a sign of recognition of the role of the American proletarian poet par excellence. Indeed, in 1935, during the (pro-Soviet) American Writers' Congress, Nadir spoke as the representative of Yiddish writers. He explained to the participants that Yiddish "has the unique distinction of having been from its inception the language of the toiling Jewish masses, as contrasted with the ancient Hebrew of the upper-class chauvinists, or the 'pure' German of the vulgar middle-class assimilationists." According to Nadir, American proletarian writers "love[d] America as one of the most beautiful flowers in the bouquet of the world Soviets of tomorrow."[129] Nonetheless, in two years' time, after the Molotov-Ribbentrop Pack, Nadir, together with a few other writers, left *Frayhayt*. At that moment Leivick, too, broke off his relations with the communist movement, with which he again collaborated during the Popular Front period, in the framework of the World Yiddish Cultural Association (IKUF)—a product of the World Yiddish Cultural Congress in Paris in September 1937.[130] That congress was a shadow of the grandiose Congress in Defence of Culture at the Salle Mutualité in June 1935, especially because the Soviet party leadership did not allow a delegation of five Yiddish luminaries—David Bergelson, Itsik Fefer, Izi Kharik, Moshe Litvakov, and Solomon Mikhoels—to take part in the forum.[131]

By that time the Stalinist Great Purges began to take their toll on Yiddish cultural circles. Immigrant literati usually had less chance to survive the repression. Among those who perished in Soviet prisons and hard-labor camps were such grand names in Yiddish literature as the poet Moshe Kulbak and the literary historian Max Erik (Zalman Merkin). Much less is known about another victim, Ziskind Lev, a novelist and playwright.[132] The gulag also swallowed up minor writers, such as Aron Yudelson, who was born in Riga, lived shortly in Vilna, but in 1928 illegally crossed the Soviet border and settled in Minsk as a rather active Soviet writer. Another of those arrested was Henekh Soloveytshik, a member of the group Yung Vilne, who had come to the Soviet Union illegally. He worked in Magnitogorsk in the Ural Mountains, where, together with another former Vilna Yiddish activist, Reuven Falk, he founded a Yiddish literary group and even staged his play *Shvartsroyt* (Black-red), with a local Yiddish troupe.[133]

Meir Wiener, one of the most significant Yiddish literary historians and a prose writer in his own right, was spared during the Great Purges. He was born in Cracow and studied in Germany, Austria, and Switzerland. In the early 1920s he lived in Berlin, visiting his friends Kvitko and Der Nister in Hamburg. Under the influence of Kvitko and other émigré Soviet writers he joined the Austrian Communist Party. Unable to find for himself a place in European Yiddish cultural circles, in 1926 he settled in the Soviet Union, working at Yiddish academic institutions in Kiev and (starting in 1933) Moscow.[134] His move to the capital was part of an effort to reinforce the Yiddish Department at the Moscow Teachers Training Institute. In the same year, Oislender also moved from Kiev to Moscow. An armchair academic, Wiener found much more in common with his Moscow colleague Aron Gurshtein than with Max Erik. In 1932 the latter moved from Minsk (where he initially lived after coming to the Soviet Union) to Kiev and headed the literary section of the Kiev Institute of Proletarian Jewish Culture. The two literary specialists were not very compatible: Erik eagerly assimilated the behavioral patterns of militant communists, whereas Wiener, albeit a committed communist, could not stand demonstrations of ostentatious loyalty.[135]

In the early 1930s three Proletpen poets went to the Soviet Union. Yosl Cohen spent a couple of years there. His book *Fun yener zayt yam* (From another side of the sea) was published in Moscow in 1932. Cohen, nonetheless, returned to America as a disillusioned communist. Interestingly, he also changed his poetic style—his 1948 book *Der morgn iz eybik* (The morrow is eternal) contains only rhymed verses, expressing strong Jewish national feelings. One of the longest poems in the books, "Ballad about the Sixteenth," was written about the first victims of Stalinist purges.

Ayzik Platner, another Proletpen poet, decided to settle in the Soviet Union. He wanted to leave America, regarding it as a place that had maimed him as a poet and where the communist literary establishment did not give young aspirants a chance to develop into professional writers.[136] While still in America, in his poem "A Greeting: To the Comrades in the Soviet Union," he wrote: Khaveyrim tayere! Mir zaynen aykh mekane, / un tseyln do mit tsiter ayer yedn tog![137] (Dear comrades! We envy you, / and count here eagerly your every day!) Platner survived the Stalinist purges of the late 1930s, but in 1949 he, then a correspondent of the Jewish Antifascist Committee, was arrested during the repression against the committee activists. He lived for only a few years after his liberation from the gulag.

Alexander Pomerantz apparently poetically wrote himself out in the early 1920s. In 1933 he went to the Kiev-based Institute of Proletarian Jewish Culture, where he prepared a dissertation on the history of Proletpen. His book *Proletpen: Sketches and Materials Concerning the History of the Struggle for Proletarian Literature in America (USA),* based on his dissertation, was published in Kiev in 1935 by the Publishing House of the Ukrainian Academy of Science. The same year he returned to America, where he produced a number of propagandist books and pamphlets that glorified the Soviet Union. However, he left the communist movement around 1950.

In general, the suppression of Yiddish culture in the post-Holocaust Soviet Union and execution of the leading Soviet Yiddish writers was a blow that decimated the ranks of American Jewish communists.[138] Only a handful of the communist poets, such as Aaron Kurts and Ber Green (A. Prints), remained contributors to *Morgn-frayhayt* in its afterlife period of mid-1950s–late 1980s. By that time, the epoch of American Yiddish communist poetry was effectively over. The literary movement, born by Lenin's October, was obliterated by Stalin's Thermidor.

CHAPTER FOUR

The New Growth

The Minsk "Young Workers"

IN THE PERIOD between the world wars, in the Soviet Union there was no other republic where Yiddish played such a prominent role as in Belorussia. A decree of 15 July 1924 confirmed that Belorussian, Yiddish, Russian, and Polish were of equal value.[1] While Belorussian was perceived as the language of the peasants, Yiddish was regarded as the language spoken by the vast majority of Belorussia's workers and artisans.[2] Indeed, the industrial proletariat, or the "hegemonic class" in early Soviet society, consisted mostly of Jews in all parts of the republic. Moreover, Jews were the most numerous ethnic group in the towns of Belorussia, including its capital, Minsk.[3] It is no coincidence that Belorussia was a stronghold of the proletarian-cum-internationalist traditions of the proletarian party Bund, whereas Ukraine, with its smaller proportion of Jewish urban and proletarian population, had a social basis for hybrid currents, more nationalist than Marxist, e.g., Labor Zionism or Territorialism.[4] The proletarian and internationalist traditions in Belorussia, on the one hand, and the Jewish particularism in Ukraine, on the other hand, developed further after the revolution. Jewish activities in Belorussia became part of the mainstream Soviet work, whereas in Ukraine they were much more compartmentalized. While the early Soviet Belorussian nation was seen as a four-headed body—Belorussian, Russian, Jewish, and Polish—Ukrainians were much more territorial. Thus, in April 1922 the Central Bureau of the Evsektsii reported to the Politburo that the party committees in many *guberniias* of Ukraine regarded local Jewish communists' activities as "a kind of exclusive, sometimes even nationalist work" rather than "a constituent of the general party work."[5]

The newly minted Belorussia had much diminished during the three years of the post-1917 civil war, especially compared with territorial claims of Belorussian nation-builders who saw their revived, independent country in the borders of the medieval Grand Duchy of Lithuania, including Vilna and some other territories of contemporary Lithuania, Poland, and Russia. However, after kaleidoscopic transitions of power—the Bolsheviks, the Belorussian National Rada Government, the German and the Polish occupations—the newborn Soviet republic was left with a small territory around its capital city of Minsk. In the mid-1920s a few more provinces acceded to Belorussia, including Vitebsk, then one of the most significant Jewish cultural centers in the Soviet Union.

Although Vitebsk did not have a prerevolutionary Bolshevik cadre,[6] a number of commissars dispatched by the new regime succeeded in Bolshevization of some part of the local population. The Jewish commissar, Sam Agurski, could also be proud of his achievements. In particular, Vitebsk became a stronghold of the Yiddish communist press. Agurski himself edited the newspaper *Der frayer arbeter* (Free worker), launched on 7 November 1918, the first anniversary of the October revolution. The short-lived Vitebsk Komsomol magazine *Khvalyes* (Waves), published August 1920–December 1921, went down in the history of Yiddish literature as one of the first periodicals whose program contained creation of proletarian Yiddish literature.[7] Agursky, himself an enthusiast of American sweatshop poets, certainly encouraged the young advocates of proletarian literature. As early as 1918 he edited a collection of poems by Joseph Bovshover, and later, after he returned from America, he was one of the main proponent of Bovshover, Morris Winchevsky, and David Edelstadt.

In Vitebsk and elsewhere, the vast majority of early Soviet Yiddish rhymesters disappeared without a trace after publishing one or two poems. Still, Mendel Abarbanel, a Vitebsk worker turned poet, became a professional Soviet Yiddish poetaster. His first poems were published in Moscow, in *Kultur un bildung* and in *Di komunistishe velt*. On 7 November 1918, his poem, written in the style of a military march, appeared in the first issue of *Der frayer arbeter*:

> Es tsitern tronen, es vign zikh kroynen,
> es gist zikh nokh blut un es rint.
> Hey, henker gekroynte, me vet aykh baloynen
> azoy nor, vi ir hot fardint.[8]

The thrones are trembling, the crowns are reeling,
the blood is still shedding and streaming.
Hey, crowned hangmen, you will be rewarded
exactly according to your deserts.

Another Vitebsk resident, Moshe Yudovin, began his literary career as a promising poet. On 29 May 1920 he published in the local communist paper *Der Shtern* (Star) one of the best poems, "[Dedicated] To the Woman," written in that time by Soviet Yiddish tyro poets:

Dayn brust tsu mayn harts!
Un shenken vel ikh dir, mayn fraynt,
dem gefil fun a broyzndn haynt,
un fargesn vestu on dem over dem shvartsn.
Ikh hob afn shpits fun mayn shverd
dir a friling gebrakht!
Nem rays zayne blumen fun dr'erd,
genis shoyn di reykhes fun friling, fun prakht!
Un loz dir nit shrekn di nakht . . .
Kh'vel khapn dem otem dem frayen,
kh'vil zen dem blits fun dayn shikern blik,
banemen dem glik fun dem lebn dem nayem.

Your breast to my heart!
And I'll give you, my friend,
the feeling of an effervescent today,
and you'll forget about the dark past.
On the spike of my sward
I brought you a spring!
Begin to pick its flowers from the earth,
[you can] already enjoy the scents of the spring, of the splendor!
And don't be afraid of the night . . .
I'll breathe in the air of freedom,
I want to see the spark of your intoxicated glance,
grasp the happiness of the new life.

In 1921 and 1922, Yudovin published in Vitebsk a couple of poetic pamphlets, but he soon gave up his literary activities and, after finishing the Vitebsk Yiddish Teachers Training College and the Moscow Teachers Training Institute, found employment as a lecturer at his Vitebsk alma mater and a compiler of readers for Yiddish schools. Incidentally, his cousin, Shlome Yudovin, was one of the remarkable Vitebsk Jewish artists, a group that included most notably Yehuda Pen, Marc Chagall, and El Lissitzky. A protégé of another prominent Vitebsker, S. An-sky, he was a member of the pre–World War I Jewish ethnographical expeditions led by An-sky. After the revolution Yudovin lived in Vitebsk and took part in the local Yiddish cultural activities.

Minsk, and in general Belorussia, boasted a rich prerevolutionary tradition of Jewish political activity. While Belorussian activists were mostly captivated by populist ideas of national revival (before 1917 in the Bolshevik party there were only two ethnic Belorussians), Jews played an outstanding role in various radical political currents. Yiddish was the language of preference for all parties propagandizing among Belorussian Jews, whose mother tongue and literacy were typically Yiddish.[9] As a Jewish cultural center, however, Minsk itself was quite insignificant. Basically, Belorussian Jews were *litvaks* and as such regarded themselves, and were regarded by the other Jewish groups, as part of the Jewish-Lithuanian subethnos, whose recognized spiritual center was Vilna. In fact, Vilna was also important as a Belorussian cultural center. It was the breeding ground for quite a few Belorussian writers, including Zmitrok Biadulia (Shmuel Plavnik),[10] who later played some role in Yiddish activities; in particular, he was one of the compilers of the *Yiddish-Belorussian Pocket Dictionary*.[11] As late as 1921, Kletzkin opened at his publishing house a special department for printing Belorussian books.[12]

After 1917, Minsk quickly became a booming Yiddish publishing center. The most important publication was the Bund newspaper *Der veker* (Alarm clock), whose first issue came out on 12 May 1917, although it continued the tradition of prerevolutionary Bund organs with the same name, most notably *Der veker,* published in Vilna in 1905–06. The Minsk paper's editorship changed hands a few times: Aron Vainshtein, Abraham Kirzhnits, and Maria Frumkin all held the post. During December 1917, *Der veker* was edited by Max Weinreich, later the foremost Yiddish linguist and organizer of Yiddish scholarship. In 1918, Frumkin returned to the editorship. Among the six Yiddish newspapers published in Minsk in 1917–18,[13] *Der veker* was preeminent as the sole Soviet Yiddish periodical launched circa 1917 and continued until June 1941. On 7 November 1925, the eighth anniversary of the October revolution, it discarded its original name, muddied with the Bundist provenance, for the more appropriate *Oktyabr* (October). All the other newspapers were short-lived. The Zionist daily *Der yid* (Jew), for example, edited by the local *maskil* Mikhl Rabinovitch, was published for only eight months, from December 1918 to July 1919. Likewise another Zionist newspaper, *Farn folk* (For the sake of people), appeared in September 1919, only to fold in January 1920. Its editor was Khaim-Dov Hurvits, a veteran Yiddish journalist and former editor of the Petrograd *Togblat*.

The publishing boom magnetized a number of intellectuals, including the poet Eli Savikovski and the literary critic Uri Finkel. Among the contributors to *Der veker / Oktyabr* was the doyen of Minsk Yiddish writers, feuilletonist Yaknehoz (Yeshaye-Nisn Goldberg), whose feuilleton "Letters from Lithuania to America" appeared in the first volume of Sholem Aleichem's *Yidishe folksbibliotek*. A few more experienced literati lived in Minsk, such as Tsodek Dolgopolsky and Daniel Marshak; both (particularly Dolgopolsky) became prolific Soviet Yiddish writers. The first homebred prose writer was Herts Maizl, who switched over from Russian to Yiddish, being inspired by the growth of Yiddish periodicals. For all that, Belorussia did not have famous literary names. Even in 1918, during the ephemeral Lithuanian-Belorussian Soviet republic—a kind of a Bolshevik reincarnation of the Grand Duchy of Lithuania—Yiddish literary celebrities such as Niger and A. Weiter rushed to Vilna rather than to Minsk. Dimanshtein, who was also in Vilna as a member of the Belorussian-Lithuanian government, wrote later, in the May Day 1919 issue of the Moscow journal *Di komunistishe velt*: "For us, Jewish revolutionaries, communists, Vilna long ago became a historical center, the heart of the Jewish spiritual liberation. It is our Moscow or Petrograd."[14] Meanwhile, the publication activities in Belorussia concentrated on producing periodicals rather than books. Between 1917 and 1922 only fifteen Yiddish books were printed there (eight in Vitebsk, five in Minsk, and two in Gomel), all of them government-sponsored publications.[15]

In the literary backwaters of Belorussia, beginners had much more elbow room than in Kiev, Kharkov, or Moscow. As a result, Belorussian towns could more easily became strongholds of Yiddish proletarian literary activities[16] and, in general, of the most iconoclastic variety of Yiddishism, whose apologists almost completely discarded Jewish traditions and prerevolutionary culture. Across the wide ideological gulf, the "amnesiac" Yiddishists shared with Zionists their disdain for all components of the shtetl life. In the early 1920s, they populated Yiddish proletarian literary and cultural circles, whose power base was in such places as Minsk and Vitebsk.

By the end of 1923 a group of fledgling writers began to concentrate at the Komsomol Minsk newspaper *Der yunger arbeter* (Young worker), published 1922–35. They were inspired by the appearance of Molodniak (Youth), the organization of Belorussian writers, founded in November 1923. Apparently, the group Yunger arbeter was initiated by Yankl Rubentshik, editor of the newspaper and one of the organizers of the Belorussian Komsomol. More or less at the same time, a proletarian literary group, Oktyabr-dor (October generation) appeared in Gomel. Among the organizers of the Gomel group were Shlome Bilov and—the group's secretary—Israel Serebreny (or Serebriani). Bilov was a former Bundist who returned to Belorussia after emigration in America, where he studied linguistics. In the 1930s he held Yiddish professorships in Odessa and Kiev, but at first he lectured at the Gomel Yiddish Teachers Training College, whose students, including Serebreny, a future Soviet Yiddish literary scholar, constituted the majority of the October Generation members. In general, the Yiddish teachers colleges in Minsk, Gomel, and Vitebsk, as well as the Yiddish faculty at the Minsk University, provided the main cadre for the literary circles. In 1924, Minsk also emerged as the first significant Yiddish academic center when a Jewish department was opened at the Institute for Belorussian Culture (Inbelkult), the precursor of the Belorussian Academy of Science.[17]

In 1925 the bureau of the Young Worker group consisted of the printer Yasha Goldman and two Minsk University students—the rising poetic talent Moshe Teif and the same Serebreny who by that time had moved from Gomel. Also taking part in the group's gatherings were a few more young people, mostly university and college students, such as the future literary critic and prose writer Rivka Rubin and the poets Mendel Lifshits, Notte Vainhoiz, Shmuel Helmond, and Hersh Kamenetski. Beginning in April 1926 the group got a regular page in the newspaper *Der yunger arbeter*. On 6 August 1926 the newspaper published the group's appeal to form an organization of proletarian writers. Local groups of Yunger arbeter were formed in a few other towns of Belorussia: Vitebsk, Mozyr, Polotsk, Mogilev, Slutsk, and Bobruisk. They were supported by the meager cadre of Jewish intellectuals. For instance, in Minsk, they benefited from seminars given to them by the linguist Khaim Holmshtok, a returnee from the United States. In Vitebsk, the literary group was guided by the lecturer of the local Yiddish teachers' college, Ayzik Rozentsvayg (who wrote often under the pseudonym of "Tsvayg").[18]

In 1925 the literary journal *Shtern*—the longest-running Yiddish magazine in the Soviet Union between the wars—was launched in Minsk. The same year a Yiddish cultural landing force arrived from Moscow to Minsk.

After studying for four years in Moscow, the Belorussian State Yiddish Theater came to fulfill its mission.[19] In addition, a few men of letters came from the Soviet capital. One of them was the poet Zelig Akselrod, who aesthetically was quite far from the proletarian poets. Ber Orshanski, a veteran Bundist turned to Communist in 1918, was invited to Minsk to head the Jewish Department at the Inbelkult. He was known as a Yiddish playwright, a few of his plays having been published in Vilna before World War I; after the revolution he continued to write plays, stories, and novels and became active as a literary critic and historian.

Nokhum Oislender became both the head of the Yiddish literary sector at the Inbelkult and became the chair of Yiddish literature at the university. By that time he had turned from poetry to literary scholarship; he was, for instance, in charge of a project (inspired by Lunacharsky but never realized) to publish a series of translations from Yiddish into Russian, including Sholem Aleichem, Sholem Asch, and Joseph Opatoshu.[20] In Minsk, he brought out, together with Uri Finkel, a book on Abraham Goldfaden. By the end of 1926 he left, having been invited to work in Kiev at the Ukrainian Academy of Science.

Yasha Bronshtein, a 1925 graduate of the literary department of the Moscow University and a graduate student at the Moscow Institute of Red Professors, was appointed to look after the Minsk Yiddish literary activities. Born in Belorussia, Bronshtein lived in Warsaw in 1914–18 and came to Soviet Russia in 1919 to fight as a Red Army soldier. In 1921 he lived in the town of Orel and worked for the local Russian newspaper *Orlovskaia pravda* (Orel truth). In the early 1920s he was a student in Kiev and, at the same time, headed a commune of young Jewish workers and unsuccessfully tried his hand at poetry.[21] Now he came to Minsk as a missionary of the Yiddish Section of MAPP. Apart from him, the Bureau of the Yiddish Section consisted of Wieviorka, Kushnirov, and Rabin. Bronshtein became a member of the Communist Party in 1925.

On 3 October 1925, Bronshtein reported to the Moscow-based Bureau's members: "I had a meeting with the Bureau of the Young Worker [group]. I acquainted myself in detail with the situation (both internal and external). The Bureau agreed with all recent resolutions of the Yiddish [Section's] Bureau of MAPP. The lads are lively, energetic young people, they waited impatiently for my arrival." A month later he was again writing to Moscow: "Our Minsk [group] is working hard. In issue 3 of the *Shtern* they have three pages of poems (there is no prose!), the collection *Kep* (Heads) will be ready by December. In addition, Teif is writing (for you) a poem 'Belorussia,' Goldman, Helmond, Lifshits, and a few [writers] from the province are writing too, though nothing but poems (it's a downright nuisance). . . . . Socially, we are a strong power here." [22]

The Minsk group became a stronghold of MAPP, and the journal *Shtern* became, in fact, the all-Soviet forum for proletarian literature. It is illuminating that the literary department of the *Shtern* was for some time edited by the Moscow-based Kushnirov and Wieviorka. The collection *Kep*, dedicated to the victims of the White Guard's terror, was published in Minsk in 1926 under the imprints of MAPP and the Minsk group Yunger arbeter. In his programmatic article "Our First Organized Appearance (*aroystrit*)," Ber Orshanski announced that the proletarian literary youth came to "smoke out" (literally to "compete out"—*oyskonkurirn*) the old literature. He criticized "Nisterism" and Dobrushin and Oislender's "national-aestheticism," and he contested the Kiev Group's rights to be regarded as the founding fathers of Soviet Yiddish literature. As early as February 1920, in his article published in the Kiev daily *Komunistishe fon* (Communist banner), he accused the Kiev Group writers of ignoring Jewish workers and targeting only "the bachelor, the *eksternik* and . . . the intellectual nudnik." [23] Incidentally, Wieviorka, although he lived in Moscow, became a strong advocate of the Minsk anti-Kiev Group line. In his controversial 1931 book *Revizye* (Revision), he argued that Soviet Yiddish literature was descended from the undeservedly defamed Shomer and the American sweatshop poets.

In 1928, Izi Kharik and Moshe Kulbak strengthened the Minsk Yiddish cultural cadre. At the same time Khatskel Dunets emerged as an active literary critic, reinforcing the ranks of the Minsk masters of invective. In 1929, Max Erik, the émigré historian of Jewish literature, settled in Minsk; he moved to Kiev in 1932. Kharik, who joined the party in 1930, would become the highest-ranking Yiddish writer, especially after his election in 1931 to the Belorussian Republic's Central Executive Committee. The fifteenth anniversary of his literary activity was marked in state, with participation of the republic's leaders and delegations from all Soviet republics. In 1936 he, together with five leading Belorussian poets, coauthored the poem "Letter from the Belorussian People to the Great Stalin." [24]

In November 1928 the Belorussian group Molodniak reformed itself into the Belorussain Association of Proletarian Writers (BelAPP), and the group Yunger arbeter joined the BelAPP as its Yiddish section. [25] The vast majority of Belorussian Yiddish writers and critics became members of this proletarian organization. Still, despite the high status of Yiddish and numerous Yiddish-speakers in Belorussia, the number of readers of Yiddish belles lettres was limited. Thus, the journal *Shtern,* which originally had a print run of seven hundred copies, reached a circulation of three thousand in 1927; however, one year later it had only three hundred subscribers and in 1929 stabilized its print run at the level of two thousand.[26]

"Simple Speech"

Although Ukraine boasted a number of heavyweight writers, young people were to occupy central positions in Ukrainian Yiddish literary circles, too. The revolution treasured young people, whereas the old-timers were considered to be suspicious and, therefore, should vanish as soon as possible.

> Fargeyt, fargeyt, ir umetike zeydes,
> mit berd tseshrokene, farlofene mit shney! . . .
> In letstn brokh, in letstn vey
> zayt ir farblibn letste eydes,—
> fargeyt, fargeyt, ir umetike zeydes!

> Pass on, pass on, you lonely grandfathers,
> With frightened beards covered with snow,
> In the last sorrow, in the final grief
> You're still here, the final witnesses.
> Pass on, pass on, you lonely grandfathers![27]

preached Izi Kharik in 1924. His Ukrainian fellow poet Itsik Fefer was one of the most prominent among the Yiddish "children of the revolution." Fefer was born in 1900 in the shtetl of Shpola, Kiev Region. His father was a teacher, and his mother was a stocking-maker. He was only seventeen years old when he became a member of the Bund and a trade union functionary. On 4 June 1918—we know the exact date[28]—he wrote his first poem. But 1919 was a stormy year in Fefer's life. He left the Bund and became a Communist; the White Guard police arrested him as a member of an underground group and incarcerated him in the infamous Lukianovka Prison in Kiev; after the liberation he volunteered for the Red Army. In prison, his cell mate was Isaac Nusinov, later a significant Yiddish—and even greater Russian—literary theorist and critic. At that time Nusinov was a recent returnee from Western Europe, where he studied at various universities. After the civil war, Fefer edited a provincial newspaper. In 1922 the Central Committee of the Ukrainian Communist Party transferred him to Kiev and placed him at the head of a trade union.

In Kiev, Fefer joined the local group of young Yiddish literary talents, called the Vidervuks (New growth). This literary nursery emerged from the ruins of the Culture League. In the hands of the Bolsheviks, as we know, this versatile, even if essentially utopian, organization, formed during the few years of Ukraine's independence, was soon reduced to an ordinary publishing house. Nusinov, who briefly played the role of the chief Jewish commissar in Kiev, was a central figure in these Bolshevization activities. At the same time, he and his circle spared no effort to construct new institutions of Yiddish cultural life. Thus, Nusinov, together with David Hofshtein and Nokhum Oislender, formed in 1921 a Yiddish publishing house, which they called Lirik (Lyric). The next year this publishing house opened an imprint, Vidervuks, for young writers. Vidervuks also became the name of the literary group associated with this imprint.

Hofshtein, who edited and prefaced the pamphlet-sized poetic collections, was the recognized leader of the group. In January 1922, Fefer wrote a letter in which he declared his affinity with the poetry of Hofshtein.[29] Later Fefer would somewhat distance himself from the master, characterizing him as a "talented poet and worthless politician."[30] Fefer, on the other hand, was a very good politician and organizer, perfectly combining two talents—of a poet and an apparatchik. In any event, the two complemented one another, and from the mid-1920s the unlikely duo worked rather harmoniously, leading the proletarian stream of the Yiddish literature of Ukraine. In this tandem, Fefer represented the first generation matured during the revolution, whereas Hofshtein, born in 1889, embodied a reformed nonproletarian talent. In 1928, the Kharkov-based Ukrainian journal for literary criticism wrote retrospectively about the orphanhood of Soviet Yiddish literature: "The young generation of [Soviet Yiddish] writers did not have living teachers. There was only their literary legacy, [but] no direct exchange of opinions and experience with the old masters of Yiddish letters." According to the article, "Yiddish proletarian literature originated in Ukraine—it had been done by the Kiev group of young Yiddish writers."[31]

Who were the other Vidervuksniks? The vast majority of them are now completely forgotten, but some of the nurslings of this group, such as Itsik Kipnis and Shmuel Halkin, were central figures in Soviet Yiddish literature. Kipnis, who moved to Kiev in 1920 from his home shtetl Sloveshne, was in a few years' time welcomed by Soviet and foreign critics,[32] and his 1926 novel *Khadoshim un teg* (Months and days) became one of only a few lasting early Soviet prose works. A few other members of the group also occupied significant places in Soviet Yiddish literary life: Ezra Finninberg, Moshe Khashchevatsky, Shaye Shkarovsky, Abraham Velednitsky, and Abraham Kahan. While literary groups generally played a significant role in postrevolutionary Russia, in Yiddish literature, with its small readership, their role was even more valuable, because such groups formed surrogate literary surroundings that stimulated creative activities.[33] The Vidervuksniks' enthusiasm for Yiddish, modernism, and the revolution formed a common denominator of their ideological and aesthetic outlooks. In 1922 the young poets' works often appeared in the literary department of the Kiev communist daily *Komunistishe fon*; in 1923 the newspaper even introduced a special department called "Vidervuks." It was arguably the most significant daily in postrevolutionary Russia, a product of the May 1919 merger of two Bolshevized Kiev papers—the Fareynikte's *Naye tsayt* (New time) and the Bund's *Folks-tsaytung* (People's paper).

But it would be wrong to see the Vidervuks only as a new growth on the stump of the Bolshevized Culture League. In reality, the group was also strongly influenced by the worker correspondent movement, organized and sponsored by the party and Komsomol. This campaign, which would ultimately recruit millions of people and be modeled by the communist press outside the Soviet Union, purported to draw newspapers closer to their readership. *Komunistishe fon* established at its editorial office the first group of Yiddish worker correspondents in 1922.[34] At that time the Central Committee of the Bolshevik Party and the Komsomol began to stimulate this drive.[35] The *Komunistishe fon* group was guided by the local bureau of the Jewish Sections. Archival documents of the bureau show that it paid a great deal of attention to the group, or—as it was called sometimes—"the school of worker correspondents." In February 1924 the Kiev worker correspondents turned against Hofshtein for signing a memorandum backing Hebrew teaching in the Soviet Union.[36] Tyro writers played an active role in this group, and many of them, including Fefer, would later emphasize their worker correspondent origin. The hybrid of the Culture League nationalist tradition, on the one hand, and the proletarian internationalism of the worker correspondent movement, on the other hand, had produced proletarian poets and prose writers who believed that blossoming forth of Yiddish literature and culture was inseparable from communism.

The appearance of Fefer's 1922 poetry collection, *Shpener* (Splinters), established him as a rising literary star. The same year he formulated his literary credo of *proste reyd* (simple speech), which would become the trademark of his work. In the early 1920s, Soviet Yiddish literature lacked prose writers. Poetry, particularly avant-garde poetry, virtually swamped the literary pages of all Soviet Yiddish periodicals. In effect, Yiddish literary circles in postrevolutionary Russia were dominated by obstinate utopians, whose philosopher's stone roughly glued together Marxism and nationalism. Despite their rhetoric about devoted service to the masses, they essentially created an ivory tower and fought against popular culture. Their publications targeted a sophisticated Yiddish reader, a rarity in post-1917 Russia. As a result, their meager readership was confined primarily to the circles of engagé intellectuals. Comprehensibility of Soviet Yiddish publications was a terrible stumbling block for the editors and critics. They were wary of the fact that the bulk of their readers could not understand newspapers, let alone modernist literature.[37] Small wonder, then, that many of them lapped up Fefer's rhymed stories, his *proste reyd,* written in the vernacular register of Yiddish, which any could understand.[38]

By 1923 some of the Vidervuksniks were already regarded as established Yiddish poets. It is illuminating, for instance, that the first anthology of young Yiddish poetry in Ukrainian translation, published in 1923, included works by Ezra Finninberg, Moshe Khashchevatsky, Itsik Fefer, Abraham Kahan, Moshe Shapiro, and Itsik Kipnis.[39] Still, their poetry was hardly proletarian poetry of "stunning revolutionary creative devices."[40] Isaac Nusinov argued later that the Vidervuksniks began as epigones of the Kiev Group's poets.[41] Writers and readers were divided into the camps of "Hoshteinists," "Markishists," and later "Feferists."[42]

Inspired by his own success and that of other Vidervuksniks, Fefer apparently began to dream about uniting young writers from other parts of the country. On 12 January 1923, Fefer published in the *Komunistishe fon* an open letter to all Yiddish worker poets:

> Dear Friends,
>
>   At the time when the Russian and Ukrainian workers already have developed large-scale activities on the cultural front, when they already have created special laboratories for forging the new proletarian literary word, we still have not even tried to collect and organize the worker literature. . . .
>
>   Now, at the time of the new economic situation, when the petty-

bourgeois current is trying to find a way in all spheres of our life, including the arts, the question about organizing the blossoming worker writers in a strong, ready-to-offer-resistance collective has to be particularly seriously raised. . . .

Write to us about the organizations you are going to create, let's put the question together and solve it together. No other authorities ever gave such possibilities to create as it does the Soviet power. Will we miss this opportunity? Will we continue to be passive?

We cannot and will not allow this to happen! . . .

Send us materials!

Let it be the first attempt to collect the dispersed reserves, the first roll-call of the worker soldiers in the artists' army. Let it be the first stone of the future association of all proletarian artists.

At the time nothing came from this appeal. Still, in the history of Soviet Yiddish literature it marked an important step on the way to *organized* Yiddish literati.

At a stretch, Vidervuks could be regarded as a proletarian group, partly because it was more iconoclastic than another Kiev literary group, Antenna. While the young "proletarians" essentially advocated mass literature for Yiddish-speaking industrial workers, the Antenna writers abhorred the idea of pandering to the taste of the mass reader. The group Antenna was formed in late 1924. Its central figures were Lipe Reznik, David Volkenstein, and Noah Lurye, who wanted to further develop the tradition of highbrow national-revolutionary literature rather than proletarian mass literature. Interestingly, among its members we find also a few former Vidervuksniks, most notably Ezra Finninberg. Antenna had much in common with the organization of Ukrainian proletarian writers called Hart (Tempering).[43] While Hart's ideological pedigree was associated with the Borot'bists (the Left Ukrainian Socialist Revolutionary Party), many of the Antenna members were former sympathizers of Jewish Territorialism or other denominations of Jewish socialism. Hart and Antenna represented the so-called national communists, or those communists who believed in a golden age of all national cultures in the Soviet Union. Paradoxically, although Antenna claimed to target all the strata of toilers rather than only the proletarians, it was an elitist group; in this bigger pool they wanted to seek out and cultivate only the sophisticated reader, whose search the Kiev Group had begun in the 1910s.

Importantly, in the mid-1920s it was not a sin to be skeptical of proletarian culture and literature, which had been rejected by Lenin and Trotsky. At that time the communist leadership did not want to delegate its hegemony to any of the literary groups, arguing that competition among them would help find the ultimate socialist method of creativity.[44] Ukrainian Yiddish writers, however, were not in a fighting mood, and in February 1925, Vidervuks and Antenna merged into the Association of Yiddish Writers in Ukraine, modeling party-sponsored endeavors to create a Federation of Soviet Writers.[45] In 1926 this association produced an almanac, *Ukraine,* whose contributors represented both groups of writers.[46]

A separate position was occupied by Moshe Litvakov, who continued to dream about a highbrow and, at the same time, ideologically loaded literature for a sophisticated reading audience. In the early 1920s he, presumably under the influence of Trotsky's pronouncements, rejected the idea of proletarian literature. Later, however, he jumped on the proletarian bandwagon, but could not accept the mass, utilitarian character of this literary movement. Thus, he regarded the worker correspondents' literary activities as a perversion of the original idea. According to Litvakov, worker correspondents had to be vigilant reporters rather than graphomaniac literary hopefuls.[47] He nourished an ambition that his criticism could stimulate writers to create highbrow works for highbrow workers. At the same time, he did not care that highbrow proletarian Yiddish readers were rather rare, arguing that Jewish workers had to rise to the necessary intellectual standard. With his head in the clouds he made numerous enemies on the ground, particularly among writers. Fefer, however, was in the good graces of the unmerciful Yiddish literary critic, who hailed him as "a real poet and, at the same time, really our poet."[48]

By 1924, Fefer already occupied one of the highest places in the hierarchy of Soviet Yiddish poetry, the leading genre in Soviet Yiddish literature. Sol Liptzin ascribed Fefer's rise to three factors: his proletarian orthodoxy, his power of invective, and his lyric talent.[49] It is also important that all the poets of the Kiev Group who were recently promoted into classics—Hofshtein, Markish, and Kvitko—were (as it turned out, temporarily, until 1925 or 1926) abroad. It is illuminating that in 1924, Fefer's poems occupied the highly privileged opening pages of the final issue (numbers 5–6) of the Moscow literary journal *Shtrom* and the inaugural issue of the Kharkov literary journal *Di royte velt.* Both publications were outlets of the *kultur-*

ligeniks, and Fefer's prominence in these journals evidenced his acceptance into this circle of former Jewish salon revolutionaries (usually of the Territorialist vintage) turned into card-carrying or fellow-traveling Bolsheviks.

Fefer was quite prolific. In 1924 his second collection, *Vegn zikh un azoyne vi ikh* (About myself and people like me), came out in Kiev. The next year he published two poetic collections, one in Kiev, *Proste trit* (Simple steps), and another in Kharkov, *A shteyn tsu a shteyn* (A stone to a stone). Vifl mentsn darf men nokh a veg bavayzn, / vifl blinde blondzhen nokh arum[50] (So many people still have to be directed, / so many blind people still wander about), made Fefer anxious in 1924, alluding apparently to one of Lipe Reznik's poems, in which he pictured the disillusioned writers as blind strolling singers.[51] He had, however, to wait until the spring of 1927. In the meantime, he, Hofshtein, and a few other Yiddish writers who had no systematic education studied as *aspirantn* (a kind of postgraduate student) under the supervision of Oislender at the Kiev-based Yiddish Chair (the precursor of the Institute for Yiddish Culture) at the Ukrainian Academy of Science.[52]

In March 1927 the time had come to unite the proletarian writers into an organization. We find Fefer among the founding members of the Ukrainian Association of Yiddish Revolutionary Writers. By the end of the year, the association was reshaped into the Yiddish Section of the All-Ukrainian Union of Proletarian Writers. Fefer became one of the leaders of the section and co-editor of its journal, *Prolit* (Pro[letarian] lit[erature]). Beginning in 1929 he was also a co-editor of the Kharkov *Di royte velt.* He was popular among Yiddish readers, although the returnees Markish, Kvitko, and Hofshtein apparently remained more in demand.[53]

An individual, with his peculiarities and his own destiny, appears rarely in Fefer's poems. The spirit of continuous revolutionary war (a just war) runs through all his poems. He writes about crowds and regiments,[54] about the impersonal masses of people who "hant tsu hant un pleytse tsu pleytse, / fis tsu fis un shinel tsu shinel" (hand to hand and shoulder to shoulder, / leg to leg and greatcoat to greatcoat) fight for the revolution.[55] The victims of the revolution are also nameless and faceless:

> Toyte goyes in shineln,
> oygn groye, shtiker ayz,
> af di heldzer nit keyn kreln,
> af di heldzer shnirlekh layz.

Dead Gentile women in greatcoats,
eyes gray, hunks of ice,
on their necks—not beads,
strings of lice.[56]

    The poet felt that the whole society around him had become impersonal and "we" had elbowed aside "I." This phenomenon was noticed by many intellectuals, such as the Russian writer Evgenii Zamyatin, who in 1921 wrote a novel called *We,* and the American Yiddish poet H. Leivick, who during his 1925 visit to the Soviet Union was bemused by the fact that people, even in his home shtetl of Ihumen, consistently used "we" rather than "I."[57] In 1926, Leivick, of course, once again heard arguments for "we" versus "I" during the dispute between Olgin and Niger.

    In 1929, Fefer, already a leading Yiddish poet in Ukraine, included in his first *Selected Works*[58] a department, containing 367 poetic lines, under the scatological title "Bliendike mistn" (Manure in full bloom). It was presented as a poetic travel log, dedicated to the author's trip to his home shtetl of Shpola. The tone was set, for those in the know, by the dedication of the whole department to the poet's father, Sholem Fefer. This was a far cry from Izi Kharik's "pass on, pass on, you lonely grandfathers."

    Although the poet meets in the shtetl an old man who reads the "whining [Shimen] Frug," he underlines that there are also old people who prefer another kind of literature: his father reads the Moscow *Der emes.* Fefer notices many signs of profound changes in his shtetl: young pioneers, members of the Komsomol, a club for workers of the clothing industry, new houses, a tannery that provides jobs for local workers. The former tavern-keeper trades in needlework rather than in liquor and girls, and her only son is in the Red Army. The poet's former *melamed* (religious teacher) has died, and his daughter ran away with a *goy.* The *shames* (synagogue sexton) dreams about obtaining a position as courier at the local party committee. Not very much is left of the old shtetl, of the "synagogue, goats, shops, and mud." Fefer is happy to see the transformation:

        Shtey ikh yontevdik un ze,
        vi in rash fun yorn
        ot-o-do in mist, in vey
        vert a velt geborn.

> I'm standing in a festive mood, seeing
> how in the noise of years
> here, in the manure, in pain,
> a world is being born.

Fefer's "Manure in Full Bloom" is a rare example of a contemporary Soviet literary work presenting a positive picture of the shtetl. In general, such festive contemplation of the shtetl was not in the mainstream of proletarian poetry, which usually sang hymns to the city.[59] Rather, it was an endeavor to cloak a nationalist agenda in a new Soviet coat. Fefer—and some other Soviet Jewish activists—obviously believed that the shtetl could be revitalized as a center of Soviet Jewish life and culture, where a new Soviet Jewish nation would be built. Later, in the 1930s or 1940s, they would pay dearly for such nation-building fantasies.

The speed with which Fefer acquired an important place in Soviet Yiddish literature does not suggest that there was much casualness about it. He won critical acclaim as a follower of Pavlo Tychina, the leading Ukrainian proletarian poet.[60] Eduard Bagritskii, Vladimir Maiakovsky, Demian Bednyi, and Heinrich Heine were also listed among Fefer's teachers.[61] In 1928–29 he, together with the Ukrainian poet Mikola Tereshchenko, toured in Poland, Germany, Czechoslovakia, and other European countries, representing Soviet literature.[62] It was one of only a few occasions when a Soviet Yiddish writer was allowed to leave the country. Another rare foreign trip occurred in 1928, when Ber Orshanski came to Berlin, although as a speaker on the perspectives of creating a Jewish republic in the Soviet Union rather than as a writer.[63]

In addition to being more talented than most of the other Yiddish proletarian writers, Fefer came to Soviet literature without any "old scores," apart from eighteen months in the Bund. According to one of his biographers, he "was perhaps the only one who had not experienced any ideological vacillations, wanderings, or doubts."[64] In one of his poems, "Ikh hob keyn mol nit geblondzhet" (I've never been lost), Fefer stated, "In all my short, happy life, I've never / been lost, nor forgotten the way I came."[65] Most importantly, Fefer came into literature as a Soviet apparatchik, with the understanding that to serve the revolution meant to serve the authorities. For them, he was a writer who could be relied on.

Indeed, he was a loyal party member, a loyal Soviet citizen, who thankfully accepted the party's and government's sponsorship of the unprecedented development of Yiddish-language education, publishing, and various other activities. He was thankful for the breathtaking prospects that Yiddish and Yiddish-speakers, he believed, had in the Soviet Union. These prospects, coupled with his own rapid transformation into a recognized, well-paid literary lion, made him see himself as a soldier of the revolution; even poetry he saw as a battlefield.

> Brigades fun dikhter!
> In marsh foroys!
> Meg Leivick and Leivicklekh shpotn . . .
> Gemutikt hot undz bolshevistisher gang,
> bagaystert undz heyser gevet hot,
> mir hobn derisn mit prostn gezang
> dem fremdn poetishn metod.[66]

> Brigades of poets!
> Quick march!
> Who cares that Leivick and his ilk mock . . .
> The Bolshevik tread has inspired us,
> the heated competition has heartened us,
> our simple song has out-voiced
> the alien poetic method.

This poem, "An entfer Kushnirovn" (An answer to Kushnirov's [letter]) was written in 1930, when the Soviet propaganda already regarded H. Leivick as a renegade of the left camp because he had distanced himself from the pro-Soviet movement, protesting against the Comintern's support of Arab riots in Palestine in August 1929.

The Kharkov "Red World"

"After the homely, Jewish atmosphere of Kiev and the friendly Jewish students' milieu of Moscow . . . , Kharkov seemed to me an alien, cold city," reminisced Hersh Smolyar, a young Jewish communist. He had been dispatched to Kharkov in the mid-1920s as a reinforcement to the local Yiddish Komsomol activists.[67] "It is a tough, industrial, not homely city," echoed in 1926 the Yiddish writer Israel Joshua Singer, sent to Russia as a correspondent of the New York best-selling Yiddish daily *Forverts*.[68] The same year, David Volkenshtein, a Kiev Yiddish writer, wrote, "Kharkov is still a desert."[69] Indeed, as a Soviet Yiddish cultural center Kharkov emerged almost ex nihilo. Very few enthusiasts of Yiddish letters lived there before World War I. It is illuminating that by 1913 the Vilna journal *Di yidishe velt,* committed to promoting modern Yiddish literature and culture, had won only seven subscribers and twenty-five regular buyers in Kharkov.[70]

In Imperial Russia, Kharkov, which was excluded from the Pale of Settlement, did not play any significant role in Jewish life. The proto-Zionist group Bilu, formed in 1881 by local high school youth and university students, is the only memorable footprint left by the city in pre–World War I Jewish history.[71] During the war, however, the Jewish population of the city increased thanks to the influx of refugees from the western areas of the empire, in particular from Lithuania and Belorussia. For instance, from Grodno to Kharkov there were evacuated the Jewish Teaching Courses (1907–18), whose graduates later played a significant role in Jewish cultural life in the Soviet Union and other countries.[72] In 1917, during the election to the All-Russian Constituent Assembly, more than 6,000 Kharkov dwellers voted for Jewish parties.[73]

In 1917 one of the Jewish refugees, Kalman Zingman, founded a publishing house named Yiddish. Apart from his own books, such as the utopian novel *In the Future Town of Edenia,* he launched a periodical called *Kunst-ring* (Art link). Its first issue came out by the end of 1917. An editorial note reassured the readers that in 1918 the *Kunst-ring* would become a monthly publication. However, its second and last issue, with a cover designed by El Lissitzky, came out in 1919. Only a few of the journal's contributors lived, at least temporarily, in Kharkov. One of them was Moshe Taitsh, who edited the first local Yiddish paper, *Kharkiver tsaytung* (Kharkov newspaper), which began to appear as a weekly in August 1918 but did not last long. Here also lived a few tyro Yiddish writers, such as Hirsh Bloshtein, a refugee from Lithuania (he would later return to Lithuania, emigrate to Argentina, and reappear in Russia as a political emigrant), and Khana Levin, a Ekaterinislav-born poet. Between 1917 and 1921, Kharkov saw a number of (usually short-lived) Yiddish periodicals of the Bund, SERP, Fareynikte (the product of the merger of the SERP with the Zionist-Socialists), and Folkspartey. All in all, between 1917 and 1921, Kharkov was the sixth-most-important Yiddish publishing center in postrevolutionary Russia, behind Kiev, Odessa, Petrograd, Moscow, and Ekaterinoslav, but ahead of Minsk and Vitebsk.[74]

Twice during the civil war the Red Army had to leave the city: first from April 1918 to January 1919, and then from June 1919 to December 1919.

Local Bolsheviks, following the example of other party organizations, formed a Jewish Section, whose main task was to conduct propaganda among the Yiddish-speaking population.[75] In March 1919 the Jewish Section of the Ukrainian Communist Party established in Kharkov its first biweekly, *Der yidisher komunist* (Jewish communist). In 1920–22, the Jewish Section published the newspaper *Der komunist* (Communist). Still, despite the fact that Kharkov, reputed as Ukraine's revolutionary center, became the capital of Soviet Ukraine, the main organ of the Ukrainian Communist Party's Jewish Section, *Komunistishe fon,* continued to appear in "nationalist" Kiev.

At the same time, Kharkov emerged as the center of Yiddish Komsomol publications: *Der yunger kemfer* (Young fighter), published 1920; *Di proletarishe yugnt* (Proletarian youth), published 1920; and *Kamfs-klangen* (Sounds of the battle), published 1921. In 1922, Aron Kushnirov, who had ripened poetically in pre–World War I Kiev and ideologically in the Red Army, edited a collection, *Yugnt* (Youth), which presented the young Yiddish poetry of Ukraine. The book appeared as a publication of the Ukrainian Komsomol in the series of "Library of a young communar." The magazine *Libknekhts dor* ([Karl] Liebknecht's generation) was another publishing attempt of the Kharkov Komsomol activists. It came out only once, in January 1923, and was later reincarnated in the Moscow *Yungvald*. In November 1923 the central Yiddish newspaper of the Ukrainian Komsomol, *Der yunger arbeter* (Young worker), began to appear in Kharkov. The next year this newspaper was relaunched as *Yunge gvardye* (Young guard), presumably because its previous name was reserved for the sister Komsomol organ published in Minsk.

In 1924 the Kiev *Komunistishe fon* was phased out, and in 1925 the Ukrainian Jewish communists were given a new daily, based in Kharkov and called *Der shtern* (Star). At the time, it was the biggest newspaper in the country; its circulation of around twelve thousand exceeded the combined circulation of the Moscow *Der emes* (seven thousand) and the Minsk *Oktyabr* (four thousand).[76] The next year another republican Yiddish newspaper began to appear in Kharkov—*Der yidisher poyer* (Jewish peasant), targeting the increasing (in number and importance) population of Jewish villagers. Kharkov continued to grow as a center of the Yiddish press as more periodicals appeared: in 1927 the paper *Der kustar* (Artisan), and in 1928 the children's paper *Zay greyt* (Be ready) and the pedagogical monthly *Ratnbildung* (Soviet education). By 1930, Kharkov had nine Yiddish periodicals.[77] In the early 1930s, a few specialized monthlies appeared in the city, with such

Soviet-speak titles as *Gezunt un arbet* (Health and work), published 1930–32; *Yunger shlogler* (Young shock worker), published 1931–32; and *Bahershn di tekhnik fun der sotsialistisher landvirtshaftlekher produktsii* (To master the technology of the socialist agricultural production), published 1932–34. In May 1933 there was launched a bilingual (Ukrainian-Yiddish) professional newspaper, called *Kooperovanyi shkirniak-Kooperirter ledernik* (Cooperated leather-dresser), an organ of the Kharkov Intradistrict Trade Union of Leather-dressers.

Like any other Soviet Yiddish publishing center, Kharkov produced predominantly periodicals and books endorsed by political organizations. No Yiddish commercial publishing houses emerged in Soviet Russia even during the NEP period, when it was allowed to open private enterprises. Predominance of partisan propagandism and modernist experimentalism was also characteristic of the contemporary non-Soviet Yiddish book market, which lagged far behind the Yiddish press.[78] Nonetheless, in no other place was the Yiddish book production so decommercialized as in the Soviet Union. In Soviet Jewish activists' eyes, entertaining literature was anathema, a sign that all their propaganda efforts were going to the dogs, and Jewish communists ruthlessly suppressed such publications. Moreover, some Soviet Yiddish functionaries regarded belles lettres as publications of minor importance when compared with political literature.[79]

In the growing population of Kharkov, Jews made up about 20 percent of the population: in 1920, there were 55,500 Jews; in 1923, 65,000; and in 1926, 81,000. By 1926 Kharkov's Jews made up the third-largest Jewish community in Ukraine, behind Odessa (153,200) and Kiev (140,300).[80] In 1925 Kharkov became the site of the second permanent Yiddish theater in the Soviet Union, after the Moscow State Theatre.[81] The Kharkov Yiddish Theater was led by Ephraim Loiter, the former head of the Culture League theater troupe.

In 1924 the question was raised of moving the Yiddish literary center from Kiev to Kharkov and of launching a capital-based Yiddish literary journal. This issue was discussed in a special memorandum of the Press Department of the Central Committee of the Ukrainian Communist Party. The head of the department, M. Ravitsh-Cherkasky, was Jewish. Motl Kiper, the head of the Ukrainian Jewish Section, backed this proposal, arguing that Yiddish literature would immensely benefit from the capital's proletarian environment, where it would liberate itself from the nationalist and Yiddishist hangups of Kiev. In reality, this idea was the party functionary's wishful thinking, because the Kharkov Jewish proletariat was more acculturated than in other parts of Ukraine: only 36 percent of the Kharkov region's Jewish trade-unionists were Yiddish-speakers, compared with 89 percent in the Berdichev region, 55 percent in the Kiev region, and 42 percent in the Odessa region.[82] In general, it was not easy to create overnight a literary center in a city that housed a number of journalists but had no literary lions. Moshe Taitsh, for instance, had been transferred to Moscow in order to reinforce the editorial staff of *Der emes*.[83] For all that, the apparatchiks' initiative resulted in creating in Kharkov a new Yiddish literary journal, *Di royte velt*.[84]

The first editors of *Di royte velt* were Henekh Kazakevich and M. Ravitsh-Cherkasky. While the latter was king for a day in Yiddish literature, Kazakevich was a remarkable figure in Soviet Yiddish journalism. A graduate of the Grodno Teachers Courses, he in 1918–24 edited various periodicals in Ekaterinoslav, Kiev, and Gomel, and in 1924 he was transferred to Kharkov. The first issue of the new journal appeared in September 1924 with a print run of two thousand. It was labeled a "politically-social, literary-scientific biweekly journal." Indeed, the first issue contained only two literary works—a poem by Itsik Fefer and a story by Shmuel Persov. The other materials were devoted to theater, politics, cosmology, and literary criticism. The journal underlined its international character. In the list of its potential contributors we find the names of the editors and writers of the New York *Frayhayt* Moshe Olgin, Morris Winchevsky, Shakhne Epshtein, Moshe Katz, and Moshe Nadir. Also, it was announced that the Vilna publishing house of Boris Kletzkin was preparing books by four Soviet writers listed among the journal's contributors: Aron Kushnirov, Moshe Khashchevatsky, Ezra Finninberg, and Nokhum Oislender.

The other four issues of the journal published in 1924 had the same polymathic character, containing some belles lettres but also articles on chemical weapons, on various technical questions, and even on the metric system, which was being introduced in the country. Khaim Abraham Finkel, a graduate of the Kharkov University and a former Zionist-Socialist, was an active writer of popular articles in the journal. In its last issue published in 1924 the editors promised to do their best to normalize the rhythm of the publication. They also announced a reduction of the subscription price.

Fifteen issues were published in 1925, although the word "biweekly" disappeared only in the double issue (numbers 10 and 11), which came out in July. Starting in 1926 the journal was published as a monthly. Another important change—the editorial board: Mikhl Levitan, now a leading functionary of the Jewish Section, was a founder of the SERP and a pioneer of Yiddish secular pedagogy; Ezra Finninberg, a former Zionist-Socialist activist and a rising Soviet literary star; David Feldman (editor in chief), a Communist functionary; Fayvl Shprakh, editor in chief of *Der shtern*; Henekh Kazakevich; and Leyb Kvitko, a recent returnee from Germany, whom the Kharkov Jewish Section "intercepted" on his way to settle in Kiev.[85] Leyb Kvitko's wife, Beti Kvitko, reminisced later:

> Kvitko was invited to become the managing editor of *Di royte velt*. The editor in chief was the communist D. Feldman, who had three other senior positions (such things happened often at that time), and Kvitko had no other choice as to take on the whole responsibility for the journal.
>
> In one of the rooms of the Ukrainian publishing house Ukrspilka [Ukrainian Trade Unions] were five editorial offices—five desks and one telephone for all of them. Kvitko occupied one of the desks. He and a proofreader, who worked also at the Tsentalfarlag publishing house, formed the whole staff of *Di royte velt*.

Overcrowded also described the Kvitkos' apartment, which they shared with three other writers and their families: one was Leyb Kvitko's Yiddish colleague Ezra Finninberg (his wife, Eva Khenkin, and Oislender's wife, the poet Mira Khenkin, were sisters), and the two remaining rooms were occupied by Ukrainian writers, one the leading Ukrainian poet Pavlo Tychina. The latter asked Kvitko to teach him Yiddish, which helped him to translate many Yiddish poems into Ukrainian. Kvitko and Tychina always remained very close friends.[86]

By the end of 1926, Feldman disappeared from the editorial board, and his place was occupied by Levitan. In the meantime, the journal concentrated on literature. The statistics published in issue 8–9 (1927) show the increase of literary materials: 36 percent of the publication in 1924, 39 percent in 1925, 45 percent in 1926, and 51 percent in 1927. In the early 1920s, when Soviet Yiddish literature was dominated by poetry, it was difficult to fill the literary pages without significant prose works. The increase of the journal's literary department indicated the appearance of prose works, written either by poets, such as Kvitko and Finninberg, or by new prose writers.[87]

In August 1927, Dobrushin, a central figure in Moscow Yiddish literary and theatrical circles, was happy to conclude that *Di royte velt* would "very soon become a successful journal."[88] Nonetheless, in January 1928 its print run was cut in half, to 1,000. Although its print run increased in November to 1,400, it fell again in December to 1,250. The circulation continued to fluctuate during 1929, rising to 1,500 by the end of the year. In the following years the journal struggled to get more readers. The following commentary in the March 1930 issue of *Di royte velt* reveals the editors' frustration: "As our readers have already noticed, the print run of this issue is 2,000 copies, which is a sign that the circulation of *Di royte velt* is increasing. None the less, it is still not enough. It will be possible to increase the circulation to 3,000 copies, if the party and Soviet organizations and individual comrades demonstrate their activity in this issue." Judging by the imprints of the journal's issues, only once (in April 1930) did it print 3,500 copies, but this was a special issue—dedicated to the collectivization.

In 1929 the journal was edited by Levitan, Kazakevich, Kvitko, and Kiper. Starting with issue 5–6, however, two new names appeared on the editorial board: Shakhne Epshtein, who became the journal's new editor in chief, and Itsik Fefer, already the main proletarian Yiddish poet in Ukraine. Issue 9 opens with photos of all the journal's editors: Kazakevich (September 1924–June 1925), Feldman (June 1925–December 1926), Levitan (December 1926–May 1929), and Epshtein, from May 1929. This iconostasis, marking the fifth anniversary of the journal, shows a peaceful succession of editors. *Di royte velt*'s editorship was Epshtein's first assignment after returning to the Soviet Union from America. He was a veteran Yiddish journalist and one of the three pre-1917 Marxist Yiddish literary critics; Shakhne Epshtein and Moshe Olgin then represented the Bundist literary thought, whereas Moshe Litvakov was the leading theorist of the Zionist-Socialist Party.

Epshtein became the fist full-time editor of the journal and its first own literary critic. He occupied this position till August 1931. Then, until December 1931 the journal was headed by the editorial board—Levitan, Fefer, Kazakevich, and Kiper. In December a new editor in chief was appointed: Khaim Gildin, the pioneer Yiddish proletarian poet in Soviet Russia. Gildin edited the journal until it was phased out after its final two issues—the quadruple 9–12 in 1932 and, eventually, the triple 1–3 in 1933.

The Civil War in Yiddish Literature

In the July 1925 issue of *Di royte velt,* Nusinov, who published in the journal his "Letters from Moscow," announced the outbreak of "the civil war in Yiddish literature," that is between the left proletarian writers, who had formed in Moscow the Yiddish Section of the MAPP and published the almanac *Oktaybr* (October), and the Moscow Collective of Yiddish October Writers, who had published the almanac *Nayerd* (New land). In addition to the confusing fact that the organization with the word "October" was not the publisher of the almanac *Oktyabr,* it is generally difficult to understand the division between the *Oktyabr* and *Nayerd* writers, except that they were two cliques. The situation is especially confusing because, according to Nusinov, two of the three "most Soviet" works, Fefer's and Kharik's poems, were published in the ostensibly less proletarian *Nayerd,* and only one, Kushnirov's story, found a place in the vehemently proletarian *Oktaybr.*[89] Granted, Nusinov was not a reliable judge of proletarian literary production. He, at that time the main literary theoretician of the journal, was an adherent of a sociological (later disparaged as "vulgar sociological") approach to creativity and did not believe that writers of nonproletarian origins could create proletarian literature. He argued that Yiddish proletarian literature had hardly any social basis because the vast majority of Soviet Jews were petit bourgeois persons trying to find their place in the new society.[90]

In fact, the civil war in Yiddish literature began earlier, in January 1922, when Moshe Litvakov, then the new editor of *Der emes,* attacked the recalcitrant "Yiddish literary emigration in Moscow." By 1925, however, literary criticism became particularly pitiless, especially because the party leadership encouraged the "hegemony of proletarian critics in assessing literary works from the point of view of their social significance."[91] Such critics as Litvakov and the younger Minsk-based literary pundit Yasha Bronshtein excelled in proletarian bloodthirstiness. The Moscow critic and writer Yekhezkel Dobrushin even asked publicly for protection from the Minsk critic's bruising attacks.[92]

The June 1925 appointment of Feldman as editor of *Di royte velt* apparently catalyzed the proletarian-nonproletarian stratification of Yiddish writers in Ukraine. A party functionary of Trotskyist persuasion, Feldman was a sharp opponent of proletarian literature, and during his tenure such "proletarians" as Gildin, Fefer, and Kushnirov had problems publishing their works in the journal. As late as 1929, Feldman argued that instead of revolutionary contents Fefer's poetry had much of revolutionary window-dressing.[93] Feldman, together with Kvitko, became a member of the Free Academy of Proletarian Literature (VAPLITE), which united "qualified writers" after the disintegration of Hart and, despite its proletarian name, opposed the All-Ukrainian Union of Proletarian Writers (VUSPP).

In 1927, during the first congress of the VUSPP, Gildin recalled how he for four years "desperately struggled" to create in Moscow a Yiddish proletarian organization. Only now he could reap his reward, but the organization remained small: it had only eighteen members—half the number belonging to the proletarian writers' organization in Belorussia. Gildin was particularly hurt when for two years he could not find a Soviet outlet for his poem *Leniniada* and initially published it in America and Argentina. (In fact, some fragments appeared in *Der emes* on 16 April 1924.) Only in 1926 did the poem came out in Kharkov. Gildin spoke also about his and other proletarian writers' boycott of *Di royte velt,* whose editors filled the journal with works by American and Polish authors.[94]

In Ukraine the proletarian-nonproletarian divide was often eclipsed by the much more serious schism between the writers who wanted to be part of the general Soviet literary process and the aggressively territorial Ukrainian writers. In the winter of 1926–27, Feldman was instrumental in founding the VAPLITE-oriented Yiddish literary group Boy (Construction) as a reincarnation of the Hart-oriented Antenna.[95] The setup of Boy brought to an end the mongrel Association of Yiddish Writers.

In the meantime, the proletarian contingent re-formed its ranks. A group of Yiddish proletarian writers, who wanted to become part of the VUSPP, surfaced in December 1927. Their meeting took place in Kharkov. The key speaker, Litvakov, came from Moscow. The main local (Kharkov and Kiev) initiators—Hofshtein, Fefer, Gildin, Abraham Kahan, and Yankel Levin—became members of the Yiddish bureau created at the VUSPP. In its resolution the meeting drew attention to a gap between their target reader—"the communist avant-garde of the Jewish proletariat"—and the petit bourgeois intellectual writer. According to Litvakov's analysis, some of the petit bourgeois intellectuals had welcomed the revolution, partly because of its nationalities politics and partly because of their hope to have also (or even predominantly) a nonproletarian readership. In the meantime, some of these intellectuals began to orient themselves on the proletariat and support the groups of young proletarian literati. Hence the "literary battles" between them and nonproletarian circles.[96] Hofshtein, one such "proletarian-oriented petit bourgeois intellectuals," was an unlikely leader of the Yiddish VUSPP. On the other hand, Dobrushin, who knew him in their Kiev and Moscow periods of activities, quoted the Yiddish saying *az esn khazer iz fet* ("if one starts eating pork, it's better to eat a fat one"), predicting that Hofshtein would join the proletarian movement in an effort to expiate his sins.[97]

In general, according to Epshtein, the vetting of candidates to the Yiddish proletarian organizations was never as rigid as in the similar Russian and Ukrainian organizations.[98] Indeed, Shmuel Niger had problems with finding distinct proletarian features in the almanac *VUSPP*, published in Kharkov in 1929.[99]

The almanac contained works by nineteen writers, including Itsik Fefer, David Hofshtein, Abraham Abchuk, Itsik Kipnis, Abraham Kahan, and Irme Druker. Nonetheless, a large group of writers in Ukraine remained outside the proletarian organization, most notably Leyb Kvitko, Der Nister, Lipe Reznik, Noah Lurie, David Volkenshtein, Ezra Finninberg, and Moshe Khashchevatsky. Such writers were sometimes called "wild" ones, or "non-organized." In Belorussia the situation was different: the vast majority of Yiddish writers had been "organized" in BelAPP, with just a handful of "wild" writers, such as the critic Ayzik Rozentsvayg and the poet Khaim Levin. All in all, judging by statistics of Yiddish books published in the Soviet Union between 1928 and 1930, the "organized" writers (with seventy-one books) outnumbered the "nonorganized" ones (thirty books).[100]

In April 1928 the VUSPP published the first issue of its Yiddish literary journal, *Prolit*. It would be, however, wrong to see this as a publication that was irreconcilably antagonistic to *Di royte velt*, especially because Fefer, one of the editors and later the editor in chief of the *Prolit*, joined the editorial board of *Di royte velt* from its issue 5–6, in 1929. Still, the journals catered different groups of writers and readers. *Di royte velt* was a highbrow periodical, modeling Russian "thick journals," whereas the *Prolit* was not ashamed to publish tyro writers—the literary yield of the worker correspondent movement. Such an openness, however, did not make the *Prolit* a mass periodical; in 1930, for instance, its circulation was fifteen hundred. The cadre of Yiddish proletarian writers, meanwhile, kept growing, from eighteen in 1928 to sixty-eight in 1931 (twenty poets, thirty prose-writers, twelve critics and essayists, and three playwrights).[101]

The climate in Yiddish literature had significantly changed by 1929. "In society as a whole 1929 marked the beginning of Stalin's autocracy. In literature it was mirrored by a political campaign, unprecedented in virulence and scale, that came to be known as the 'Pilnyak and Zamyatin Affair.' The pretext was the publication abroad of works by the two writers: [Yevgeny] Zamyatin's novel *We*, [Boris] Pilnyak's short novel *Mahogany*." [102] In this climate, Soviet Jewish functionaries made much less penetrable the barriers between Soviet and non-Soviet literary milieus. One of the signs of the change became the castigation of Shmuel Gordon, then a young Yiddish writer, for sending his poems to the Warsaw weekly *Literarishe bleter*.[103] Granted, also before 1929 writers were criticized for publishing their works in noncommunist foreign periodicals. For instance, in issue 3 (1928) of *Prolit*, Markish had to repent of publishing his poem in *Literarishe bleter*. Nonetheless, it was Gordon whom Soviet media turned into an object lesson. (Gordon, after a few public acts of repentance, was given a chance to graduate from the Moscow Teachers Training Institute; later he became an established writer of prose.)

Relations with the West became even more confrontational in the aftermath of Abraham Reisen, H. Leivick, Isaac Raboy, and Menakhem Boreisha's resignation from *Frayhayt*. Paul (Pesakh) Novick, the *Frayhayt* journalist (and later its editor), was at that time in Kharkov and reported about the meeting of local Yiddish literati, condemning the defectors. Markish and particularly Kvitko stood out as the sharpest denouncers and initiators of a wordy resolution, which stressed the rupture of their relations with the anti-*Frayhayt* group: "We cannot have any relations with the defenders of the bloody attack in Palestine of the Zionists, who support the British imperialism; with those who allowed to be drawn into the chauvinist-nationalist hysteria, fabricated by the yellow-black press as a weapon in the fight against the revolutionary labor movement, against the Soviet Union."[104] Yet Markish wrote to his American colleague and friend David Opatoshu, arguing that he was not directly involved in the campaign:

I was not in Kharkov [at that time]. It was in Yalta where I read the protest with my signature under it. I also read there my speech that someone had delivered on my behalf. Nonetheless, not [that] this is, of course, important, but Leivick, who was popular in the Soviet Union, really popular, even if somewhat less than [Abraham] Reisen . . . In general, we don't know which end is up anymore. The atmosphere here is one of striving for being ostentatiously proletarian and 100% kosher, and it has revealed plenty of lie, cowardice, and wavering; it's becoming quite impossible to work.[105]

Peretz Markish was lambasted for his story "Khaveyrim kustarn" (Comrades artisans), published in 1928 in issues 10 and 11 of *Di royte velt*. The protagonist of the story, Koplman, is a propagandist working with Jewish artisans. A communist and a demobilized Red Army soldier, he is always, even on the hottest day, dressed in a military overcoat, thus remaining ready to return to his regiment. He does not react to the typist Bella's persistent flir-

tation because he respects only one woman—Rosa Luxemburg. He successfully fulfils his mission of converting a synagogue into an artisans' club
named after his beloved heroine of the German revolution. Small wonder,
then, that vigilant critics accused Markish of ridiculing Jewish party activists.[106] Judging by Markish's January 1927 letter to his Warsaw friend
Melekh Ravitsh, he indeed was rather sarcastic about Litvakov and, generally, the Jewish functionaries. Litvakov, he argued, was "more tragic than
communist." Markish was also skeptical about the audience for Yiddish activities. Yiddish intellectuals were becoming a caste, catering to the most
backward part of the Jewish population.[107] Markish also did not hide his
disdain for the "proletarian parasite" Gildin, who lived in Kharkov and was
busy denouncing his colleagues; in particular, he denounced Markish for
having a Polish passport.[108] In the meantime, the Kharkov *Yunge gvardye* accused Markish of being a money-grubber, demanding ten rubles for an appearance at a factory. Litvakov ostensibly berated the Kharkov newspaper
for digging up dirt on Markish, but by quoting the accusation in *Der emes* he
actually spread it among his readers.[109]

Bickering became sharper among Soviet writers. Thus, Lipe Reznik complained of being accused of mysticism (by Hofshtein) and decadence (by
Fefer) and of receiving general sharp criticism of his writing (by Abchuk). As
a result, he had been able to publish only two poems during the last two
years.[110] Zelig Akselrod, whom literary pundits (e.g., Abchuk) accused of
modeling Esenin's epicureanism, did not publish any books during the whole
decade between 1922 and 1932.[111] Litvakov, Bronshtein, and a few other
critics sharply criticized Der Nister's 1929 book *Gedakht* (Imagined). But
Litvakov, an old admirer of Der Nister, held his ground and managed to
combine criticism of the writer's symbolism with praise for his talent:

> [Der Nister's] Symbolism reveals his ideological outlook with a clear attrac-
> tion towards the other world and mysticism. At the same time, however,
> Symbolism has a pure technical side, it has its technical methods to general-
> ize things and phenomena. Such methods are used by the bourgeois for re-
> moving those things and phenomena from our contemporary world. The
> proletarian art, none the less, can undergo transformation according to its
> own ways and needs, therefore it can also use Symbolic methods of collect-
> ing, applying, and organizing lexical material, and, as a result, enriching the
> intellectual and ideological vocabulary of the language. By rejecting in Der
> Nister Der Nister's ideology, I maintain that from the point of view of word-

interlacing (*verter-geveb*) and of striving for artistic generalization, Der Nister represents a higher stage than Sholem Aleichem.[112]

In other words, in 1930, Litvakov was still keen to find a hybrid between Der Nister's mysticism and prescribed realism. He was not fated to live to see how Der Nister would a decade later realize his dream—as well as the dream of the two other leading critics of the Kiev Group vintage: Dobrushin and Oislender. Der Nister's novel *Di mishpokhe Mashber* (The Mashber family), with "mystic layers hidden under its realistic façade," "had summed up the ideological and aesthetic search of Soviet Yiddish intellectuals in the 1920s." [113] In the meantime, however, Der Nister remained fair game for criticism. Rakhmiel Fish, an editor of *Der emes* who reviewed N. Oislender and L. Goldin's *Leyenbukh farn drintn yor* (Reader for the third grade, published in Kharkov in 1933), was not happy to find in the book an "obscure" fairy tale by Der Nister.[114]

In 1930, Fefer listed the effects of proletarian critics' attacks: Dobrushin had left the field of literary criticism and concentrated on writing plays; Oislender had given up his endeavors "to head the belated Yiddish Symbolism" and worked as an academic; Markish, Finninberg, Orland, and Daniel had "moved to the left," whereas Der Nister and Reznik had "moved to the right"; Akselrod and Volkeshtein "had fallen silent." [115]

The greatest scandal, however, was created around Kvitko's poetic *sharzhn* (caricatures), particularly the *sharzh* that depicted Litvakov as a "stink bird Moyli," sitting unattainably high on the roof and poisoning with its stink people's lives. Kvitko published his caricatures in *Di royte velt* (5–6, 1929) and included them in his book *Gerangl* (Struggle), published the same year in the Kharkov Tsentrfarlag, whose editor was his friend Henekh Kazakevich.[116] Ironically, these caricatures, which would be treated as a protest against the party guidance of literature, came out soon after a conference at the Ukrainian Communist Party's Jewish Sections, dedicated to the party's leading role in literary life. Significantly, during that conference Gildin emphasized that Litvakov did not represent the general line of the party.[117] Kvitko, Epshtein, Kazakevich, and other opponents of Litvakov's one-upmanship apparently did not realize that an open attack against the central Yiddish daily's editor could provoke accusation of a serious violation of party discipline. In any case, after the two publications of Kvitko's fables, events followed thick and fast. In September 1929 the Yiddish Section of the

VUSSP convened an extraordinary meeting to discuss Kvitko's "anticommunist pasquinade" and demanded the author be sacked from his position at *Di royte velt*.[118] Indeed, after the October 1929 issue Kvitko's name disappeared from the journal's imprint. He ended up working as apprentice lathe operator at the Kharkov Tractor-Building Factory.

Many writers saw Kvitko's case as a signal that Litvakov and his ilk wanted to achieve full control over Soviet Yiddish literature. Litvakov did not hide his intention, condemning the Ukraine writers' "literary protectionism" and their literary "fiefdom." [119] Hofshtein, whose relations with the VUSPP began to deteriorate even before Kvitko's case, sent a circular letter (it was eventually published in *Der emes*)[120] in which he argued that, although Kvitko had been out of line, it was not right to humiliate him, especially because Litvakov was well known for bullying other writers and for his dictatorial character. Epshtein, too, tried to protect Kvitko, arguing that the poet could not be treated as a Yiddish Pilnyak.[121] Markish also felt impelled to raise his voice, writing an open letter to Litvakov.[122] Kiper was against carrying Kvitko's ostracism too far. Moreover, he used Kvitko's case to justify the closing down of the Jewish Sections, which—he argued—became a breeding ground for turf battles.[123] As a sign of rehabilitation, a poem by Kvitko opened the September 1930 issue of *Di royte velt*. In January 1931, an article on the Kiev Yiddish readers' demand revealed that Kvitko was the fourth most popular Soviet Yiddish writer, behind Bergelson, Markish, and the younger prose writer M. Daniel.[124] Kvitko used as fodder for his writing his experience working at the factory, publishing in 1931 a new book— *In trakter-tsekh* (In tractor shop).

The "proletarian" camp, however, was not ready to pardon Kvitko. The young proletarian critic Shmuel Zhukovski defined Kvitko's case as a "relapse" (*retsidiv*—a popular word in Soviet Speak) of petit bourgeois views. According to Zhukovski, this case helped get rid of the petit bourgeois abscess in Yiddish literature. The VUSPP could not deal directly with Kvitko, who was not its member, but it expelled his "accomplices," Hofshtein and Itsik Kipnis, and censured Abraham Kahan, who in a letter to *Der shtern* (published on 17 September 1929) had admitted his "creative and ideological failure." [125] Beginning with the November-December 1929 issue of *Prolit*, Hofshtein's name disappears from the list of its editors.

Litvakov, who chronicled the development of Kvitko's case, diagnosed it as a symptom of the Kharkov (most notably Epshtein's) dissidence. He presented it as one of the three concurrent "literary mutinies against the com-

Leyb Kvitko

munist guidance": (1) Pilnyak's mutiny in Soviet Russian literature; (2) Kvitko's in Soviet Yiddish literature; and (3) Leivick, Boreisha, Reisen, and Raboy's mutiny in the American communist literature and press.[126] Litvakov's revenge shows through in the 1931 Russian anthology of Yiddish poetry, which he prefaced: Kvitko is represented with only one poem, whereas other poets of his stature were represented with seven poems.[127] In the introduction to Kvitko's 1933 book, published in the Emes Publishing House, we read,

> The book *Gerangl*, which came out in the year of the Bolshevik offensive on all fronts and of sharpened class-struggle (1929), once again mirrored the poet's vacillations. The same book contains motifs of revolutionary labor struggle in Germany, motifs of struggle against the petite bourgeois, private-owning elements and, at the same time, the infamous "Caricatures," which expressed class-alien views concerning the party guidance of the literature.
>
> From 1930 L. Kvitko's poetic route becomes straighter directed toward an organic understanding, and reflecting in his creative work, the revolution and Soviet reality.[128]

Ultimately, Kvitko was saved by the leading Russian children's writer Kornei Chukovski, who during the 1933 Kharkov conference on children's literature recognized in him a unique talent and later helped him to become a household name, *Lev* Kvitko. His books in Russian, Ukrainian, and other translations had print runs of many millions.[129] In general, non-Yiddish literary circles sometimes had their own yardstick and ignored opinions of the muscular Yiddish critics. For instance, the much-criticized Markish's story "Comrades Artisans" was translated into Ukrainian and published as a separate book.[130] Likewise Kipnis's *Months and Days* appeared in Russian.[131] Sholem Asch, who was almost a nonperson for Soviet Yiddish publishers, was available to Russian readers thanks to his collected works in seven volumes, published in 1929.[132] It seems that such experts as Nusinov and Gurshtein, both influential people in Russian literary circles, could overpower those Yiddish critics whose power base was confined to the readership of *Di royte velt, Prolit, Shtern,* and other Yiddish periodicals.

Di royte velt survived a bit longer than the *Prolit,* whose last issue came out in June 1932. In January 1933, Yiddish writers in Ukraine were given a new periodical, *Farmest* (Challenge), which soon swallowed *Di royte velt.* Consolidation was the key word of the literary 1930s, aside from the fact that the combined readership of a few thousand could not justify the existence of two literary periodicals. *Di royte velt* was arguably the most significant Soviet Yiddish literary periodical (and one of the first long-running Yiddish literary journals in the world) published in the relatively pluralist period of the late 1920s. Essentially, it was pluralism of "cliques masked with ideological principles."[133] The clique around *Di royte velt* represented predominantly the circles of Yiddish literati formed in Kiev in the 1910s and 1920s. Their squabbles, too, were mainly with the "Kievans," most notably with Litvakov, a central figure in Jewish literary life in Kiev in 1907–21.

After pre–World War I literary experiments, the post-revolutionary almanacs *Eygns* and *Baginen* produced in Kiev in 1918–20 and the short-lived Moscow journal *Shtrom,* the literary circle—developed in Kiev—eventually got a state-sponsored forum, *Di royte velt.* In marketing terms, all these publications, including *Di royte velt,* were failures. The general Yiddish reader was conservative; he was not remotely interested in the literary theories, debated ad nauseam in the journal, or in modernist poetry, which dominated in its literary departments. At the same time, *Di royte velt* was the most significant Soviet Yiddish literary creche, especially if we believe Nusinov, who argued that until 1924 there had been virtually no Yiddish literature written in

Moshe Litvakov

the Soviet Union.[134] Compared with *Prolit,* where fast-rising cub writers could mature into future socialist realists, *Di royte velt* played an important role in Soviet transmogrification of established writers, such as Kvitko, Markish, and Der Nister. The critics, too, transformed year after year. Nusinov, for example, stopped negating proletarian literature and began to argue that a Yiddish section at a proletarian association could be the only acceptable form of Yiddish writers' organization.[135] In the 1930s he would head the Yiddish section at the Soviet Writers' Association.

A unique role in the Ukrainian Yiddish literary life was played by Itsik Fefer, who placed himself above the divide between *Di royte velt* and *Prolit,* serving on the editorial boards of both journals. It is hardly a coincidence, then, that he headed the unified *Farmest,* with Gildin and Kvitko among the members of its editorial board. Fefer's role underlines the fact that the two Kharkov literary journals existed and later merged as complementary forums of Soviet Yiddish literature, which was in the making in the 1920s and early 1930s.

After 1934, when Ukraine's capital was transferred to Kiev, Kharkov saw an out-migration of Yiddish writers and journalists, primarily to Kiev and Moscow. It was, in any case, a makeshift literary center.

CHAPTER FIVE

Toward Socialist Realism

Soviet Classics

IN 1934 THE BOLSHEVIK REGIME was still young—just over sixteen. However, the Jewish branches of the ubiquitous Soviet apparatus had already reached the apogee of their development. Some of them, notably the Bolshevik Party's Jewish Sections, had died off earlier, but—in general—the Soviet Jewish subapparatus would stagger on until 1937–38. Meanwhile, an event in spring 1934 raised the expectations of the Soviet Jewish activists.

On 7 May, the Soviet government declared that the Birobidzhan Jewish National District (*raion*) had been raised to a higher status, that of Jewish Autonomous Region (*oblast'*). This change was widely regarded as a step toward a Jewish Autonomous Republic. In the steeply stratified Soviet hierarchy of ethnic groups and their autonomies, any upgrading of the Birobidzhan "Zion" signified wider opportunities for Jewish culture and its elite.[1] It is hardly a coincidence that 7 May 1934 was also the opening of the most representative forum in the history of Soviet Yiddish-language planning: the Kiev Yiddish Language Conference.[2]

Yiddish literature, too, was on the upswing. It is illuminating that—apart from the three Slavonic languages, Russian, Ukrainian, and Belorussian—only Georgian, Armenian, and Yiddish were regarded as languages of Soviet peoples with long-established literary traditions. As a result, for instance, they had not been deprived of their own writing systems during the campaign of general Latinization. Yiddish writers were full-fledged members of the Soviet literary community, particularly in Kiev, Kharkov, Minsk, and Moscow. Soviet Yiddish literary critics and scholars—notably Isaac Nusinov, Aron Gurshtein, Yasha Bronshtein, and Meir Wiener—played a visible role in the stormy discussions on proletarian literature and, after 1933, on socialist realism. Khatskel Dunets, the Minsk-based Yiddish critic, was even vice minister

136

of education in the Belorussian government from 1933 until 1935. In August 1934, twenty-four people represented Soviet Yiddish literature during the grandiose parade of unity between men of letters and the party leadership—the First All-Union Congress of Soviet Writers: Moscow was represented by David Bergelson, Peretz Markish, Shmuel Godiner, Yekhezkel Dobrushin, Aron Kushnirov, Moshe Litvakov, Isaac Nusinov, Ezra Finninberg, Josef Rabin, and Alexander Khashin; Ukraine by Itsik Fefer, David Hofshtein, Leyb Kvitko, Hirsh Orland, Moshe Alberton, Abraham Wieviorka, and Notte Lurye; Belorussia by Izi Kharik, Moshe Kulbak, Yasha Bronshtein, Zelig Akselrod, Ziskind Lev, and Khatskel Dunets; and the Caucasus by Shmuel Bregman.[3] Moshe Olgin came from New York as a correspondent of the American (English and Yiddish) communist press. The congress marked a new era in Soviet literary life. From then on a Soviet writer could be a member of only one organization—the Soviet Writers' Union.

Characteristically, Litvakov played a marginal role among the Yiddish delegates to the congress: he did not make a speech, although his archenemies Dunets and Bronshtein addressed the congress as general theorists of socialist realism.[4] Litvakov never recovered from the Kharkov assault, which was continued in the pages of *Di royte velt*. According to Epshtein's analysis, Litvakov's method combined formalism with Yiddishist nationalism and had little to do with Marxism.[5] Litvakov's situation was particularly difficult because he was attacked also by Yiddish critics from Minsk. The scandal around Litvakov became so noisy that in May 1930 it attracted the attention of the leaders of the All-Union Association of Proletarian Writers, VOAPP. In its resolution it protected Litvakov from his ruthless Minsk opponents (e.g., Dunets), who accused him, for instance, of praising the "raging petit bourgeois" poet Shmuel Halkin. Although the literary apparatchiks admitted Halkin's "nationalist tendencies," they condemned Dunets's description of his poetry as "a voice of a petty bourgeois who went berserk." Litvakov, too, was condemned for arguing that nationalism in Yiddish literature was less dangerous than national bolshevism.[6] Still, after 1929 Litvakov's influence waned. In 1930 his newspaper, *Der emes,* whose existence was always rather precarious,[7] lost its affiliation as the central organ of the party's Jewish Sections, which had been closed down. At a result, Litvakov was left suspended in midair after losing his position of the Jewish Sections' literary authority. His final collection of critical articles, *Af tsvey frontn* (On two fronts, 1931), was mainly a counterattack on his Kharkov and Minsk opponents.

In November 1931 the VOAPP returned to the issue of Litvakov in its resolution on concurrent discussions in Yiddish literary circles. The resolution criticized Yiddish literati for paying too much attention to Litvakov's persona. The Soviet literary leadership was not happy that Litvakov became the whipping boy in Yiddish literature and argued that the Minsk critics had overshot the mark in their criticism of the Moscow editor. At the same time, the resolution praised proletarian Yiddish writers for such positive achievements as their repulse of Kvitko's and Hofshtein's "reactionary pronouncements against the party leadership in literature," "unmasking of the reactionary, nationalist essence of works by Der Nister, Kipnis, Reznik, Halkin, and some other writers," and unmasking "Feldman's Trotskyist theories" and "anti-Marxist mistakes of Nusinov, Epshtein, and Litvakov." [8] The VOAPP's resolution, however, could not protect Litvakov from further attacks. In 1932 and 1933, *Di royte velt* continued to inveigh against Litvakov for his approach to Yiddish literary heritage (Abchuk) and for lack of "serious Marxist education" and "literary taste appropriate for a communist" (Gildin). [9]

On 2 December 1933, the Commission on Yiddish Literature at the Organizational Committee of the Soviet Writers Association listened to the reports on the state of affairs in Ukraine (Fefer), Belorussia (Dunets), and Russia (Nusinov). [10] The commission was glad to hear that cliquishness (*gruppovshchina*) was disappearing form the Yiddish literary circles. At the same time, Yiddish critics were reprimanded for lack of interest in socialist realism. In effect, Bronshtein, secretary of the Belorussian Writers' Union (he occupied this high position from 1932 until 1937), was the only Yiddish critic who had published an article on this topic. The Moscow Yiddish writers were also criticized for missing a chance to organize a literary soirée with Kvitko, who had moved from Kiev to Moscow a few months earlier, especially because Kvitko "latterly set an example of considerable transformation." The dearth of Russian writers interested in translating Yiddish poetry into Russian was also mentioned during the meeting; David Brodsky and Osip Kolychev were mentioned as the only Russian writers seriously committed to such translations. [11]

During the meeting, Markish, and later Godiner, spoke with fervor about the decline of Yiddish readership. They argued that the "denationalized" young Jewish reader did not want to read Yiddish books, being satisfied with Russian writers such as Mikhail Sholokhov and Fedor Panferov. As a result, some Yiddish writers began to think about switching over to Russian. Nonetheless, a number of the participants from Ukraine and Belorussia, most notably Kharik, Bronshtein, Fefer, and Rafalsky, diagnosed Markish's and Godiner's pessimism as a sickness characteristic of the Moscow-based writers, who were cut off from the mass of Yiddish speakers. True, the cited average print run of Yiddish books spoke for itself—2,000 to 3,000 for belles lettres; only school textbooks were printed in runs of 50,000 copies.

On 5 August 1934, shortly before the First Congress of Soviet Writers, an All-Union Conference of Yiddish Writers emphasized the fact that Soviet Yiddish literature became the first and only (worldwide) Jewish literature liberated from the Jewish question. Mirroring the reconstruction of the entirety of Jewish life in the Soviet Union, the literature had covered a huge distance—from the Pale of Jewish Settlement to Birobidzhan.[12] In 1935, Dmidrii Mirskii, a scion of a Russian aristocratic family who returned to Russia in 1932 as an established western literary critic and historian, hailed David Hofshtein, Leyb Kvitko, and Peretz Markish (whom he read in Osip Kolychev's translation) as the poets whose importance exceeded the bounds of Yiddish literature. He was particularly impressed with Markish's "monumental poetry." In summary, he said that Yiddish poetry was one of the most powerful branches of Soviet poetry.[13]

On the eve of the congress, Litvakov boasted that Soviet Yiddish literature had managed to draw into its ranks such a first-class master as Bergelson, who settled in the Soviet Union in the beginning of 1934.[14] Bergelson, however, corrected Litvakov, emphasizing the fact that he had been influenced by "the whole Soviet literature, the whole practice of socialist construction, led by the Communist Party" rather than by Soviet Yiddish literature alone.[15] During the congress, Bergelson was a few times hailed by his Soviet Yiddish colleagues. Dunets praised Bergelson's plays.[16] Fefer stated, "Our prose is headed by the prominent master David Bergelson. He leads our prose ahead. He, for example, gave us such an excellent work of Soviet Yiddish prose as *Bam Dnyeper*."[17] Bronshtein concentrated on the new phenomenon in Soviet literary life—creative self-criticism ("autocritique") of former fellow travelers whose works used to be crowded with reactionary characters. Following the method of self-criticism, such reformed retrogrades created new works, also populated with the same kind of characters, but the writers used merciless criticism to "guillotine" them and free themselves from their old errors. Bergelson's *Bam Dnyeper* was, according to Bronshtein, a striking example of such self-purification in Yiddish literature.[18] It might be added that Bergelson also "purified" his earlier stories, recasting them for the Soviet reader and critic.[19]

Bergelson was the only former Yiddish fellow traveler who was permitted to take the floor of the congress. In his speech, he argued that Soviet literature, the leading literature of the whole world, could no longer use the technique of western writers, because the contents of Soviet life and the subject matter of Soviet writings had become incompatible with non-Soviet life and literature. Bergelson reserved his most sharp criticism for Hamsun, in whose shadow he had been living for twenty-five years. Hamsun, argued Bergelson, had failed to show in his Nobel Prize–winning novel *The Growth of the Soil* a link between capitalists and farmers.[20] Bergelson welcomed the directive, given to Soviet writers by Stalin, "the great leader of the world proletariat," to use the method of socialist realism and to work as "engineers of human souls."[21]

In 1933, Bergelson explained the changes his methods of writing had undergone:

> During the last decade Bergelson has been working in a more organized manner and was more independent of his "Muse." . . . Bergelson explains that [before] he could not see the aim of his work clearly, for what and for whom he was writing, though perhaps it had also to do with lack of writing technique. Now Bergelson can successfully write two works at a time. Last year, for instance, he was writing concurrently *Birebidzhaner* (Birobidzhaners) and the second volume of *Bam Dnyeper.* . . . In recent years he has set himself a rate—5,000 characters a day [about two pages], with one free day a week. In former years he used to rewrite his works many times, but now it is different.[22]

The book *Birebidzhaner* (Moscow, 1934) was based on the travel notes Bergelson had made during his visits to the Far Eastern Jewish territorial unit, particularly in November 1932.[23] This was the first book Bergelson wrote as a *real* Soviet writer: in 1933 he finally left Germany and, after a short stay in Copenhagen, came to live in the Soviet Union. Apparently he was expected to settle in Birobidzhan—the showcase of Soviet Jewish policy—and to become a symbol of Yiddish culture there. Soviet Yiddish literary lions did not want to go to the remote Far Eastern borders, however, and tried to recruit for this mission returnees from the West. Bergelson kept promising to move to Birobidzhan,[24] but this plan never materialized.

Birebidzhaner puzzled Yiddish critics in the West. Meisel, who was always very charitable to Bergelson, wrote of it a decade later that in the process of mastering the new life in Birobidzhan, Bergelson had radically changed his mode of creativity.[25] It is difficult to agree with Meisel's opinion, however, because Bergelson's correspondence from 1926 can be seen as drafts for his Birobidzhan story. On the other hand, this was indeed the first *book* that marked a radical change, most obviously in the language it employed. Bergelson's *Birebidzhaner* is peppered with such Soviet Yiddish coinages as *fabzavutsh* (factory school), *fargezekshaftlekhn* (to socialize/collectivize), *fizkulturnik* (athlete), *kolvirt* (collective farm), and *komyugist* (member of the Komsomol). It appears that he generally changed the register of his language, preferring the vernacular style. For linguists he has a special gift—the verb *skompanyen zikh* (to associate), a unique example of a Yiddish verb formed with a Slavonic prefix.[26] However, the use of numerous colloquialisms does not save the story as a whole from being contrived. The characters are schematic, divided into three clearly demarcated groups: heroes, antiheroes, and the masses led by the heroes. In effect, the story in many places is as superficial as the 1936 Soviet film *Seekers of Happiness,* produced by Belgoskino (Belorussian State Film Studio).[27]

The majority of the characters are "the déclassé *shtetl* raw material," to borrow Litvakov's cynical definition.[28] The antiheroes are incorrigible, including Zayvl Brodsky, a former producer of fruit drops, and his son Zuzya, an accountant, who grew up speaking Hebrew. Zuzya came to Birobidzhan as a Zionist "to solve the Jewish question" rather than to build Soviet Jewish life. Another incorrigible character is Mendel Lifshits, who used to make money writing anti-Soviet letters and publishing them in an American Yiddish newspaper. The heroes are for the most part young people, members of the Komsomol. It is obvious that Bergelson knows very little about them, and they act like animated Soviet propaganda posters, especially when the book is compared with the competent prose of Moshe Alberton, the pioneer of the Birobidzhan topic.[29] At the same time, it is clear that Bergelson really likes these people. Niger, in his 1934 review of *Birebidzhaner,* pointed to this new trait in Bergelson's writing: in portraying young Birobidzhaners, Bergelson "learns to love," Niger suggests, whereas his previous creative work "was usually an act of hatred." Strictly speaking, this is inaccurate. The young Red Army soldier Pinke Vayl, a protagonist of in *Mides-hadin,* was a precursor of the young characters in *Birebidzhaner.* Niger also argues that *Birebidzhaner* was Bergelson's first book to contain some open and some hidden humor.[30] This comment suggests that Niger probably did not want to believe that Bergelson could be so uncritically naïve, and so attributed his unqualified enthusiasm to "hidden humor."

But there is hardly any humor in Bergelson's utopian vision of Biro-bidzhan. The future city of Birobidzhan is depicted as rivaling the great European capitals: the tributaries of the River Bira will cut through the Jewish city just as the canals of the Spree cut through Berlin or the Seine cuts through Paris. A cable railway, like those in the Swiss Alps, will run from the city to the hill (*sopke*), where there will be a sanatorium for workers and a very tall monument to Lenin. The Jewish capital itself will be "a big, noisy city with a lot of factories on the outskirts, a completely socialist city in a classless society." The Birobidzhan trademark will be known all over the world: "in New York and in Paris people will come to stores and ask: 'Please give me a jar of Birobidzhan honey.' " Such rapturous imagery also appears in the pamphlet *Birobidzhan: A General Overview of the Jewish Autonomous Region,* which Bergelson penned five years later in collaboration with the young Yiddish writer Emanuel Kazakevich. For instance, the writers concentrate on the sun that shines in Birobidzhan. It is an exceptionally warm and healthy sun, three times more powerful than the sun in Berdichev, Minsk, or Kiev. "This sun, coupled with the sun of the Socialist Homeland, make the [Jewish] people healthy and strong." [31]

Similarly, Birobidzhan emerged as a fairyland in works by other Yiddish writers. Fefer dedicated one of his poems to the Birobidzhan rose colored marble, which would adorn stations of the Moscow metro. [32] Kushnirov depicted Birobidzhan as a land flowing with milk and honey: Un milkh genumen trifn hot fun groz un grin, / un honik hot genumen trogn undz di bin [33] (And milk began to trickle from grass and verdure, / and the bee began to bring us honey). Moreover, according to Kushnirov, it was also a place where men had an extraordinary potent sexuality. The poet overheard whispers of ·a lovemaking couple, and their whisper did not fade the whole night: un nokh a mol, un biz es nemt shoyn togn . . . / A froy vet do fargeyn in trogn [34] (and once again, until it's already getting light . . . / A women will become pregnant here).

Another Birobidzhan miracle was recorded by David Khait, a prolific Russian Jewish prose writer: even by the mid-1930s the younger generation knew very little about Jewish religious traditions and were bemused when a group of *subbotniks,* or Russian converts to Judaism, settled in one of the collective farms of the Jewish autonomous region. Some Jewish collective farmers even offered in jest their services as *shabes-goyim,* or Gentiles hired to perform domestic chores forbidden to Jews (and the godly converts) on the Sabbath. [35] Importantly, the Birobidzhan *shabes-goyim* qualified as socialist Jews even by the standards of Khaim Zhitlovsky, the noncommunist Yiddishist guru: "When a Jew satisfies his spiritual-cultural needs in Yiddish, reads a Yiddish newspaper, a Yiddish book, goes to a Yiddish lecture, to a Yiddish theater, discusses a Jewish or a general problem in Yiddish, listens to the Yiddish radio hours, sends his child to a modern Yiddish secular school, he is beyond doubt a Jew who belongs to the Jewish people." [36]

Although Bergelson's *Birebidzhaner* is set in 1928, the events of his *Penek* take place at the end of the nineteenth century. The novel *Bam Dnyeper* was originally conceived as a saga in five volumes,[37] but only two of them ultimately came out: the first volume, *Penek,* in 1932; the second—despite Bergelson's Stakhanovite productivity of 5,000 characters a day—only in 1940; there was never a third volume. Both *Birebidzhaner* and *Penek* mark Bergelson's inaugural Soviet work. Bergelson followed Dobrushin's behest and combined his own "intellect of a constructor and feelings of an artist." As an artist, Bergelson arguably achieved in *Penek* the summit of his stylistic technique. On the other hand, his characters lost much of their independence from the author's volition. This Hamsunesque independence, peculiar to his first works,[38] now impeded the functions of the characters, which were predetermined by the ideological imperatives of the novel's construction. As a result the impressionist narrative articulated through the vision of the protagonist became implausible when Bergelson overloaded the boy hero, Penek, with the sententious statements required to convey the writer's chief message: the assertion that offspring of a rich family could grow up in close contact with the people and, in consequence, be fully equipped to assimilate into a proletarian society. The quintessence of this message was concentrated in the following phrase: "Penek [the unloved, uncherished son of the wealthy merchant Levin] spent day after day in the [poor] backstreets *[hintergeslekh]* and, unwittingly, looked at everything with eyes of the backstreets." [39] No doubt this represented Bergelson's own personal message—from the very beginning of his literary career he had regarded himself as a "man of the people" *(mentsh fun folk).*[40]

Although *Penek*—and *Bam Dnyeper* as a whole—was later included in the Soviet literary canon as arguably the major Soviet Yiddish novel and went through five Yiddish and four Russian editions, many contemporaries were aware of its halfway character. Markish, for instance, characterized it as a national rather than a proletarian work.[41] Lamed Shapiro late in life argued that the older generation had failed to write proletarian prose because for them it was a terra incognita where they could not compete with talented younger writers who had an intimate knowledge of proletarian surroundings. *Penek* was, in Lamed Shapiro's opinion, the highest achievement in proletarian prose by an older writer. Bergelson's success, however, was based on familiar, old material, although "he bought some new paints and daubed with them, leaving stains here and there." [42] For all that, *Penek* was much more suitable as a Soviet classic novel than was Kipnis's *Months and days,* Markish's *Dor ayn, dor oys* (A generation leaves, a generation comes), and other contemporary works set during the civil war, because the anti-Jewish atrocities depicted in these works might stigmatize the gentile population, most notably the Ukrainians, as incorrigible anti–Semites. Topically, *Penek* was very well matched with other Yiddish novels about the joyless life of children before the revolution that had already been sanctified by Soviet literary watchdogs, most notably Sholem Aleichem's *Motl Peysi dem khazns* (Mottel the cantor's son) and Kvitko's *Lyam un Petrik* (Lyam and Petrik). [43]

Socialist realism, this very Soviet Newspeakism, has been interpreted and ridiculed countless times. In fact, the writers had to take part in creating a looking-glass world of model characters and situations; their "duty was to describe as realistically as possible what did not exist—at least not yet— namely a socialist society." [44] Meir Wiener formulated this principle in his 1935 article on the general problems of socialist realism: "The authentic reality is directed into the future, into development, into *revolutionary* development. . . . To see and recognize the authentic reality means to see and recognize the inevitable future in its more or less developed embryo, even if it categorically contradicts the visible 'reality.' " [45]

However it is defined, socialist realism was not merely an abstract concept or a method of creative work, particularly of writing. It was also an occupation; all Soviet writers were obliged to be socialist realists. A writer could not be "wild" anymore. Only "organized" writers and people striving to become "organized" (or, in fact, state-employed) had the opportunity to get into print. In "organized" Soviet society, hierarchies permeated all domains of life, including letters. Petr Pavlenko, a notorious figure in the Stalinist literary world, saw writers standing "as a pyramid rather than shoulder to shoulder." [46] Yiddish literature, too, was provided with an appropriate pyramid, arranged according to the writers' "significance," the highest level of which was "All-Union." [47] On this scale, Fefer was a "poet of the All-Union significance." A 1933 list of forty-five leading Yiddish authors of the Ukrainian Republic shows that Fefer stood first in the pecking order. Moreover, two of the listed literati, Moshe Dubilet and Shlome Bilov, were then writing studies on Fefer's poetry.[48] During the First Congress of Writers, Fefer was the only Yiddish writer to serve as a member of the congress presidium; he and Izi Kharik represented Yiddish literature on the inaugural *pravlenie* (board) of the Soviet Writer's Union. Together with David Hofshtein, Fefer also represented Yiddish literature in the Ukrainian Writer's Union.[49]

Although Fefer occupied the leading position in the Ukrainian Yiddish literary hierarchy and Kharik played a similar role in Belorussia, Markish became the first-in-command Yiddish writer in Moscow. Markish's talent and charisma helped him to avoid the marginalization suffered by most Soviet Yiddish writers; he was rather well known outside the Yiddish literary world and became, like Michoels, a member of the general Moscow bohemian circles. Anticipating events, I will mention here the Order of Lenin, the highest Soviet decoration, conferred on him in 1939, whereas Fefer and Hofshtein got Signs of Honor, or decorations two grades lower, and such writers as Bergelson and Der Nister never held any order.

In 1931, Abraham Wieviorka, a prolific Yiddish playwright and essayist, published his book *Revision*.[50] This retrospect of literary history should prove that communist (or proletarian) Yiddish literature originated from two sources: the sweatshop poetry of Morris Rosenfeld, Morris Winshevsky, and their kind; and the popular prose of such best-selling novelists as Shomer, whose writings were in the late 1880s condemned by Shimen Dubnov and Sholem Aleichem as trashy, or *shund,* works. No doubt, Wieviorka's main objective was to question those theorists who canonized Kiev as the cradle and a few Kievans—most notably Sholem Aleichem, Osher Shvartsman, and David Bergelson—as the fathers of Soviet Yiddish literature. It would be a mistake, though, to see *Revision* only as an artifact of the internecine strife within the communist literary circles. Wieviorka could also detect that the Soviet surroundings were propitious for a new form of the *shund* literature, especially because similar writings already blossomed in Russian literature.

Shomer and his fellow writers of the nineteenth-century Yiddish *shund* usually did not exploit sex and crime in order to pander to the taste of their readership. Rather they produced moralistic novels with happy endings, which were, in a sense, part of the *maskilic* drive to modernize East European Jews. Soviet Yiddish literati, who also sought to educate the masses, revitalized the *shund* literature, using its technique of creating contrived plots with happy and/or instructive ends. Such works were populated by stilted characters of three categories: (1) impossibly positive communists; (2) incorrigibly bad enemies of the Soviet regime; and (3) those who were not very positive but could mend their ways. According to the master Yiddish critic Shmuel Niger, the Jewish communists pursued a sort of neo–*Haskalah* cultural policy, because, like *maskilim,* their objective was to reform and bypass traditional Jewish life.[51] The end justified the means, therefore the reality depicted in their ostensibly realist works was more often than not embellished (for Soviet settings) or darkened (for non-Soviet settings) in order to create the desired result.

In the first half of 1934, Markish published his novel *Eyns af eyns* (One on one), which the same year appeared in a Russian translation, titled *The Return of Nathan Becker.*[52] Judging by the novel, it was not the same Markish who in 1926, then a recent returnee, was thinking about leaving the Soviet Union because the Soviet Yiddish literary establishment treated him as an outsider.[53] Also, *Eyns af eyns* was a far cry from his 1929 novel *Dor oys, dor ayn,* written in the style of revolutionary romanticism. By the early 1930s, Markish had already mastered devices of proletarian *shund* writing and could write a novel like *One on One,* depicting the Soviet Union as a superior society that, among other things, reforms immigrants from the West.

One of the main missions of communist writers was to blacken the conditions of life outside the Soviet Union. Such works were especially expected from those writers who had spent time abroad. Kvitko published a book of stories, *Riogrander fel* (Rio Grander Pelt), based on his experience of living and working in Hamburg.[54] Moshe Kulbak in his 1933 long poem *Disner Tsharld Harold* (Childe Harold of the Desna), depicted two different Berlin worlds: one of them was the world of the struggling proletarians, while another—of the inhabitants of decaying bourgeois neighborhoods—was characterized by such "European" permanent fixtures as "a dog, a gonorrhoea, and a pair of pyjamas."[55] Bronshtein praised Kulbak's "break with the past," demonstrated in this poem, "which was directed against the emptiness and futility of Jewish bohemianism of the petit bourgeois decadents who collected their 'spiritual treasures' in the backyards of European culture."[56]

In 1932, a talkie (film) titled *Nosn Beker fort aheym* (Nathan Becker goes home), known in English as *The Return of Nathan Becker,* was released by Belgoskino (four years later the same studio would produce *Seekers of Happiness,* again about returnees, but this time from Palestine to Birobidzhan) with Michoels starring as Nathan's father. The film was written by

Israel Joshua Singer

Markish, but its plot significantly differed from that of the novel: in the film, Nathan comes to Russia with an African American friend who does not appear in the novel; the setting chosen for Nathan's cinematographic reforging is, to all appearances, Magnitogorsk, whereas the novel's protagonist settles in Ukraine; Nathan's home shtetl is shown in the film as a write-off without any future, whereas the novel underlines the shtetl's revitalization; in the film, it is Nathan's wife who adapts more easily to the Soviet surroundings, but in the novel Markish has transformed her into a primitive housewife.[57] Interestingly, an antipode novel—also a formulaic one—was written in 1938 by Markish's former close friend Israel Joshua Singer (the last time they apparently saw each other was in 1926). Singer's *Khaver Nakhman* (Comrade Nakhman) tells the story of a Polish Jewish communist, whose escape to the Soviet Union brings misfortune to him and his family.

The main hero of Markish's novel, Nathan, who has been living for twenty-eight years in New York, working as a virtuoso bricklayer and loving America "like a servant loves his boss's horse," suddenly sees the light during a communist meeting. He decides to return home, where his father still lives in their home shtetl in Volhynia. He spends a short time in his shtetl, where he sees that it has been transformed into a socialist settlement with a mixture of industrial enterprises and collective farms. The revised picture of the shtetl mirrored another attitude toward such settlements, spelled out, for instance, in Itsik Fefer's pronouncements and in projects of Elie (Ilia) Veitsblits, who headed the Department of Social and Economic Studies at the Kiev-based Institute for Proletarian Jewish Culture.[58] Then Nathan moves to Kharkov, having been invited to share his professional experience with builders of a new factory. There he meets a new, enigmatic breed of Soviet workaholics, whose enthusiasm at first puzzles and then infects him.

Soon Nathan even begins to hate his wife, Meyke, whose interests are limited to housekeeping. At the same time he fancies Natta, a young Jewish communist, who came from Poland together with the retreating Red Army. In general he likes "the young Soviet women-workers with fresh red kerchiefs on their windy *(vintike)* heads, with yummy faces—jolly, mischievously *(sheygetsdik)* snub-nosed." Still, Markish remains somewhat conservative. He endows Natta with characteristics of a Gentile young woman rather than making Nathan fall in love with a non-Jewish girl, although interethnic love affairs and intermarriages were part and parcel of Soviet Yiddish literature.

Markish underlines the rejection of Jewish traditions—a popular topic in Soviet Yiddish literature. Thus, Hershl Shamay, the protagonist of Abraham Abchuk's eponymous proletarian novel, rejects the Jewish tradition to such an extent that even his thoughts about how "it is so lovely outside and there is a holiday in my heart, as if it were the First of May" are political and uninfluenced by his national background. Abchuk wanted to make his readers believe that in the mind of an elderly man, such as Shamay, the image of the May Day proletarian holiday could supplant, for instance, Passover.[59] In reality, even the Yiddish writers could not brainwash themselves so easily. Irme Druker reminisced that Itsik Fefer called him *bal-shakhres* (cantor officiating at the morning service) and for Notte Lurye Fefer had another nickname, but also from a religious register—*bal-moysef* (miracle worker).[60]

Markish's hero, Nathan, is angry with Meyke for wanting to celebrate Purim. The word "Palestine" sounds to him even stranger than, for instance, the name of the Ukrainian town of Konotop. Secularization improves the former synagogue-goers. The new healthy lifestyle of a worker plays a therapeutic role: Khil Stelnik, one of the reformed "rubbish" *(khlam)* people, who came from the "rubbish dump" *(smitnik)* of the traditional Jewish life, gets rid of lameness and piles. (Old Ukrainian traditions are also harmful. The veteran Bolshevik Kholodenko, who is director of the factory and also Natta's boyfriend, cannot stand the "stink" of the Ukrainian musical instruments, *kobza* and *bandura*.) Soviet workers appear physically different, people of another bearing—while Nathan is used to work in a stooping position, his Soviet colleagues work with straight backs. Even Nathan's father, who is sixty-eight, looks as if he is younger than his son (this detail echoes Bergelson's 1926 essay "Moscow," one of whose characters argues that he is four times sixteen rather than sixty-four). Markish concludes the novel when Nathan is halfway to becoming a proper *homo sovieticus*; in any case he understands that he has a lot to learn and his professional experience of a capitalist worker cannot be easily used in the progressive Soviet environment.

Sovetish

On the eve of the First Congress of Soviet Yiddish Writers, Yiddish literati were at pains to demonstrate that they already understood what the authorities expected to find in their writings. Two almanacs, *Soviet* and *Almanac of Soviet Yiddish Writers,* were brought out—the former in Moscow and the latter in Kiev—as proof of their ideological maturity. The almanac *Sovetish* (Soviet), published by the central Yiddish publishing house Emes, was provided with the imprint of the newly created Association of the Moscow Yiddish Soviet Writers at the Organizational Committee of Soviet Writers. The almanac was edited by Shmuel Godiner, Isaak Nusinov, and Josef Rabin. This unnumbered literary collection became, in effect, the first volume of the almanac *Sovetish,* whose first numbered issue, number 2, appeared in 1935; its last, issue, number 12, dedicated to Sholem Aleichem, concluded this series in 1941. After the war, in 1947 and 1948, its tradition was continued by the Moscow almanac *Heymland* (Homeland), and in 1961–91 by the Moscow journal *Sovetish heymland* (Soviet homeland).

Although Markish did not edit *Sovetish,* he appears in it as its central writer: his two poems open the almanac, and Dobrushin's article "Markish's Ascent" underline the poet's key role. In *Sovetish,* Markish appears as a traditionalist, especially compared with Fefer. Markish's poems are dedicated to contemporary Jewish characters rather than to polar explorers or other generally Soviet, anational groups of heroes that we will find in Fefer's poem's, published in the Kiev almanac. Ezra, the hero of the poem "Moscow," is a party or government functionary, perhaps the same communist Ezra who had gone though purgatory of the civil war in Markish's novel *A Generation*

Leaves, a Generation Comes. This time the poet introduces him to us when Ezra is returning at midnight after an important meeting through the Red Square to his office. The tired functionary (in Soviet writings, high-ranking officials are always overworked) thinks about the enormous project of creating the new society, and his dreams are fed with Messianic imagery of the final battle that brings the reign of light and everlasting peace.[61] It is true that Markish's secular redemption of the world is limited to the "bones" of the living Moscow (i.e., Soviet) denizens and does not include the resurrection of the dead:

> S'vet yedes harts, s'vet yeder trot,
> s'vet yeder lebediker eyner
> fun frishndiker Moskve-shtot
> aribertrogn zayne beyner
> in land fun tsukunft un fun glik,
> in land fun ufgevekte troymen,—
> es tut zikh on di vayt mit blit,
> es efenen zikh uf di roymen,
> es mekt shoyn op zikh yeder grenets,
> es geyt shoyn tsu der letster shlakht,
> az umetum shoyn zol derbrent zayn
> di letste shternloze nakht!

> There will every heart, there will every step,
> there will every one who lives
> in the refreshing city of Moscow
> transfer his bones
> into the land of future and of happiness,
> into the land of wakened dreams,—
> the horizon is putting on blossom,
> the realms are opening,
> the borders are vanishing,
> the final battle is getting closer,
> let the last moonless night
> burn out everywhere as soon as possible!

During the 1920s, the Soviet Jewish population had stratified into three groups. The first group, which can be called "Soviet allrightniks," consisted of members of the party, Komsomol, and trade unions who had access to the most prestigious and lucrative positions in society. This group was quickly growing; for instance, the number of Jewish communists had quadrupled during 1922–30, reaching 76,000.[62] Still, the "allrightniks" continued to constitute a minority of the general Jewish population. The second group represented temporary beneficiaries of the NEP, including numerous fly-by-night profiteers, who were forced out in the late 1920s. The third, largest group, the "losers," consisted of people, notably shtetl inhabitants, who professionally or/and ideologically could not or did not want to adapt to the new regime. Joseph Roth learned during his 1926 visit to the Soviet Union that "Of the 2.75 million Jews in Russia, there are 300,000 organized workers and employees; 130,000 peasants; 700,000 artisans and self-employed. The remainder consists of (a) capitalists and déclassé individuals, who are described as 'unproductive' elements; (b) small traders, middlemen, agents, and hawkers, who are seen as unproductive but proletarian individuals."[63] In his story "A Shklov Moon in the Arbat" (not included in Sovetish), Shmuel Godiner portrayed a typical déclassé: a previously well-off accountant from Shklov who had lost everything and ended up as a street trader in Moscow.[64] Like many other Jews hit by the revolution, Godiner's character, formerly a rather secularized semi-intellectual, became a follower of the Lubavitcher Rebbe, R. Joseph Isaac Schneerson, who headed the underground Committee of Rabbis of the USSR.[65]

Although the Soviet functionary Ezra in Markish's work is certainly an "allrightnik" (with a strong chance of either perishing or spending a long stretch in the gulag), the hero of the second Markish poem published in Sovetish, "Anshel the Ironmonger," is a "loser." Once a shopkeeper in his home shtetl, he is forced to move to a rural settlement, where he drags out a miserable existence. He thinks the whole time about his former happy life and cannot forgive the Soviet regime the destruction of his habitat. He particularly misses the routine of Friday preparations for the Sabbath. There is little hope that Anshel can be reformed into a citizen of full value. But Markish, obviously, does not care. Nor does the doctor, who is called when Anshel becomes seriously ill. He advises the use of bankes (cupping-glasses), but says to apply them to the window rather than to Anshel's body (an allusion to the Yiddish saying helfn vi a toytn bankes, meaning that such a treatment is as effective as applying cupping-glasses to a dead body). At the same time, Anshel's children are already typical Soviet citizens: his son-in-law is a Red Army officer, whose photos appear in newspapers, and his son is an accountant at a cooperative. Shmuel Halkin discusses a similar "fathers and children" situation in his poem "Keeping Pace with the Children" and comes to the conclusion,

> . . . lomir reydn ofn:

> Dos lebn geshtelt tsu der vant hot,
> di orems fardreyt ahinter:
> oder in trot mit di kinder,
> oder tsum opgrunt a shpan ton.

> . . . let's speak open:

> life put [the parents] up against the wall,
> the hands tied up behind:
> either they keep pace with their children,
> or they head toward the abyss.

In fact, all the characters of the almanac *Sovetish* represent two kinds of people—the Ezras and the Anshels, the "people of our side" and the enemies, or, at best, the ballast. The two groups even speak differently. Only the ballast/enemies use such derogatory words as *goy* for Gentiles and *zhid* for Jews. Anshel thinks about *goyim* (peasants). The same word is in the vocabulary of the rich Jewish peasant Hirsh Arav in the story "Ingul-Boyaro" by Eli Gordon, a writer on village topics. In the same story, the Ukrainian bandits use the word *zhid,* which is also current among the narrow-minded people depicted in the story "A Bridge" by Abraham Frumkin, better known as an editor at the Emes Publishing House. A positive hero thinks and speaks mainly about the revolution and production plans. One of the two main characters of Frumkin's anodyne story, the Jewish communist Dan, is overfilled with emotions toward his papermaking machine (he works as its operator):

> He was still very young when a picture became engraved on his memory
>   and for ever remained before his eyes. How:
> cylinders and shafts play with rays of sunlight, they wash themselves in the
>   rays, jump in drops . . .
> And how:
> cloths and sifters stretch from underneath, stretch from above—and
>   flattened-out hoses carry ribbons of paper on their shoulders.
> A machine—a song.

Positive heroes use in their language new, Soviet words, such as *fabkom* (factory committee), *partey-kemerl* (party cell), *shediker* (saboteur), and *spets-freseray* ("specialist baiting"—showing a negative attitude toward all specialists of nonproletarian origin). Soviet reality also forces people to reconsider their family relations. Thus, the wage worker and trade unionist Meir Yelin, the protagonist of Yudel Yoffe's story *On the Direct Road*, leaves his beautiful and, until recently, beloved Jewish wife Berta and her petit bourgeois family who tried to lure him into a private business; he finds happiness with Natasha, a young non-Jewish communist.[66] While Markish only implies that Nathan may eventually leave Meyke, Dan's Russian friend, Vladimir Snorovkin, a communist of the Lenin enrollment (i.e., the mass enrollment that followed Lenin's death), breaks with his wife and, in general, with her milieu of old believers.

An engineer with a nonproletarian mentality is the fall guy for Soviet writers of that period, despite the official rejection of indiscriminate "specialist-baiting." After the 1928 trial of a group of mining engineers and technicians from the Shakhty area of Donbass (Donets Basin, Ukraine), the term "bourgeois specialist" became a byword for a "wrecker." In the spirit of the time, Dobrushin and Nusinov's play *The Specialist,* about a member of an anti-Soviet group of wreckers, was premiered in March 1932 in the Moscow State Yiddish Theater.[67] In Frumkin's "A Bridge," the engineer Miron Soloveichik ridicules a useful invention made by Snorovkin. His rejection of Snorovkin's warning that "the babbit has cracked on the left bearing of the right knee-shaft" brings a disaster. Technical meticulousness is one of the features of Soviet industrial prose. Moshe Alberton, for instance, listed ninety-three newly coined terms used in his proletarian novel *Shakhtes* (Mines), filling such lexical lacunae as "bearing," "timberer," and "sleeve joint." [68]

In their proletarian collectives young Soviet people had to pass a test for their social and political fitness. Jewish communists paid particular attention to the miners and factory workers of the Donbass. Jewish apparatchiks were happy to report that, despite the initial failures to recruit the shtetl youth to work at the Donbass mines, in 1931 there were already almost 5,000 Jewish miners among the Ukrainian trade unionists.[69] Alberton's *Shakhtes*, published in Moscow in 1931 and 1934, was praised as one of the most significant Soviet Yiddish prose works. Images of Jewish miners also inspired other Soviet Yiddish writers. In the words of Aron Kushnirov (from the poem "My Second Hero," published in *Sovetish*),

Tsi hobn zikh zeydes dos forgeshtelt,
tsi hot zikh dos tates gekholemt,
ba shtolene kopers,
    ba shakhtisher shvel
yunge fun Shklov un fun Shpole.
In ayzerner shtayg es trogt zey hast
un ful mit zey yeder zaboy vert . . .
In shmelts-oyvns heyse
kokht iber Donbas
dos dozike mentshishe royvarg.

Could their grandfathers imagine,
could their fathers dream:
at the steel twills,
    on the threshold of mines—
youth from [the Belorussian shtetl of] Shklov and from [the Ukrainian
    shtetl of] Shpola?
In iron cages they are carried quickly
and every pit-face is full of them . . .
In hot smelting furnaces
the Donbass reforges
this human raw material.

Granted, this process of social engineering also produces "slag." In Kushnirov's poem, twin brothers come to the Donbass. One of them successfully passes the "reforging," but his brother runs away to Moscow, where he gets a less demanding job as a builder at the Moscow Car Factory.

Purges were an important part of the reforging process. During such purges, special commissions interrogated members of the party and Komsomol, deciding whether to renew or cancel their membership. The almanac *Sovetish* contains two works whose protagonists pass a purge. One is the story "Three Encounters and a Fourth One" by Josef Rabin, whose hero, a Jewish worker, ideologically grows up under the influence of a Russian Bolshevik. The second story is "Motherland" by Shmuel Godiner, written in the name of a young Jewish woman, Freyda, whom the purge commission ostensibly advised to commit to paper the story of her life. This genre partly justifies the low quality of the story penned by one of the best Soviet Yiddish prose writers. In a rather convoluted form, Godiner depicts the tragic lives of three Jewish girls. One of them, Freyda's mother, is left pregnant when her fiancé went to America and soon died after falling from the tenth floor while washing the windows of a skyscraper. Surka, another girl, becomes pregnant after being raped by the nephew of the owner of the glass factory where the girls work. A mute girl, also a glass factory worker, is raped by the son of the owner. A central role in the story is played by a middle-aged Jewish woman, Liba, who is a spontaneous rebel. She is brave enough to defy convention and help the unlucky girls. Illegitimate children were apparently regarded as a good reservoir of revolutionaries. In any case, another almanac author, Shmuel Rosin, poeticises a story of a non-Jewish revolutionary, Mishka ("Sons and Daughters"), who was born out of wedlock—his mother had been impregnated by her employer, a landowner.

Ziskind Lev and Meir Wiener, both emigrants from the West, published in *Sovetish* works set in a non-Soviet environment. Lev (spelled *Lyev* in *Sovetish*), who worked as a Comintern agent in a few European countries before settling in the Soviet Union, writes, in his story "Franz Ksantops Sells His Son," about an unemployed Berlin widower with five children who, driven to despair, sells his five-year-old son Kurt to an adoption agency. Meir Wiener combined two careers—as a significant Yiddish literary historian, critic, and theoretician, and as a prose writer. In *Sovetish* he published chapters from his historical novel *Kolev Ashkenazi,* which the same year came out in Moscow in book form (a revised second edition was published in 1938). The novel is set in medieval Poland, and Wiener draws a clear parallel between the societal stratification among the ruthlessly suppressed Gentile and Jewish populations.

The *Almanac of Soviet Yiddish Writers*

The *Almanac of Soviet Yiddish Writers,*[70] edited by Itsik Fefer, contains works by twenty-eight authors, mostly Ukraine-based Soviet Yiddish writers. Like the almanac *Sovetish,* the Kiev almanac appeared without any introduction, but Fefer's poem "Between Sky and Ice," glorifying the Arctic expedition of the SS *Cheliuskin,* played this role. Later, in his speech to the First All-Union Congress of Soviet Writers, Fefer argued that the "heat" or ardor of the Arctic heroes had to become a model for Soviet literature.[71] In 1933 and 1934, the polar expedition of the *Cheliuskin,* which was crushed in the ice attempting the "northern passage," [72] attracted the attention of many millions and gave rise to a vast body of writing. The events became extremely sentimentalized and emotionally colored. Even the (then émigré) Russian nonconformist poetess, Marina Tsvetaeva, went into raptures about the expedition.[73] This Arctic adventure took place at a time when the party functionaries, literary critics, and writers were desperately looking for a philosophers' stone of Social Realism. The Arctic subject matter fitted perfectly into the socialist-realist thematic base: mastery over nature, technical advance, patriotism, optimism, leadership of the party, Stalin, and heroism.[74] Small wonder that Fefer, whose "mission as a communist poet" was "to formulate popular opinion,"[75] wrote a *Cheliuskin* poem, too.

In "Between Sky and Ice," Fefer stressed the leading role of communists, who stared danger in the face ("In a shaggy, snow-covered cloak / the communist rose to his full height"). The head of the expedition, the "Commissar of Ice" Otto Shmidt, became an icon of Soviet mass culture.[76] Tsvetaeva called him "the second Shmidt in Russian history,"[77] drawing a parallel with Petr Shmidt, a hero of the 1905 revolution. Fefer, in his turn, used the Yiddish meaning of *shmid* (blacksmith) to create the image of a communist with an iron will: "The heroes stand like a wall / forged by Shmidt's [or: the smith's] skillful hand." There is even a moment of miracle, also associated with Shmidt: "The icebergs swing around / now the communist Shmidt works!"

Fefer obviously wanted to stress the epic character of his poem. According to the current discourse of Soviet literary officialdom, various folkloric forms—including epic and heroic songs—were welcome in works of socialist realism.[78] Thus it is no coincidence that Fefer wrote a substantial part of the poem in trochaic tetrameter, which, in Russian literature, was widely used for imitations of fairy tales.[79]

Although the whole country is troubled about the polar expedition, the main decision maker is, of course, Stalin:

> Der kremlsher zeyger klingt oys a banakht,
> bam firer iz shtendik gants fri,
> er zitst un er tseylt di vegn fun shlakht
> mit ayz-berg in frostikn gli.
> . . . .
> Er shteyt in zayn groyskayt, der firer un hert
> vi s'klapt itst dos harts funem land,
> er zet shoyn di vegn, vos firn di erd
> un vayzt ir dem veg mit zayn hant.

> The Kremlin clock strikes midnight,
> for the leader it is always morning,

he sits and draws the ways of the battle
with icebergs in frosty glow.
· · · · · · · · · · · · · · · · · · · ·

He stands in his grandeur, the leader, and hears
the heart of the country beating,
he already sees the directions which the world will follow
and shows it [the world] the way with his hand.[80]

Starting in 1934 exaltation of Stalin's genius became common in Soviet writings.[81] Soviet Yiddish writers did not lag behind other literati in finding a new approach to presenting people's worship of the leader, who embodied the best qualities of Soviet men. A few years later, the pregnant heroine of Abraham Gontar's poem would look at Stalin's photo, following the popular belief that a child may be born similar to the person that the woman sees during her pregnancy.[82]

It was not politically correct to mourn those who fell for their country and for communism. Death was not part of Bolshevik culture, because the communist cause and idea were immortal.[83] In a contemporary Soviet Yiddish novel we read, "Do not bemoan the heroes! Their names will never be forgotten!"[84] Fefer, too, promises that the only victim of the expedition will not be forgotten. He even reveals the future: the drowned member of the expedition, who—in Fefer's poetic interpretation—serves as the *Cheliuskin*'s underwater guard, will be found; the drowned Arctic explorer "will stretch out, like a tree branch, his bone-hand" and "we will pin a medal to his lapel." Still, happiness in the communist martyr's afterworld cannot compete with the joy of life in the Soviet Union: "We cannot live without joy / as [we cannot live] without toil and bread" are the concluding lines of the poem. Buzi Olevski, who will be killed in action in the early period of the war with Nazi Germany, echoes Fefer in his unnamed poem, published in the Moscow almanac:

A toyt iz do—a tsikhtiker vi shney,
a toyt, vos iz nit yedern bashert . . .
Ikh vil nor zayn a nutslekher vi zey,
ikh vil nor epes ufton far der erd! . . .

A death is here clean like snow,
a death that not everyone is given . . .
I want only to be as useful as they were,
I want only to do something for the world!

Fefer and Olevsky were not the only Yiddish poets captivated by *Cheliuskin* mania. For instance, Izi Kharik's poem "Karina Vasilieva" (not included in the *Almanac*)—about the girl who was born during the expedition and saved by the Soviet pilots—"demonstrated that the contemporary Soviet Yiddish poets lived in tune with the heroic daily life of the whole country." [85]

The pilots who eventually evacuated the expedition became the first Soviet men to receive the title "Heroes of the Soviet Union." Their heroism was the apex of the herculean mission to master both the Arctic and the air. While the pilots play a secondary role in Fefer's panoramic poem, they appear as the central protagonists in "On the Verge of Death" by the former Vitebsk proletarian poet Mendel Abarbanel, another *Cheliuskin* poem published in the *Almanac*. "To the Future Man" by Motl Hartsman and "We are Still Alive" by Moshe Khashchevatski also glorify Soviet conquerors of the stratosphere. Hartsman's main hero, however, is the Great Leader, Stalin, "our kith and kin, our helmsman," whose participation in a funeral for pilots killed in a crash turned the grief into an "enormous joy."

✳   ✳   ✳

Khaim Gildin was the oldest *Almanac* contributor. The last editor in chief of *Di royte velt* and now a member of the editorial board of *Farmest,* the central Yiddish literary periodical in Ukraine, he was second after Fefer in the Ukrainian hierarchy of Yiddish writers.[86] Gildin's story "Mendel Graf," published in the *Almanac,* deals with another theme that, like the *Cheliuskin* saga, was pertinent in 1934: the "reeducation" of criminals in the Soviet labor camps. The highest-profile case was the construction of the White Sea–Baltic Canal (Belomorkanal), officially named in Stalin's honor. This gigantic project, which cost the lives of tens of thousands of prisoners, began in 1931 in Karelia. Twenty months later, in May 1933, a 227 kilometer canal connected Lake Onega with the White Sea. The White Sea–Baltic Canal became a model for the network of "constructions of communism," in which millions of prisoners toiled in the subhuman conditions of the gulag. In the early 1930s, however, Soviet propaganda still presented the labor camps as places where various lawbreakers were reformed and "born again," thanks to the miracles of Soviet social engineering.

In August 1933, Maxim Gorki, the guru of the Soviet literary world, led 120 Soviet writers to visit the canal. In this assorted group, Fefer represented Yiddish literature.[87] Gildin also seems to have been a member of the entourage. It was not, of course, merely an excursion; the writers had to deliver

results. Indeed, the "achievements" of the gulag social engineers were represented in a spate of publications and performances, which marked the official completion of the canal. Suffice it to say that of the plays produced in
Moscow theaters in the 1934–35 season, 22 percent of the characters were
builders of the canal.[88]

Gildin's hero, Mendel Graf, a safecracker, is also a gulag prisoner. There,
together with thousands of counterrevolutionaries, thieves, prostitutes, and
bandits, he has to be educated, both vocationally and ideologically, in order
to return home as a citizen enjoying equal rights—a useful *homo sovieticus*
rather than a hated outlaw. However, Mendel refuses to work and plays
cards for days on end. Still, he is not so hopeless as, say, czarist engineers.
One of the latter, Verzhbitski, now a reformed saboteur, retains the habit of
screwing up his left eye. According to Gildin, this reveals that Verzhbitski ac-
cumulates secret thoughts on the left (sinister) side of his brain.

Despite his murky past, Mendel is a much better candidate for reform
because he comes from a pure, proletarian family. His father was a poor,
tubercular chimney sweep. His sister was sold to a Buenos Aires brothel. In
addition to having the correct social origins, Mendel is also a talented musi-
cian. Firin, the camp chief, promises Mendel a new *baian* (accordion) if he
starts working. Soon, the former criminal becomes an enthusiastic builder of
the canal. Firin does him the honor of inviting him to play the *baian* for the
camp officers and dine with them. Mendel is in seventh heaven, especially
because the prisoner-waiter turns out to be the czarist governor of the
province where Mendel's family used to live. At the end, Mendel performs a
feat of valor and, instead of serving out his ten years, is sent to the Leningrad
conservatoire.

The hero of the story, however, is really "the creator" Firin rather than
"the raw material" Mendel: "An enigma always smiled in the corners of his
[Firin's] red, tightly compressed mouth. His look was very concentrated and
earnest, though at the same time it was shining with the joyful reflections of
a life full of great struggle."

Early Soviet literature eulogizing the gulag was, in essence, literature
about the heroic *chekists*—officers of the Soviet punitive apparatus.[89] Gildin
chose a high-profile real-life model—Semen Firin, the son of a Jewish peasant, who went through fire and water to become the gulag's deputy head. (He
received the Order of Lenin in 1933 and was executed as a "counterrevolutionary" in 1939.[90]) In October 1933, Firin (the real one) argued that he and
his colleagues used "mainly means of persuasion" and that, under the ame-

liorating influence of work of social utility, many former criminals had been transformed into useful and honest Soviet toilers.[91] The poem "A Born-Again Man," by the Odessa poet Shlome Lopate, published in the *Almanac,* is about a Jewish thief from Odessa, Boris Ginzburg, reformed during the construction of the canal. Ginzburg, who had five previous convictions, was awarded the Order of the Red Banner of Labour as the organizer and leader of a brigade of prisoners.

Firin was also one of the editors of the notorious "history" of the White Sea–Baltic Canal.[92] In this volume—or to be precise, in the chapter "Rothenburg, or the History of the Man Reforged"—Gildin could find the prototype for his Mendel Graf, or at least some of his traits. In the autumn of 1933, Abram Rothenburg, formerly a thief and a swindler, was awarded the Order of the Red Banner of Labour for his heroic work on the construction of the canal. Another "reforged" man depicted in the volume was Kvasnitzky, a Jewish thief from Odessa. Because we know that Firin led the tour of 120 writers and fed them with stories of how he and his colleagues had reeducated the inmates, the main source for Graf may have been a character in one of Firin's stories. In general, the *baian* story is a striking illustration of the thesis that the state and the party, rather than the writers, were the real authors of works of Social Realism.[93] Indeed, the same *baian* plot was used by the Russian playwright Nikolai Pogodin and the Belorussian prose writer Mikhas Lynkov, in whose story Firin became Pirin.[94] Apart from many parallels between the general schemes of Gildin's story, Pogodin's play *Aristocrats,* and Lynkov's story "Baian," their reformed characters—Mendel Graf, Kostia "Captain," and the "Ataman" Andrei Andreevich—are carbon copies of one another.

In one of his *Almanac* poems about the accomplishments of the First Five-Year Plan (with the refrain: "If a cannon—it [must be] of the most powerful calibre!"), the much-criticized (but by 1934 apparently reformed) symbolist poet Zelig Akselrod mentions the canal. The poet justifies the death toll taken by the construction: "Each new, further turn / always costs people's lives." By that time Akselrod's modernism had surrendered to Stalinist philistinism, one of whose principles was "the end justifies the means." For being more pliant to the party guidance, Akselrod was promoted in 1932 to the editorial board of the Minsk journal *Shtern,* and his poetic collections began to appear in the Minsk-based State Publishing House.

* * *

"Between Sky and Ice," a poem without Jewish characters, and the story "Mendel Graf," with its protagonists' nominal Jewish backgrounds, are extreme cases of the "national in form and socialist in content" Soviet Yiddish literature. As a rule, the characters created by Yiddish writers were Jewish. In the *Almanac,* too, there are dozens of Jewish characters: members of a new agricultural commune "Red Star" organized on the outskirts of Kharkov in the documentary account "Two Miles from Kharkov" by M. Daniel; counterrevolutionary shtetl intellectuals in "My Enemy," a play by Abraham Weiviorka; a vigilant Soviet surgeon in the story "A Usual Operation" by Abraham Kahan; builders of an industrial giant in the play "White and Black," by Aron Kushnirov; etc. These characters performed in two types of setting: multiethnic (usually the construction of an industrial project) and the exclusively Jewish shtetl or village. This was in keeping with the dual program of *yidishe arbet,* formulated in 1926 by Maria Frumkin.

Rural topics were subject to less criticism than shtetl-related literature, which was often branded "petit bourgeois" and "nationalist." "It is wrong and harmful to dream about a shtetl Jewish environment," lectured a character in the contemporary industrial novel *Zayd* (Silk) by Tsodek Dolgopolski.[95] Although the Jewish apparatus officially turned its "face to the shtetl," [96] modeling the party's 1924 "face to the countryside" turn,[97] many of the apparatchiks, particularly in Belorussia (where the proportion of Jewish shtetl-dwellers was smaller than in Ukraine and the apparatchiks proper were more dogmatically proletarian), still regarded the shtetl as a malignant tumor on the healthy body of Soviet society. True, there was still a danger of being accused of parochialism, which for militant critics was synonymous with nationalism. Stories set only in Jewish villages might be categorized as "parochial." It was important to show the class struggle among the peasants. In the *Almanac* we find the story "Daniel Karsunivski's Worry" by Meir Oranski, about saboteurs of collectivization.

Another theme welcomed by critics was the "productivization" of former shtetl residents and most particularly of the so-called *lishentsy*—people deprived of suffrage and some other civil rights, including access to higher education, on account of their social origins or occupation (mainly tradesmen, clergy, and artisans). In the second half of the 1920s, the *lishentsy* sometimes composed the largest group among the shtetl Jewish population.[98] As a result, migration of the Jewish population from shtetls to villages was often motivated by social reasons: people wanted to escape the stigma of being *lishentsy.* Some day a study will be written about various devices invented by the Jewish youths to allow them to clean their biographies from the genealogical stain of nonproletarian origins. Oral history evidence describes one such unorthodox exit from disenfranchisement: "My older brother disowned my parents in the newspaper, because it was impossible to get jobs if your parents were disfranchised. He announced that he did not recognize them as his parents, because they belonged to the clergy. Of course, my father permitted him to do so, otherwise he would have never ever done anything like that." [99] My own father, born in the Ukrainian shtetl of Krasilov, was close to being thrown out of the Yiddish department of the Zhitomir Teachers Training Institute because a vigilant student, a native of a nearby shtetl, remembered a shopkeeper named Estraikh. Fortunately for my father, he could prove that the shopkeeper was his cousin many times removed—sufficiently removed to save him from the purge.

Velvel, a character in Daniel's "Two Miles from Kharkov," decided to join the "Red Star" commune only because he was afraid of losing his children, especially after two of them—pupils at the Yiddish school—left their parents' home and wrote a letter to the local authorities, the shtetl soviet, "to liberate them from their capitalist father." It is well known that the "third generation," or children born after the revolution, played an important role in the paranoid Soviet society. The Siberian village boy Pavlik Morozov, the denouncer of his own father, became a role model for many pioneers—members of the teenagers' Communist organization. [100] Jewish children born into that "third generation" had to be freed from fundamental national traditions.

Leyb Kvitko published in the *Almanac* a few of his very popular poems, including one about a swineherd and her pink-and-white suckling pigs. The next year this poem, *Khazerlekh* (Small suckling pigs) was published in Odessa in three languages: Yiddish, German, and Ukrainian. While the former two editions had a print run of 3,000, the Ukrainian version—translated by the first chairman of Ukraine's Writers Union, Yiddish-speaking Ukrainian poet Ivan (Israel) Kulik—had a print run of 10,000. No doubt, Kvitko's interest in this daring topic was part of the campaign—fuelled by ideological rather than purely economic reasons—to introduce pig-breeding among the Jewish peasants. Kvitko did not pioneer pig-breeding in Yiddish literature. In 1928, Abraham Kahan's short story *A khazer* (A pig) was published in book form. [101] Kahan's hero, Yoilek, fifty-five years old, recently resettled from a shtetl to a Jewish village. The local department of the Agro-Joint (a subsidiary of the American Joint Distribution Committee) allots him a pig. This happens on the eve of the Yom Kippur, and the next day Yoilek fasts and prays together with the *minyan* of other traditional men, while the younger villagers and the women continue to work. In the meantime, Yoilek cannot stop thinking about the pig, who is hungry because his wife still does not want to pay any attention to the Agro-Joint's present, regarding it wrong to keep a pig in a Jewish household. When Yoilek comes home, he first of all feeds the pig; his wife eventually relents, accepting her husband's arguments.

Tsodek Dolgopolski, who wrote satiric poetry under the pseudonym Horodoker, argued in one of his poems:

> khazeyrim ba undz iz a naye problem,
> "khazeyrim"(bazunders yorkshirer gebirt)
> dos vort iz a nayer,
> arayngefirt ersht farayorn . . . [102]

> pigs represent for us a new problem,
> "pigs" (particularly of the Yorkshire breed)
> is a new word,
> introduced only last year . . .

Horodoker-Dolgopolsky was right: Yiddish did not excel in pig-related terminology. For instance, Soviet Yiddish language-planners argued as to the proper calque for the Russian *oporosit'sia* (to farrow): *oporosen zikh* or *opkhazern zikh*; or for the Russian *svinomatka* (sow): *khazer-muter* or *muter-khazer*.[103] In the meantime, pig-breeding was spreading among Jewish peasants, particularly in the Crimea, where more than seven thousand pigs were kept by Jewish peasants and kolkhozs.[104] Agronomist M. Druyanov published a number of Yiddish pamphlets instructing how to work with pigs and rabbits (another nonkosher animal).[105]

Pig-breeding apart, the Yiddish writers' attraction to rural settings can only partly be attributed to ideological considerations. More importantly, such a setting allowed the writers to depict Yiddish-speaking characters, whose life and language they really knew. Non-Jewish characters presented difficulties and lacked clarity and color, particularly in comparison with the same authors' Jewish types.[106] A typical example is Adamov, a Russian functionary in the story "Two Miles from Kharkov." Daniel, much praised for his 1930 novel *Julius* (whence the name of his son, the dissident Russian writer Iulii Daniel), created a stilted character, a cliché of the virtues ascribed to a Soviet apparatchik: hardworking, unpretentious, principled. Adamov's woodenness is particularly conspicuous against the backdrop of colorful images of the would-be Jewish farmers, like Velvel, trying to adjust to the new life.

In general, the farther the writers moved from the traditional Jewish surroundings into the supranational "socialist content," the harder it was to employ the vocabulary and stylistic devices used by their precursors at the turn of the century. Some of the linguistic problems were later analyzed by David Bergelson. In 1937 he complained that Yiddish literature of his day lacked the vocabulary to describe such unconventional domains as for example a landscape, weather conditions, the charms of nature, and the beauty of women. Bergelson argued that Yiddish writers, who made skillful use of folk idioms and oral constructions when they depicted the traditional mode of life, evinced little skill when their characters found themselves outside the shtetl surroundings.[107] Indeed, it is difficult to believe that the "industrial novel" *Agglomerate* was written by Hershl Orland, the celebrated author of the novel *Hreblyes* (Dikes, 1929), which is based on Orland's own experience as a land-reclamation worker in the Ukrainian Polesie. The except from *Agglomerate,* published in the *Almanac* under the title "Winds from the Village," is a poorly conceived story about a Crimean Tartar girl who does not want to be the concubine of a rich landowner and finds her happiness among the young communist builders of a factory.

Together with other Soviet literatures, Yiddish literature was subjected to constant censorship of certain topics and literary devices. In particular, socialist realism was hostile to satire. A smile or touch of irony was looked at with suspicion. Nusinov, for instance, argued that in Soviet literature satire was essential only for fellow travelers who had to compensate for their own past. As for the proletariat, its laughter was muffled by the dominant revolutionary enthusiasm and pathos.[108]

Fayvl Sito is the only satirist in the two almanacs. His story "What Has Happened?" represents the optimistic satire of socialist realism. Sito's hero is a nameless seventeen-year-old news writer for a Soviet Yiddish daily. He exaggerates minor incidents in order to fill his column, headed "What Has Happened?" Meanwhile, the boy dreams about a real sensation, like the suicide of a beautiful young girl. One fine day the editors decide to drop the column. This decision radically changes the young journalist's life. He no longer wishes to write about suicides or other dark sides of Soviet life and comes to understand that his column was in general out of step with the times. Indeed,

Jewish colonists in
the Crimea, 1926–27

now is the time to glorify only organized heroic sacrifices and condemn a disorganized, egoistical step like suicide.

In his *Almanac* article on the young Soviet Yiddish prose writers, Irme Druker could not agree with those critics who referred to humor as a "charitable and forgiving" device; accordingly, he completely rejected it in proletarian writing. At the same time, he was ready to admit that Soviet proletarian humor had nothing to do with the humor of Sholem Aleichem and Anton Chekhov, whose aim was to "distract the readers from their bitter thoughts about death and ruin." On the contrary, Soviet humor had to represent the resounding, joyful, and enthusiastic laughter of the victorious proletariat. Various remnants of the old society were the only objects that Druker would allow to be laughed at. Discussing socialist realism in the *Almanac,* Oyzer Holdes, another Yiddish critic, argued that there was no longer any need for

Sholem Aleichem's "laughter through tears," because Soviet humor and satire professed optimism. As an example of such a positive approach, he mentioned Fefer's 1932 trivial poetic raillery "A Panegyric to the Diacritic," which ridiculed the small-mindedness of some Yiddish linguists.

In 1930, Shmuel Niger was *surprised* to find irony in the then-popular Soviet novel *Hershl Shamay* by Abraham Abchuk.[109] The dryness of Soviet Yiddish literature was directly associated with its nature: rather than being a product of literary imagination, it was a manifestation of politically correct discourse. It is no coincidence that a list of Yiddish writers discussed in a newspaper article (with their novels, poems, kolkhoz sagas, and plays focusing on construction of hydroelectric stations, factories, the Moscow subway, and so on), resembles a Soviet production plan.[110]

Indeed, in his programmatic *Almanac* article on Soviet literature in Yiddish, Dunets, who two years earlier published a book on transplanting into literature the spirit of the Magnitogorsk construction,[111] a flagship of the first Five-Year Plan, argued that problems of industrialization and collectivization were already dominating Soviet Yiddish literature. According to Dunets, literature had to be regarded as a "weapon;" its mission was to present and defend current politics. In other words, the discourse of Soviet literature was equated with the discourse of the authorities. As a result, writers and, especially, editors got used to the idea that literary work was worthless, or even dangerous, unless it was in line with the aims approved by the highest echelons of Soviet bureaucracy. In fact, the majority of the writers and editors sincerely believed in communism as the blessed future of the Jewish people. As for the present, they were sure that they enjoyed more real freedom than did their foreign colleagues. In 1932, Shmuel Halkin proudly formulated the Soviet writers' credo: "mir shraybn vos mir viln— / mir shraybn vos me darf" (we write what we want to— / we write what we have to).[112] A similar recipe of socialist realism is found in Hofshtein's *Almanac* poem "A Moment":

> Vi heystu?
> Nit muze!
> . . . .
> derfilt un dershpirt,
> az alts in mayn land
> tsu lebn un ufshtayg gefirt un getsoygn
> vert shtendik fun libe fun groyser
> fun groysn farshtand!

What is your name?
It is not Muse!
. . . .
Sense and detect
that everything in my country
is being led and drawn to life and raising
only by the great love
and the great judgement!

The Era of Muses was over. Soviet authors, including those writing in Yiddish, had to face the Era of Judgment.

Epilogue

IN THE MID-1930s the tight-knit world of Yiddish communist writers, journalists, and critics was populated by hundreds of people. Some of them were eminent literary figures. Their Mecca was in the Far East of Russia, and it was called Birobidzhan (or sometimes, in Yiddish, Birebidzhan). Only a handful of writers and journalists settled there, predominantly young people such as the poets Khaim Levin and Henekh Shvedik, both migrated from Belorussia. The poet Lyuba Vaserman came to Birobidzhan from Palestine in 1934. Henekh Kazakevich was the oldest among the Birobidzhan literati. He left Kharkov in 1932 to became the editor of the local newspaper *Birobidzhaner shtern* (Birobidzhan star) and the head of the local writers' organization, which replaced the BiroAPP (Birobidzhan Association of Proletarian Writers) formed in 1931.[1] His son, Emanuel Kazakevich, was a precocious poet, whose first collection of poems, called *Birebidzhanboy* (Birobidzhan construction), appeared in Birobidzhan in 1932. After Henekh Kazakevich's death in 1935, Josef Rabin, the pioneer proletarian writer, was sent from Moscow to lead, in 1936–37, the local writers' organization. In 1936, Birobidzhan was provided with its own quarterly for literature and politics, *Forpost* (Outpost), with Rabin and Bergelson serving among the members of its inaugural editorial board. For all that, the majority of authors in Birobidzhan, who penned numerous glowing poems and prose works there, would come only as pilgrims. Bergelson never moved into the house that was built for him at one of the *sopkas* (mounds).[2]

Not only was Birobidzhan far away from the "historical habitat" of European Jews, but there was something artificial in the whole project: creating a place that proletarian Jews were supposed to regard as their hearth and home but avoiding any national slogans. Khaim Sloves, initially a French Yiddish communist and later an angry anti-Soviet writer, compared such a task with squaring the circle.[3] Soviet communists also appreciated the paradox of

their party's national politics. Shimen Dimanshtein wrote about the "temporary contradiction" of fighting against nationalism, on the one hand, and
stimulating nationalism, on the other hand.[4] Yiddish writers tried to solve
this puzzle by introducing non-Jewish characters in their Birobidzhan works.
Thus, in Fefer's "Birobidzhan *freylekhs*" (cheerful Jewish dance), Jews are
not the only dancers: "Tantsn yidn un koreyer, pionern, roytarmeyer" (There
dancing Jews and Koreans, pioneers, Red Army soldiers).[5] For all that, a conference scheduled for 1937 was intended to mark Birobidzhan as the official
center of Soviet Jewish culture. Among the announced papers was Bergelson's
"The Language of Literature." However, the purges of the année terrible
1937 annihilated the plan to convene the conference.[6] Among the people arrested in Birobidzhan in the late 1930s was Rabin, but he was lucky to be released during World War II. A quarter of a century later he would write the
first Soviet Yiddish novel on Stalinism, *In yenem yor* (In that year), which was
published posthumously in *Sovetish heymland*.[7]

It is hard to understand the murderous logic of the Stalinist inquisition.
Yet the general impression that one gets from studying lists of Yiddish
writers imprisoned in the gulag is that the 1937 wave of arrests fell predominantly upon the most militant intellectuals: Moshe Litvakov, Yasha Bronshtein, Khatskel Dunets, and Abraham Abchuk were among those arrested.
In a black farcical finale, Litvakov was accused of leading an anti-Soviet ter-
rorist group in Minsk—with his archenemies Dunets and Bronstein among
its members. He was brought to Minsk and executed there in December
1937.[8] Kharik and Kulbak also perished in the gulag.

The novelist Eli Shekhtman described the atmosphere of that time in his
autobiographical novel *Ringen oyf der neshome* (Rings on the soul). Shekhtman recalls how he once spent an evening with two Yiddish poets, Motl
Hartsman and Moshe Pinchevsky, drinking wine in a Kiev bar. Late in the
evening they came out into a street with a huge portrait of Stalin on one of
the walls. Hartsman looked at the portrait and said, "A shlekhter mentsh! (A
bad man!)" Pinchevsky immediately vanished into thin air, but the next
morning he came to Shekhter and asked him to sign a memorandum about
Hartsman's anti-Soviet behavior. Shekhter, however, wrote his own version
of the story, arguing that Pinchevsky walked a few steps behind and therefore misheard Hartsman's words, which were, "Shlekht gemolt! (Badly
painted!)" Fortunately, the meeting of Hartsman's Komsomol cell, convened
on the same day, accepted Shekhtman's version.[9]

In Belorussia, Yiddish circles suffered much more than they did in

Moscow or Ukraine.[10] After 1938, Yiddish was no longer an official language of the republic, although the newspaper *Oktyabr,* the journal *Shtern,* and Yiddish books continued to appear in Minsk. Nonetheless, the editorial board of *Shtern* became completely unrecognizable: a few journalists, including the last editor of *Der yunger arbeter* (phased out in 1935) Zalman Tsirlin; the poetess Sora (Sarah) Kahan; and two communist refugees from Warsaw—the journalist David Rikhter and the writer Binem Heller. At the same time, the Kiev literary journal *Farmest* only changed its somewhat cheeky name (meaning "challenge") into the more austere *Sovetishe literatur* (Soviet literature), but otherwise it represented the same group of writers. As for the Moscow *Sovetish,* it lost Litvakov but did not need to change its name.

Many other writers and critics who had been severely criticized for years as symbolists, nationalists, and petit bourgeois remained unscathed. These included, in addition to the one-of-us Fefer, Hofshtein, Der Nister, Kvitko, Markish, and Bergelson. Why? Perhaps the regime still needed Yiddish literature, especially because Yiddish-speakers constituted a great proportion of some foreign communist parties. Inside the country, meanwhile, it was a traumatic time for all Soviet Yiddish activists, not only because of the arrests but also because the government began a radical reduction of education in Yiddish.[11] In two years' time, however, the pre–World War II Soviet expansion reinforced the position of Yiddish. In September 1939, in accordance with the Soviet-Nazi pact, eastern Poland came under Soviet rule; in 1940, the Baltic countries likewise became Soviet republics, and the annexations of Bessarabia and northern Bukovina were made at the expense of Romania. The Soviet Jewish population swelled from three million to more than five million. As a result, the decrease of Yiddish activity was somewhat reversed; the Soviet regime made use of Yiddish education and media in these areas with deep-rooted Jewish life.

In October 1940 a new Yiddish "political and literary" monthly *Ufboy* (Construction) began to appear in Riga. The newspaper *Vilner emes* (Vilna truth) originally contained only translations and reprints, but it soon began to publish poems by Abraham Sutzkever and works by other local writers. The almanac *Bleter 1940* (Pages 1940), published in Kovno under the imprint of the Yiddish Writers' Union of Lithuania, featured works by such authors as Khaim Grade, Abraham Sutzkever, Hirsh Osherovich, Meir Yelin, and Yakov Josade. Kovno also had its own *Emes* and a Komsomol weekly, *Shtraln* (Rays). An active group of Yiddish writers had concentrated in Bialystok, where the newspaper *Bialistoker shtern* (Bialystok star) began to appear in September 1939.[12] Binem Heller and David Rikhter, who became editors of the Minsk *Shtern,* also lived in Bialystok. Zelig Akselrod, who was not arrested in 1937, often visited Bialystok, where he met and soon married I. M. Weissenberg's daughter, Perl.

David Sfard, the former secretary of the Linke shrayber-grupe in Poland and now the chief functionary among the Bailystok-based Yiddish writers, distinguished two parallel lines toward the national minorities in Soviet politics. On the one hand, the central authorities wanted to minimize the national culture's influence on the corresponding national group, but at the same time they stimulated further development of the culture proper.[13] A token national culture of an assimilated ethnic group was the strategy pursued by the authorities from the late 1930s. This may give us another possible explanation why many vociferous advocates of Yiddish mass literature vanished in the gulag, whereas their counterparts from the camp of highbrow and middlebrow Kievers were granted a decade's grace. In Belorussia the repression was stronger, probably because the authorities wanted to remove Yiddish from the mainstream and compartmentalize it like in had always been in Ukraine.

In 1939 six Yiddish writers, predominantly former members of the Kiev Group, became holders of high Soviet decorations: Peretz Markish, Leyb Kvitko, David Hofshtein, Itsik Fefer, Yekhezkel Dobrushin, and Shmuel Halkin. The older generation continued to foster younger writers. In 1938, almanacs in Moscow and Kiev targeted the Komsomol youth; some of the authors were also young, including Aron Vergelis, a beginner poet, brought from Birobidzhan to study in Moscow.[14] In 1940 the former Vidervuksnik Abrahan Kahan and the younger poet Abraham Gontar edited a collection of works by tyro Yiddish writers.[15] However, this situation does not mean that the secret police stopped arresting Yiddish writers: for example, Khaim Gildin disappeared in the gulag in 1940 and Zelig Akselrod was arrested in 1941. However, in the years before the World War II, Soviet Yiddish literature was licensed to live.

The Yiddish writers began to annoy the regime both during and particularly after the war, when the Jewish Antifascist Committee, in which they played a central role, began to change the committee's original design of a pure propagandist agency into a communal organization, pursuing (or, in the eyes of the secret police, plotting) territorialist plans of reviving the Birobidzhan or Crimean projects.

The writers treasured the secular variety of Jewishness, formed, with their help, in the Soviet Union—the Jewishness of being "no worse than any-one else," that is to eat pork, work on the Sabbath, but also speak Yiddish and read Sholem Aleichem and Itsik Fefer. In other words, a socialist realist kind of Jewishness—in form but not in content. The Holocaust had ruined the habitat of their constituency, most notably the shtetl and the five Jewish national districts in the Crimea and Ukraine, and they, old hopeless dream-ers, believed that the regime would allow them to relocate thousands of sur-vivors in order to preserve the Soviet Jewish nation. At the end of the day, they lived in a country where rivers had been linked and peoples resettled. Their literature's license expired in the late 1940s, when many Yiddish literati, including virtually all surviving Kiev Group writers, were arrested and some of them executed; five writers—Bergelson, Kvitko, Hofshtein, Markish, and Fefer—were killed on 12 August 1952.[16]

By an eerie coincidence, the day of their execution was Bergelson's sixty-eighth birthday. His prosecutors were not interested in knowing that he was not the same Bergelson who, longer than many other writers, tried to find his place in Soviet literature. Now he knew perfectly well how to create a social-ist realist story. His last significant work, *Tvey veltn* (Two worlds),[17] mod-eled the scheme that had been tested in *The Return of Nathan Backer* and *Seekers of Happiness*. It is set in Birodizhan, where an American professor arrives to find the girl he used to love many years ago, back in his home shtetl. Of course, the professor is a complete duffer at Soviet life, and the process of his becoming familiar with the reality provides a vehicle for the writer to glorify the Soviet system in general and Birobidzhan in particular. It was a perfect example of socialist realist *shund,* one of many pliant works that still could not save the Soviet Yiddish milieu from destruction.

In the 1990s, the publication of some archival materials and particularly the appearance of Aleksand Borshchagovskii's book *The Indictment of Blood*[18] dealt a blow to the posthumous reputation of Fefer. He began to be presented as a villain rather than a victim, or—at best—as a victim of his own dishonesty. It is true that, as the archives witness, in 1944 he became an informer of the Soviet secret police and later, during the prosecution of the Jewish Antifascist Committee, his testimonies served as the linchpin of the prosecution's case. Still, it is important to bear in mind that Fefer's collabo-ration was a natural, inescapable concomitant of his position at the Jewish Antifascist Committee—while Solomon Mikhoels chaired the committee, Fefer ran the committee as its main functionary. In the paranoid Soviet soci-

ety, particularly during the war, any position involving contacts with foreigners could not be occupied without clearance from the secret police. Such
functionaries also had to report to the secret police.

Fefer, the master of "simple speech," perceived himself and was praised
by critics as a poet for the masses. Indeed, he was popular among Yiddish
readers both in the Soviet Union and in the milieu of western Yiddish left-
wingers. At the same time, he was one of many Soviet court poets, who provided the media with easily understood and remembered texts for glorifying
Stalin and Stalinism. The Yiddish court poets remained useful as long as the
Soviet Union had considerable Yiddish-speaking masses and the regime regarded the Jews as a minority with its own language and culture. In the late
1940s, however, after the Holocaust and assimilation had decimated the
Yiddish-speaking contingent of the Soviet population, Fefer and his ilk became
redundant. Moreover, they were seen as an obstacle for further assimilation.

In 1946, Fefer wrote his poem "Epitaph":

S'hot yeder mentsh a troym, vos lebt mit im ineynem,
amol vi heyse fraynt, amol vi kalte shkheynim.
Eyn troym, eyn groyser troym bagleyt mikh in mayn gang,
er lebt in mir, vi s'lebt mayn harts un mayn gezang:
Ven blaybn mit der hoyler erd vel ikh aleyn nor,
ven s'vet der yidisher besoylem mayne alte beyner ufnemen,
zol der farbaygeyer, bamerkndik mayn tsam,
derzeendik dos groz, vos heybt zikh fun mayn shtam,
a zog ton far dem lebedikn vint:
—Er iz geven a mentsh, er hot zayn folk gedint![19]

Everyone has a dream that lives with him together,
sometimes like faithful [literally "hot"] friends, sometimes like cold
     neighbors.
One dream, one big dream follows me in my life,
it lives in me, like my heart and my song:
When I remain on my own with the naked earth,
when the Jewish cemetery takes my old bones,
I hope a passer-by, noticing my fence
and seeing the grass which grows from my body,
will tell the living wind:
—He was a mensch, he served his people!

The regime, however, did not need poets who dreamed of being buried in a Jewish cemetery. They had done their duty.

By the end of the 1950s, the government once again allowed some token forms of Yiddish culture, most notably the Moscow Yiddish literary journal *Sovetish heymland,* launched in August 1961. However, this begins a different story—a story of Soviet Yiddish literature's life from Nikita Khrushchev to Mikhail Gorbachev.[20]

NOTES
BIBLIOGRAPHY
INDEX

Notes

Prologue

1. Norbert Wiener, *I Am a Mathematician* (London: Gollancz, 1956), 45.

2. Leo Wiener, *The History of Yiddish Literature in the Nineteenth Century* (New York: C. Scribner's Sons, 1899), viii, ix, 9, 110, 199.

3. For an analysis of Russian Jewish literacy, see Shaul Stampfer, "What Did 'Knowing Hebrew' Mean in Eastern Europe?" in *Hebrew in Ashkenaz: A Language in Exile,* ed. Lewis Glinert (Oxford: Oxford Univ. Press, 1993), 129–40; and Joel Perlmann, "Russian Jewish Literacy in 1897: A Reanalysis of Census Data," in *Papers in Jewish Demography in Memory of U. O. Schmelz,* ed. Sergio DellaPergola and Judith Even (Jerusalem: Hebrew Univ. of Jerusalem, 1997), 123–37.

4. David Shavit, "The Emergence of Jewish Public Libraries in Tsarist Russia," *Journal of Library History* 20, no. 3 (1985): 239–52.

5. Zalman Reisen, "Tsu der statistik fun yidishn bukh," *YIVO Bleter* 1, no. 2 (1931): 182–83.

6. Dan Miron, *A Traveler Disguised: The Rise of Modern Yiddish Fiction in the Nineteenth Century* (New York: Syracuse Univ. Press, 1996), 24.

7. Sholem Aleichem, *Oysgeklibene briv, 1883–1916* (Moscow: Emes, 1941), 47.

8. Reisen, "Tsu der statistik fun yidishn bukh," 184.

9. Rose Bachelis, *Undzer foter Shomer* (New York: Ikuf, 1950), 157.

10. See Shimen Dubnov [Kritikus], "Literaturnaia letopis'," *Voskhod* 7, no. 5 (1887): 6–21; idem, "Literaturnaia letopis'," *Voskhod* 7, no. 7 (1887): 12–15; idem, "O zhargonnoi literature voobshche i o nekotorykh noveishikh ee proizvedeniiakh v chastnosti," *Voskhod* 8, no. 10 (1888): 21; idem, *Fun 'zhargon' tsu yidish un andere artiklen: literarishe zikhroynes* (Vilna: B. Kletzkin, 1929), 84–85.

11. Sholem Aleichem, *Shomers mishpet, oder der sud prisyazhnikh oyf ale romanen fun Shomer* (Berdichev: n.p., 1888), 3–4.

12. David G. Roskies, "Ayzik-Meyer Dik and the Rise of Yiddish Popular Literature" (Ph.D. diss., Brandeis Univ., 1974), 124.

13. Ken Frieden, *Classic Yiddish Fiction: Abramovitsh, Sholem Aleichem, and Peretz* (Albany: State Univ. of New York Press, 1995), 139.

177

14. Yekhezkel Dobrushin, *Gedankengang* (Kiev: Kultur-lige, 1922), 107.

15. Shmuel Niger, *Lezer, dikhter, kritiker* (New York: Yidisher kultur farlag, 1928), 1: 22.

16. See also Dan Miron, *Sholem Aleykhem: Person, Persona, Presence* (New York: Columbia Univ., 1972).

Chapter One: Kiev

1. Joseph Pennell, *The Jew at Home* (London: William Heinemann, 1892), 91, 92, 102.

2. Sholem Aleichem, *Ale verk,* vol. 4 (New York: Sholem Aleichem folksfond, 1925), 9.

3. G. Gurevitsh, "Di kiever yidishe kehile in di yorn 1906–16," *Shriftn far ekonomik un statistik* 1 (1928): 104.

4. "Kiev," *Evreiskaia entsiklopediia* (St. Petersburg: Brokhaus-Efron, 1906–13), 9: 526.

5. See Alexander B. Tager, *The Decay of Czarism: The Beiliss Trial* (Philadelphia: The Jewish Publication Society of America, 1935).

6. Heorhii Kas'ianov, *Ukraïnska intelihentsiia na rubezhi XIX–XX stolit'* (Kiev: Lybid', 1933), 35.

7. "Kiev," 526–27; Michael F. Hamm, *Kiev: A Portrait, 1800–1917* (Princeton, N.J.: Princeton Univ. Press, 1993), 128–29. For a history of the Brodskys, see Alexandra Fanny Brodsky, *Smoke Signals: From Eminence to Exile* (London and New York: Radcliffe Press, 1997), 3–17.

8. Brodsky, *Smoke Signals,* 3.

9. Sholem Aleichem, *Oysgeklibene briv,* 49, 57. For a vivid description of the reaction of Jewish literati to the unheard-of honoraria, see Shmuel Leyb Zitron, *Dray literarishe doyres* (Warsaw: S. Sreberk, 1920), 1: 23–42.

10. Y. L. Peretz, *Di verk fun Yitskhok Leybush Perets* (New York: Yidish, 1920), 1: 28.

11. For a description of the "sages of Kiev," see Nakhman Meisel, *Undzer Sholem Aleykhem* (Warsaw: Yidish bukh, 1959), 23–42.

12. Sholem Aleichem, *Ale verk,* 12: 59–67.

13. Ibid., 16: 231.

14. Barbara A. Anderson, *Internal Migration During Modernization in Late Nineteenth-Century Russia* (Princeton, N.J.: Princeton Univ. Press, 1980), 167, 170.

15. In 1911 the average percentage of (3,602) Jewish students at all ten Russian universities was 9.7 percent; see F. Gets, "Shkol'noe obuchenie u russkikh evreev," *Zhurnal Ministerstva narodnogo prosveshcheniia,* 51 (1914): 27.

16. Brodsky, *Smoke Signals,* 13.

17. David Zaslavsky, "Materyaln tsu der geshikhte fun kiever organizatsye fun Bund," *Royter pinkes* 1 (1920): 27–35.

18. A. Litvak, *Vos geven* (Vilna: B. Kletzkin, 1925), 96–112.

19. A. Litvak, *Geklibene shriftn* (New York: Veker, 1945), 164–65.

20. Cf. Jan Assmann, *Religion und kulturelles Gedächtnis* (Munich: C. H. Beck, 2000), 15.

21. Az., "Zhargonnaia literatura v 1905 g.," *Voskhod* 26, no. 1 (1906): 48.

22. Moshe Mishkinsky, "Regional Factors in the Formation of the Jewish Labor Movement in Czarist Russia," in *Essential Papers on Jews and the Left,* ed. Ezra Mendelsohn (New York: New York Univ. Press, 1997), 78–100.

23. See A. L. Patkin, *The Origins of the Russian-Jewish Labour Movement* (Melbourne: F. W. Cheshire Pty, 1947), 222–28, 237–41; Alfred Abraham Greenbaum, *Tenu'at ha-tehiyah ("vozroz'denyah") u-mifleget ha-poalim ha-yehudit-sotsyalistit* (Jerusalem: Merkaz Dinur, 1988).

24. Litvak, *Vos geven,* 137; Daniel Charney,"Tsu der kharakteristik fun der yidisher literatur inem ratnfarband," *Fraye shriftn farn yidishn sotsyalistishn gedank* no. 6 (1929): 78–79.

25. Christoph Gassenschmidt, *Jewish Liberal Politics in Tsarist Russia, 1900–14: The Modernization of Russian Jewry* (Basingstoke: Macmillan, 1995), 70.

26. On *Kievskaia mysl',* see A. A. Goldenveizer, "Iz kievskikh vospominanii, 1917–21," *Arkhiv russkoi revoliutsii* 4 (1922): 173; M. Cherepakhov and E. Fingerit, *Russkaia periodicheskaia pechat', 1895–1917* (Moscow: Gosudarstvennoe izdatel'stvo politicheskoi literatury, 1957), 112.

27. Gennady Estraikh, "Languages of 'Yehupets' Students," *East European Jewish Affairs* 2, no. 1 (1991): 63–71.

28. Abraham Kirzhnits, *Der yidisher arbeter: khrestomatye tsu der geshikhte fun der yidisher arbeter, revolyutsionerer un sotsialistisher bavegung in Rusland* (Moscow: Tsentrfarlag, 1927), 3: 87; Sofia Dubnov-Erlich, "Yosef Leshtshinsky (Y. Khmurner): zayn lebn un shafn," in *Kmurner-bukh* (New York: Unzer tsayt, 1958), 76.

29. Nakhman Syrkin, *Geklibene tsionistish-sotsyalistishe shriftn* (New York: Central Committee Poale Zion, 1925), 1: 87.

30. Cf. Walker Connor, *The National Question in Marxist-Leninist Theory and Strategy* (Princeton, N.J.: Princeton Univ. Press, 1984), 19–20.

31. Dubnov-Erlich, "Yosef Leshtshinsky," 64.

32. Shimeni, "Di geshikhte fun a shul," *Literatur un lebn* 3 (1914): 142–436; Khaim Kazdan, *Fun kheyder un "shkoles" biz tsisho* (Mexico: Shlomo Mendelson fond, 1956), 187–91; Elias Schulman, *A History of Jewish Education in the Soviet Union* (New York: Ktav, 1971), 22.

33. Yeshue Liubomirsky, "Farblibn in zikorn: a bleter zikhroynes vegn Osher Shvartsman," *Sovetish heymland* no. 1 (1965): 135–36.

34. "Literarish-kinstlerishe khronik," *Literarishe monatshriftn* no. 3 (1912): 96–97.

35. Nokhum Oislender, "Yugnt, yugnt! Vi a shpilndike vel," *Sovetish heymland* no. 2 (1980): 129–30.

36. Aron Vergelis, "Di goldene keyt fun der yidisher literature," *Sovetish heymland* no. 4 (1963): 104.

37. Abe Finkelshtein, "Vegn eynem a briv," *Sovetish heymland* no. 8 (1973): 168.

38. Dvoire Khorol, "Lirishe heftn," *Sovetish heymland* no. 9 (1975): 153.

39. Khaim Tamarkin, "Durkh yorn un gesheenishn," *Sovetish heymland* no. 4 (1983): 120.

40. Sol Liptzin, *A History of Yiddish Literature* (New York: Jonathan David, 1985), 189.

41. Nakhman Meisel, *Dovid Bergelson* (New York: Kooperativer folks-farlag, 1940), 35–36, 46; see also "Materyaln tsu D. Bergelsons bio-bibliografye," *Visnshaft un revolutsye* nos. 1–2 (1934): 70.

42. Nakhman Meisel, *Forgeyer un mittsaytler* (New York: Ikuf, 1946), 223. On Meisel's family, see his *Bleter zikhroynes* (Kibbutz Alonim: n.p., 1978).

43. Elkhanan Kalmanson, *Dos lebedike vort* (Kiev: n.p., 1910), 10.

44. Hillel Kazovsky, "Shtetl versus megapolis v tvorchestve evreiskikh poetov i khudozhnikov v Amerike," *Zerkalo* nos. 17–18 (2002): 171–83.

45. David Bergelson, "Leksik-problemen in der yidisher literature," *Forpost* no. 2 (1937): 140–53.

46. See in particular M. Lirov's introduction to *Sbornik evreiskoi poezii,* ed. I. S. Rabinovich (Moscow and Leningrad, 1931), 1; Hersh Remenik, *Shtaplen: portretn fun yidishe shrayber* (Moscow: Sovetskii pisatel', 1982), 15, 25; Seth Wolitz, "The Kiev-Grupe (1918–1920) Debate: The Function of Literature," *Yiddish* 3, no. 3 (1978): 97–106. Cf. George S. N. Luckyj, *Literary Politics in the Soviet Ukraine, 1917–34* (Durham, N.C.: Duke Univ. Press, 1990), 30.

47. Bal-Makhshoves, *Shriftn* (Vilna: B. Kletzkin, 1928), 4: 37.

48. Khaim Beider, "Fun Yekhezkl Dobrushins arkhiv," *Sovetish heymland* no. 1 (1976): 128.

49. Uri Finkel, "Moyshe Khashchevatsky," *Folks-shtime,* 8 June 1957.

50. Jacob Glatstein, *In tokh genumen: eseyen 1945–47* (New York: Matones, 1947), 42–43.

51. Genrikh Agranovskii, "Evreiskoe knigopechatanie v Vil'ne v 60-70-e gody XIX stoletiia," *Vestnik Evreiskogo universiteta v Moskve* 15 (1995): 115.

52. Khone Shmeruk, "Aspects of the History of Warsaw as a Yiddish Literary Centre," in *From Shtetl to Socialism,* ed. Antony Polonsky (London: Littman Library of Jewish Civilization, 1993), 120–33; Stephen D. Corrsin, *Warsaw Before the First World War: Poles and Jews in the Third City of the Russian Empire, 1880–1914* (New York: Boulder, 1989), 75.

53. George Y. Shevelov, *The Ukrainian Language in the First Half of the Twentieth Century, 1900–41* (Cambridge, Mass.: Harvard Univ. Press, 1989), 40.

54. See obituary of Yakov Slonim in *Folks-shtime,* 2 July 1958.

55. See Viktor Kel'ner and Dmitrii Eliashevich, *Literatura o evreiakh na russkom iazyke, 1890–1947* (St. Petersburg: Akademicheskii proekt, 1995).

56. Hrihorii Hrigor'ev, *U staromu Kievi* (Kiev: Dumka, 1961), 151–52.

57. Max Weinreich, "Yidish," in *Algemeyne entsiklopedye* (Paris: Dubnov-fond, 1940), Yidn/B: 27.

58. On the Czernowitz conference, see Joshua A. Fishman, *Yiddish: Turning to Life* (Amsterdam: J. Benjamins, 1991), 231–90; Emanuel S. Goldsmith, *Modern Yiddish Culture: The Story of the Yiddish Language Movement* (New York: Fordham Univ. Press, 1997). See also

Abraham Novershtern, "Sholem-Aleykhem un zayn shtelung tsu der shprakhn-frage," *Di goldene keyt* 74 (1971): 164–88.

59. Benjamin Pinkus, "La participation des minorités nationales extra-territoriales à la vie politique et république de l'Union Soviétique, 1917–39," *Cahiers du monde russe* 36, no. 3 (1995): 299; Gassenschmidt, *Liberal Jewish Politics,* 70.

60. Bachelis, *Undzer foter Shomer,* 96, 101.

61. Oislender, "Yugnt, yugnt!" 136.

62. B. Gorin, "Di oyfbliung fun der yidisher literatur in Amerike," *Di tsukunft* no. 7 (1902): 340–43.

63. See M. Shalit's statistics and analysis in *Der pinkes: yorbukh far der geshikhte fun der yidisher literatur un shprakh, far folklor, kritik un bibliografye,* ed. Shmuel Niger (Vilna: B. Kletzkin, 1913), 277–306.

64. N. M. Sheikevitsh, *Di amerikanishe glikn: a roman fun yidishn lebn in Amerike* (Vilna: Katsenelson, 1912), 3.

65. Gitl Meisel, *Eseyen* (Tel Aviv: I. L. Peretz, 1974), 23.

66. Nakhman Meisel, *Kegnzaytike hashpoes in velt-shafn* (Warsaw: Ikuf, 1965), 319–20.

67. Ibid., 314. For more on *At the Depot,* see Mikhail Krutikov, *Yiddish Fiction and the Crisis of Modernity, 1905–14* (Stanford, Calif.: Stanford Univ. Press, 2001), 38–45.

68. Shmuel Niger, "Briv fun Dovid Bergelson," *Zamlbikher* 8 (1952): 85; Nosn Hertsman, "Der vald hot oysgeshpign a ban," *Folks-shtime,* 5 Dec. 1959; Oislender, "Yugnt, yugnt!" 136; Y. Rapoport, *Zoymen in vint* (Buenos Aires: Alveltlekher yidisher kultur-kongres, 1862), 380.

69. See Sh. Brianski, *D. Bergelson in shpigl fun der kritik, 1909–32* (Kiev: Institut far yidisher proletarisher kultur, 1934), 13.

70. Z. Ratner and Y. Kvitni, *Dos yidishe bukh in f.s.s.r. far di yorn 1917–21* (Kiev: Tsentr-farlag, 1930), 14.

71. Khaim Kazdan, "Undzer literatur far kinder," *Bikher-velt* nos. 4–5 (1919): 29.

72. Finkelshtein, "Vegn eynem a briv," 168.

73. Edvardas Vidmantas, "Sotsial-demokraticheskaia pechat' i rabochee dvizhenie v Litve v 1895–1907 gg" (candidate diss., Vilnius Univ., 1976), 61, 80a, 86a.

74. In the 1910 and 1911 editions of I. V. Volfson, *Adresnaia i spravochnaia kniga: gazetnyi mir* (St. Petersburg: n.p.), Boris Kletzkin's enterprise is listed as a printing shop (Vilna, 33 Zaval'naia Street) specializing in producing newspapers and books rather than a publishing house.

75. B. Rivkin, *Grunt-tendentsn fun der yidisher literatur in Amerike* (New York: Ikuf, 1948), 145.

76. Esfir Bramson-Alperniene, "Der Vilner yidisher farlag un zayn grinder Boris Kletzkin," *Jiddistik-Mitteilungen* 27 (2002): 3–6.

77. For the circumstances of the arrest and exile of A. Weiter (Aizik Meir Devenishski), see Khana Gordon Mlotek, "Der toyt fun A. Vayter un zayne nokhfolgn," *YIVO Bleter* 2 (1994): 48.

78. Susanne Marten-Finnis, "Wilna als Zentrum der jüdischen Parteiliteratur 1896 bis 1922," *Aschkenas* 10, no. 1 (2000): 208–9.

79. Tsivyon, "Di ershte yidishe sotsialistishe teglekhe tsaytung in Vilne," in *Vilne,* ed. Ephraim H. Jeshurin (New York: Vilner Brentsh 367 Arbeter Ring, 1935), 191.

80. Arcadius Kahan, "Vilne—a sotsial-kultureler profil fun a yidisher kehile tsvishn beyde velt-milkhomes," *YIVO Bleter* 2 (1994): 27–42.

81. See Ber Borokhov's 1913 programmatic article "Di oyfgabn fun der yidisher filologye," in Ber Borokhov, *Shprakh-forshung un literatur-geshikhte* (Tel Aviv: I. L. Peretz, 1966), 53–75.

82. See Ewa Geller, *Warschauer Jiddisch* (Tübingen: Max Niemeyer, 2001), 31–33.

83. Peretz Hirshbein, *In gang fun lebn* (New York: Tsiko, 1948), 147.

84. See J. Anilowicz and M. Joffe, "Yidishe lernbikher un pedagogik, 1900–30," *Shriftn far psikhologye un pedagogic* 1 (1931): 483–88.

85. See David Bergelson, "A zun-bashaynter riz," in *Osher Shvartsman: zamlung gevidmet dem XX yortog fun zayn heldishn toyt,* ed. Aron Kushnirov (Moscow: Emes, 1940), 10–14.

86. Kazdan, "Undzer literatur," 29; Khone Shmeruk, "Sholem-Aleykhem un di onheybn fun der yidisher literatur far kinder," *Di goldene keyt* 112 (1984): 48. On children's Yiddish literature in pre-WWI Russia, see also A. Slutskii, "Detskaia literatura na razgovorno-evreiskom iazyke," *Vestnik Obshchestva rasprostraneniia prosveshcheniia mezhdu evreiami v Rossii* 13 (1912): 29–45; S. Korsyna and E. Shabad, "Ob izdanii detskoi literatury na razgovorno-evreiskom iazyke," *Vestnik Obshchestva rasprostraneniia prosveshcheniia mezhdu evreiami v Rossii* 22 (1913): 55–62.

87. A. Gornfel'd, "Zhargonnaia literatura na russkom knizhnom rynke," *Evreiskii mir* (Jan. 1909): 68–69.

88. Wolitz, "The Kiev-Grupe Debate," 97.

89. The Vilna University was destroyed as a punishment for its students' participation in the anti-Russian revolt in Warsaw in November 1830; see James T. Flynn, *The University Reform of Tsar Alexander 1, 1802–35* (Washington, D.C.: Catholic Univ. of America Press, 1988), 187.

90. See the publications in *Novyi put'* no. 7 (1917): 34; no. 18 (1917): 4–5, 8.

91. M. Kleinman, "Der kumendiker yid," in *Untervegs* (Odessa: Moria, 1917), 158–70.

92. Shmuel Niger, *Shmuesn vegn bikher* (New York: Yidish, 1922), 39.

93. Morris Myer, *A yidishe utopye: a plan fun rekonstruktsye farn yidishn folk* (London: Tsayt, 1918), 3–5.

94. Shimon Dubnov, "Zhitlovskis 'avtonomism," in *Zhitlovski-zamlbukh* (Warsaw: H. Bzshozo, 1929), 193; Jonathan Frenkel, "The Dilemmas of Jewish National Autonomism: The Case of Ukraine, 1917–20," in *Ukrainian-Jewish Relations in Historical Perspective,* ed. Howard Aster and Peter J. Potichnyj (Edmonton: Canadian Institute of Ukrainian Studies, 1990), 263–64.

95. Kh. D. Hurvits, *Yidishe klasn un parteyen: a sotsyalistisher etyud* (Petrograd: Geule, 1918), 35.

96. Shmaryahu Gorelik, "Kunst un natsyonale oyslebn," *Der yidisher almanakh* (Kiev: Kunst-farlag, 1910), 85.

97. Nathan Birnbaum, "Di absolute idee fun yidntum un di yidishe shprakh," *Di yidishe velt* no. 1 (1912): 45–52.

98. A. D. Karalnik, "Evreiskaia problema vlasti," *Novyi put'* no. 32 (1917): 10.

99. Ben-Yakov, *In der tsukunft-shtot Edenya* (Kharkov: Yidish, 1918).

100. Cf. Khaim Zhitlovsky, *Yidn un yidishkayt* (New York: Kh. Zhitlovsky farlag-komitet, 1939), 17.

101. Ben Adir, *Undzer shprakh-problem* (Kiev: kultur-lige, 1918), 45.

102. Nokhum Shtif, *Yidn un yidish, oder ver zaynen "yidishistn" un vos viln zey? Poshete verter far yedn yidn* (Kiev: Onhoyb, 1919), 65–96.

103. See in particular Bal-Dimyen, *Humanizm in der elterer yidisher literatur: a kapitl literatur-geshikhte* (Kiev: Kultur-lige, 1920), 62; Dobrushin, *Gedankengang*, 8.

104. Moissaye J. Olgin, *A Guide to Russian Literature, 1820–1917* (New York: Harcourt, Brace, and Howe, 1920), 11.

105. See for example Assmann, *Religion und kulturelles Gedächtnis*.

106. Mikhail Krutikov, "Soviet Literary Theory in the Search for a Yiddish Canon: The Case of Moshe Litvakov," in *Yiddish and the Left,* ed. Gennady Estraikh and Mikhail Krutikov (Oxford: Legenda, 2000), 231–32; Moshe Litvakov, *In umru* (Kiev: Kiever farlag, 1919), 76.

107. Dobrushin, *Gedankengang*, 29, 31.

108. Yekhezkel Dobrushin, "Yidisher kunst-primitiv un dos kunst-bukh far kinder," *Bikher-velt* nos. 4–5 (1919): 13–23; Oswald Spengler, *The Decline of the West* (London: G. Allen and Unwin, 1959), 174.

109. Krutikov, *Yiddish Fiction*, 211.

110. I. Z. Eliashev, "Narodno-evreiskaia literatura s XIX-go veka," in *Otechestvo. Puti i dostizheniia natsional'nykh literatur Rossii. Natsional'nyi vopros,* ed. J. N. Baudoin de Courtenay et al. (Petrograd: M. V. Petrov, 1916), 1: 331.

111. Nakhman Meisel, ed., *Briv un redes fun Y. L. Peretz* (New York: Ikuf, 1944), 379.

112. Quoted from a reprint in Leo Kenig, *Shrayber un verk* (Vilna: B. Kletzkin, 1929), 70–72.

113. Rivkin, *Grunt-tendentsn fun der yidisher literatur,* 163.

114. Iv. Bondarenko, "Z istoriï natsional'noho pytannia: K. Marksa Zur Judenfrage," *Literaturno-naukovyi vistnyk* (June 1909): 485.

115. Reprinted in 1919 in Litvakov, *In umru,* 30.

116. Joseph Tenenbaum, "Di yidishe shprakh oyf der tog-ordenung fun der sholem-konferents in Paris, 1919," *YIVO Bleter* 41 (1957–58): 219, 229.

117. Solomon I. Gol'del'man, *Zhidivs'ka natsional'na avtonomiia na Ukraïni* (Munich: Institut zur Erforschung der UdSSR, 1963); Adelina Gritsenko, *Politychni syly u borot'bi za vladu v Ukraïni* (Kiev: Institut istoriï Ukraïny AN Ukraïny, 1993).

118. M. P. Khodos, *Materialy po statistike naseleniia Kieva* (Kiev: n.p., 1926), 148–49.

119. Mikhailo Rybakov, ed., *Pravda istoriï. Diial'nist' evreiskoï kul'turno-prosvitnyts'koï organizatsiï "Kul'turna Liha" u Kievi, 1918–25* (Kiev: Kyi, 2001), 4, 13.

120. Hillel Kazovsky, "The Art Section of the Kultur Lige," *Jews in Eastern Europe* 3 (1993): 6–7; Hillel Kazovsky, *The Artists of the Kultur-Lige* (Jerusalem and Moscow: Gesher, 2003), 34–42.

121. Ben Adir, *Undzer shprakh-problem*, 27.

122. Wolitz, "The Kiev-Grupe Debate," 98.

123. David Bathrick, "Die Berliner Avantgarde der 20er Jahre: Das Beispiel Franz Jung," in *Literarisches Leben in Berlin, 1871–1933*, ed. Peter Wruck (Berlin: Akademie, 1987), 2: 49.

124. Quoted in Abraham Abchuk, *Etyudn un materyaln tsu der geshikhte fun der yidisher literatur-bavegung in fssr, 1917–27* (Kharkov: Literatur un kunst, 1934), 10.

125. Israel Joshua Singer, "A briv fun Amerike," *Forverts*, 7 June 1942.

126. Kazovsky, *The Artists of the Kultur-Lige*, 63.

127. Hillel Kazovsky, "Jewish Art Between *yidishkayt* and Civilization," in *The Shtetl: Image and Reality*, ed. Gennady Estraikh and Mikhail Krutikov (Oxford: Legenda, 2000), 88.

128. G. Meisel, *Eseyen*, 41.

129. Peretz Markish, "Af di vegn fun yidisher dikhtung," in *Trep* (Ekaterinoslav: Kultur-lige, 1921), 37.

130. Sergei Esenin, *Sobranie sochinenii v trekh tomakh* (Moscow: Sovetskii pisatel', 1987), 3: 126–27.

131. Peretz Markish, *Nakht-royb* (Moscow: Lirik, 1922), 28.

132. Nokhum Oislender, "In 1917," *Sovetish heymland* no. 9 (1969): 130.

133. Melech Ravitsh, *Dos mayse-bukh fun mayn lebn: yorn in Varshe, 1921–34* (Tel Aviv: I. L. Peretz, 1975), 375–77.

134. Nokhum Shtif, "An ekspeditsye fun aeroplan oyf di gimalayen fun undzer moyekh," *Dos fraye vort* no. 3 (1923): 32–36.

135. See a reprint in Litvakov, *In umru* (Moscow: Shul un bukh, 1926), 61–73. Although the Yiddish title of the 1919 article is "Dikhtung un gezelshaftlekhkayt," which literally translates as "Poetry and Society," Bergelson used the word *dikhtung* in the sense of any literary creativity. See Rivka Rubin, *Shrayber un verk* (Warsaw and Moscow: Yidish bukh, 1968), 246.

136. Régine Robin, "L'itinéraire de David Bergelson," in David Bergelson, *Autour de la Gare suivi de Joseph Shur* (Lausanne: L'Age d'homme, 1982), 26.

137. Bal-Dimeyn, "Der yidisher komunist, di kultur-lige, un dos yidishe bukh," *Di tsukunft* 28, no. 1 (1923): 32.

138. Abchuk, *Etyudn un materyaln*, 18.

139. T. Draudin, *Ocherki izdatel'skogo dela v SSSR* (Moscow and Leningrad: Gosudarstvennoe sotsial'no-ekonomicheskoe izdatel'stvo, 1934), 166. For a bibliography of the Culture League's publications, see Rybakov, ed., *Pravda istoriï*, 176–87.

Chapter Two: Moscow

1. 36 Yiddish titles were published in Moscow in 1917, 32 in 1918, 28 in 1919, 11 in 1920, and 3 in 1921. Ratner and Kvitni, *Yidishe bukh in f.s.s.r.*, 16.

2. Abchuk, *Etyudn un materyaln.*

3. Daniel Charney, *A yortsendlik aza, 1914–24* (New York: Tsiko, 1943); Menashe Halpern, *Parmetn: zikhroynes un shilderungen* (Saõ Paolo: Alveltlekher yidisher kultur-kongres, 1952).

4. Zalman Reisen, *Leksikon fun der yidisher literatur, prese un filologye* (Vilna: B. Kletz-kin, 1928–29), 1–4; 1956–81. *Leksikon fun der nayer yidisher literatur* (New York: Tsiko, 1956–81), 1–8.

5. Published in *Sovetish heymland* no. 11 (1966): 141–46; no. 12 (1966): 134–40; and no. 4 (1967): 139–45.

6. On the expulsion from Moscow, see O. B. Goldovskii, *Evrei v Moskve: stranitsy iz is-torii sovremennoi Rossii* (Berlin: n.p., 1904); S. Vermel', *Moskovskoe izgnanie* (Moscow: Mir, 1924).

7. Mark Kupovetskii, "Evreiskoe naselenie Moskvy, XV–XX vv," in *Etnicheskie gruppy v gorodakh evropeiskoi chasti SSSR,* ed. Igor' Krupnik (Moscow: Geographicheskoe obshch-estvo, 1987), 64.

8. Reuven Brainin, *Fun mayn lebns-bukh* (New York: Ikuf, 1946), 284.

9. Kh. Braude, "Iz evreiskoi rabochei statistiki," *Novyi put'* nos. 26–27 (1917): 9–14.

10. Dmitry A. Elyashevich, *Pravitel'stvennaia politika i evreiskaia pechat' v Rossii, 1797–1917* (St. Petersburg and Jerusalem: Gesharim, 1999), 512–16.

11. "Literaturnaia khronika," *Novyi put'* no. 7 (1917): 31.

12. See the following Shmuel Agurski works: "Di antshteyung un antviklung fun der yidisher komunistisher prese," *Der veker,* 3 Mar. 1923; "Di antshteyung fun der ershter komu-nistisher tsaytung in yidish," *Komunistishe fon,* 7 Mar. 1923; *Der yidisher arbeter in der komu-nistisher bavegung, 1917–21* (Minsk, 1925), 2; "Di ershte yidishe sovetishe tsaytung," *Folks-shtime* 7 Nov. 1967.

13. See the publications in *Evreiskaia nedelia* nos. 9–10 (1922): 5–6; and nos. 11–12 (1922): 23.

14. Daniel Charney, "Tsu der geshikhte fun der yidisher komunistisher prese," *In shpan* no. 1 (1926): 132.

15. "Vospominaniia Leo Keniga," publication of Hille Kazovsky, *Vestnik Evreiskogo uni-versiteta* 2 (1999): 331.

16. Cf. Vladimir Lapshin, *Khudozhestvennaia zhizn' Moskvy i Petrograda v 1917 godu* (Moscow: Sovetskii khudozhnik, 1983), 86.

17. Charney, *A yortsendlik aza,* 293–94.

18. Arlen Blium, *Evreiskii vopros pod sovetskoi tsenzuroi, 1917–91* (St. Peterburg: Peter-burgskii evreiskii universitet, 1996), 29–30.

19. E. I. Pivovar et al., *Rossiia v izgnanii: sud'by russkikh emigrantov za rubezhom*

(Moscow: Institut vseobshchei istorii RAN, 1999), 349. On the Soviet attitude toward Zionism, see Michael Beizer and Vladlen Izmozik, "Dzerzhinskii's Attitude toward Zionism," *Jews in Eastern Europe* no. 1 (1994): 64–70.

20. Jeffrey Veidlinger, "Let's Perform a Miracle: The Soviet Yiddish State Theatre in the 1920s," *Slavic Review* 52, no. 2 (1998): 380–84; Aleksandr Kamensky, *Chagall: The Russian Years, 1907–22* (London: Thames and Hudson, 1989), 278, 329.

21. Charney, "Tsu der kharakteristik fun der yidisher literatur," 74. According to the Vilna-based monthly *Di naye velt,* the vast majority of Yiddish books published in Russia in 1918 had a print run of 3,000–4,000, while the circulation of periodicals was 5,000–8,000; quoted in *Sovetish heymland* no. 10 (1969): 146.

22. "Statistika evreiskoi literatury v 1915 g.," *Novyi put'* no. 18 (1916): 7–9.

23. Ratner and Kvitni, *Yidishe bukh in f.s.s.r.,* 12. See also Khone Shmeruk, "Nokhem Shtif, Mark Shagal un di yidishe kinder-literatur in vilner kletskin farlag," *Di pen* 26 (1996): 1–19.

24. Ziva Amishai-Maisels, "The Jewish Awakening: A Search for National Identity," *Russian Jewish Artists in a Century of Change, 1890–1990,* ed. Susan Tumarkin Goodman (Munich: Prestel, 1995), 60; Nikolai Gudzhiev, *Stat'i ob avangarde* (Moscow: RA, 1997), 1: 237.

25. Draudin, *Ocherki izdatel'skogo dela v SSSR,* 52.

26. These included Chagall, Lissitzky, Abraham Brazer, Isaak Brodskii, Joseph Tchaikov, Mark Epshtein, Robert Falk, Evgenii Katsman, Abraham Manievich, Yssachar-Ber Rybak, David Shterenberg, and Shlome Yudovin. The tradition of such exhibitions started with the first exhibition of Jewish artists, organized in Berlin in 1907. In Moscow, exhibitions of this kind were held in the spring and summer of 1917. See "Vystavka evreev-khudozhnikov," *Novyi put'* 13–15 (1917): 32; L. M. Antokol'skii, "Evreiskaia khudozhestvennaia vystavka v Moskve," *Evreiskaia nedelia* 25 (1917): 33; A. K., "Yidishe kunst-oysshtelung," *Der emes,* 8, 9, and 11 Aug. 1918.

27. In December 1920, MCYMA held an evening in An-sky's memory (see *Der emes* 12 Dec. 1920).

28. For information about the Polish period of Broderzon's life, see Gilles Rozier, *Moyshe Broderzon: Un écrivain yiddish d'avant-garde* (Saint-Denis: Presses Universitarires de Vincennes, 1999).

29. There, after the Polish occupation of the city in April 1919, Niger escaped death by a hair's breadth (on April 21, Polish troops executed his fellow writer A. Weiter). Mlotek, "Der toyt fun A. Vayter un zayne nokhfolgn," 49–56. Soon after, Niger settled in New York.

30. I. Abramskii, "Eto bylo v Vitebske," *Iskusstvo* 10 (1964): 69–71; Sophie Lissitzky-Küppers, *El Lissitzky: Life, Letters, Texts* (London: Thames and Hudson, 1968), 20; Kamensky, *Chagall,* 264; Hillel Kazovsky, *Artists from Vitebsk: Yehuda Pen and his Pupils* (Moscow: Imidzh, 1992).

31. Lev Trotskii, *K istorii russkoi revoliutsii* (Moscow: Izdatel'stvo politicheskoi literatury, 1990), 160.

32. Richard Sakwa, *Soviet Communists in Power: A Study of Moscow During the Civil War, 1918–21* (Basingstoke: Macmillan, 1988), 35–36.

33. Der Nister, "Moskve: a shvere dermonung," *Di royte velt* nos. 7–8 (1932): 125, 132, 133.

34. Russian Center for the Preservation and Study of Documents of Contemporary History (RCPSDCH), f. 445, op. 1, d. 29, p. 42.

35. Borokhov, *Shprakh-forshung un literatur-geshikhte,* 348.

36. Gregory Aronson, *Rusish-yidishe inteligents* (Buenos Aires: Yidbukh, 1962), 251; see also Z. Wendroff, "Di 70-yorike milkhome," *Sovetish heymland* no. 3 (1966): 149–53, and Moshe Notovich, "Yugnt—zayn oytser," *Sovetish heymland* no. 1 (1967): 69–73.

37. Vladislav Ivanov, *Russkie sezony teatra Gabima* (Moscow: Artist. Rezhiser. Teatr, 1999), 60–74, 240.

38. *Bor'ba* nos. 9–12 (1920): 12.

39. RCPSDCH, f. 445, op. 1, d. 97, p. 119.

40. Roman Timenchik and Zoia Kopel'man, "Viacheslav Ivanov i poeziia Kh.N. Bialika," *Novoe literaturnoe obozrenie* 14 (1995): 106.

41. David Bergelson, "Moskve," *Frayhayt,* 5 Sept. 1925; Singer, "A briv fun Amerike."

42. Osher Shvartsman, *Ale lider* (Moscow: Sovetskii pisatel', 1961), 77, 150.

43. Cf. Gennady Estraikh, *Soviet Yiddish: Language Planning and Linguistic Development* (Oxford: Oxford Univ. Press, 1999), 117–22.

44. M. Shulman, "Vos iz azoyns proletarishe poezye?" *Di komunistishe velt* no. 2 (1919): 18–22.

45. First printed in *Di komunistishe velt* nos. 6–7 (1919): 32, and in *Sovetish heymland* no. 6 (1976): 150.

46. Cf. Kurt Johansson, *Aleksej Gastev: Proletarian Bard of the Machine Age* (Stockholm: Almqvist and Wiksell International, 1983).

47. See Ber Orshanski, *Di yidishe literatur in Vaysrusland nokh der revolutsye* (Minsk: Tsentr-farlag, 1931).

48. Reprinted in *Sovetish heymland* no. 3 (1961): 101.

49. *Sovetish heymland* no. 9 (1965): 144.

50. Aron Kushnirov, *Vent* (Kiev: Melukhe-farlag, 1921), 9–10.

51. Mordechai Altshuler, ed., *Briv fun yidishe sovetishe shraybers* (Jerusalem: Hebrew Univ., 1979), 194.

52. Charney, "Tsu der geshikhte," 131.

53. Khaim Tamarkin, "Moskve in di tsvantsiker yorn," *Sovetish heymland* no. 8 (1985): 126–27, 130–32.

54. Aron Yerusalimski, "Di 'mayrevke'— undzer 'kleyner internatsional,' " *Sovetish heymland* no. 2 (1974): 168–73.

55. Itshe-Meir (Isaac) Shpilrein, who in 1922–24 also headed the Yiddish Language Commission of the Commissariat of Education, was essentially a lover of Yiddish. He is better

known as an authority on psychotechnics; see V. A. Kol'tsova et al., "I. N. Shpil'rein i sovetskaia psikhotekhnika," *Psikhologicheskii zhurnal* 11, no. 2 (1990): 111–33. Another untrained Yiddish linguist, Aizik Zaretski, who combined teaching mathematics for the Proletkult with masterminding the 1920 Soviet Yiddish spelling reform, moved to Kharkov in 1921 to study linguistics with the Ukrainian professor Leonid Bulakovskii. He returned to Moscow in 1926.

56. Joseph Rabin, "Hert mikh oys: fun mayne zikhroynes," *Sovetish heymland* no. 8 (1984): 140.

57. Gabriele Freitag, "Evreiskoe naselenie Moskvy v fokuse politiki kommunisticheskoi partii v otnoshenii natsional'nykh men'shinstv," *Tirosh* 3 (1999): 180.

58. Kharik was born in the shtetl of Zembin, Belorussia.

59. RCPSDCH, f. 445, op. 1, d. 120, p. 2–3.

60. Litvakov's outlook in the early 1920s is analyzed on the basis of his 1926 collection of articles, *In umru,* and his Russian article "Ob uprostitel'stve i popustitel'stve," *Pechat' i revoliutsiia* no. 7 (1923): 68–75. See also Elias Schulman, *Di sovetish-yidishe literatur* (New York: Bikher, 1971), 81–96.

61. On the influence of Plekhanov's aesthetic legacy, see Burton Rubin, "Plekhanov and Soviet Literary Criticism," *The American Slavic and East European Review* 15, no. 4 (1956): 527–42.

62. Shakhne Epshtein, ed., *Di yidishe kinstlerishe literatur un di partey-onfirung* (Kharkov: Melukhe-farlag, 1929), 44.

63. Yavneh was the location in Palestine where the Jews began to rebuild their religious and national life after the Romans destroyed the Temple in Jerusalem. There the Jews began developing a new *masorah,* Hebrew for "tradition."

64. Anatolii Lunacharskii, "Svoboda knigi i revoliutsiia," *Pechat' i revoliutsiia* no. 1 (1921): 5.

65. Moshe Litvakov [M. Lirov], "Sholom-Aleikhem," *Kievskaia mysl',* 9 May 1916.

66. Nakhman Meisel, Bergelson's old friend, was of the same opinion; see his book *Dos yidishe shafn un der yidisher shrayber in sovetnfarband* (New York: Ikuf, 1959), 176–77. Dobrushin also considered Bergelson as "Sholom Aleichem's organic successor;" see Yekhezkel Dobrushin, "Sholem-Aleichem's alie," *Shtrom* no. 2 (1922): 59.

67. Moshe Litvakov, "Nayes fun der yidisher literatur," *Der emes,* 25 Apr. 1924.

68. Yasha Bronshtein, "Der stiln-kamf inem period fun militerishn komunizm," *Prolit* nos. 11–12 (1929): 66.

69. This and a few other letters of Dobrushin of that period are preserved in the personal archive of the Yiddish writer Khaim Beider (1920–2003), to whom I am indebted for providing me with copies of these letters. On Litvakov's argumentative character, see also Hersh Smolyar, *Fun ineveynik* (Tel Aviv: I. L. Peretz, 1978), 288–90.

70. Rabin, "Hert mikh oys," 144.

71. See Moisei Belen'kii, "Put' pisatelia," in Joseph Rabin, *Izbrannoe* (Moscow: Khudozhestvennaia literatura, 1984), 4.

72. *Lenin. Troyer-tog. 27 yanvar 1924* (Moscow: Kultur-lige, 1924).

73. "Yidishe kultur-tuer kegn kemfndikn hebraizm," *Der emes,* 12 Feb. 1924.

74. "Yidishlekher ongrif un Dovid Hofshteyn," *Der emes,* 19 Feb. 1924.

75. Mordechai Altshuler, ed., *Briv fun yidishe sovetishe shraybers,* 125, 167–68.

76. David Shneer, "An Ambivalent Revolutionary: Izi Kharik's Image of the Shtetl," *East European Jewish Affairs* 32, no. 1 (2002): 117.

77. See Ivanov, *Russkie sezony teatra Gabima.*

78. "Der mishpet iber Yungvald," *Der emes,* 1 Nov. 1925.

79. Mordechai Altshuler, ed., *Briv fun yidishe sovetishe shraybers,* 19.

80. Isaak Nusinov, "Af farfestikte pozitsyes," *Di royte velt* no. 9 (1926): 105–6.

81. Charney, "Tsu der kharakteristik fun der yidisher literatur," 77.

82. Sh. Strazh, "Der ufshtand fun masnleyener," *Oktyabr* no. 1 (1925): 107–8.

83. Nakhman Meisel, "Der krizis fun yidishn bukh," *Literarishe bleter* no. 56 (1925): 1. Nakhman Meisel, "Dos yidishe bukh in 1925," *Literarishe bleter* no. 87 (1926): 2–3.

84. Ben-Yakov, *In der tsukunft-shtot Edenya.*

85. RCPSDCH, f. 445, op. 1, d. 172, p. 23–24.

86. See Herman Ermolaev, *Soviet Literary Theories 1917–34: The Genesis of Socialist Realism* (Berkeley: Univ. of California Press, 1963), 36–54.

87. Shneer, "An Ambivalent Revolutionary," 101.

Chapter Three: Offshore Soviet Literature

1. Cf. Krutikov, "Soviet Literary Theory," 228.

2. Luckyj, *Literary Politics,* 55.

3. *Albom lekoved dem yoyvl fun progresivn yidishn vort in Argentine* (Buenos Aires: n.p., 1973).

4. Sara Lapitskaia, "Publitsisticheskaia deiatel'nost' Bera Gal'perina v Parizhe," in *Evrei Rossii—immigranty Frantsii,* ed. W. Moskovich, V. Khazan, and S. Breuillard (Jerusalem and Moscow: Mosty kul'tury, 2000), 144–51.

5. Joseph Sherman, "With Perfect Faith: The Life and Work of Leibl Feldman," in Leibl Feldman, *Oudtshoorn: Jerusalem of Africa* (Johannesburg: Univ. of the Witwatersrand, 1989), 15.

6. Nakhman Meisel, *Geven amol a lebn: dos yidishe kultur-lebn in Poyln tsvishn beyde velt-milkhomes* (Buenos Aires: Tsentral farband fun poylishe yidn, 1951), 23–66.

7. *Albatros* 1 (1922): 16.

8. David Sfard, *Mit zikh un mit andere* (Jerusalem: Yerusholayimer almanakh, 1984), 52–69; presumably also written by Sfard, "Der virklekher zin fun der provokatsye kegn der progresiver yidisher tsaytung in Poyln *Fraynd*," *Folks-shtime,* 4 Dec. 1958. On Yung Vilne, see Justin D. Cummy, "Tsevorfene bleter: The Emergence of Yung Vilne," *Polin: Studies in Polish Jewry* 14 (2001): 170–91.

9. Leo Fuks and Renate Fuks, "Yiddish Publishing Activities in the Weimar Republic, 1920–33," *Leo Baeck Institute Year Book* 33 (1988): 421. See also Susanne Marten-Finnis and

Heather Valencia, *Sprachinseln: Jiddische Publizistik in London, Wilna, und Berlin 1880–1930* (Cologne: Böhlau, 1999), 115–37.

10. Nakhman Meisel, "Dos yidishe bukh in 1925."

11. Maren Krüger, "Buchproduktion im Exil: Der Klal-Verlag," in *Juden in Kreuzberg. Fundstücke, Fragmente, Erinnerungen* (Berlin: Berliner Geschichtswerkstatt, 1991), 421–26; Vladimir Naumov, ed., *Nepravednyi sud: Poslednii stalinskii rasstrel* (Moscow: Mezhdunarodnye otnosheniia, 1994), 80.

12. G. Meisel, *Eseyen,* 24.

13. Israel Rubin, "Bay di tishlekh fun romanishn kafe," *Literarishe bleter* no. 3 (1930): 53–54.

14. Abrahan-Nokhum Stencl, "Arop funem yarid . . . ," *Loshn un lebn* nos. 10–11 (1968): 25; Delphine Bechtel, *La Renaissance culturelle juive: Europe centrale et orientale, 1897–1930* (Paris: Belin, 2002), 206f.

15. B. Kvitko and M. Petrovskii, *Zhizn' i tvorchestvo L'va Kvitko* (Moscow: Detskaia literatura, 1976), 129–31.

16. From a letter cited in Delphine Bechtel, *Der Nister's Work 1907–29: A Study of a Yiddish Symbolist* (Bern: P. Lang, 1990), 15.

17. Delphine Bechtel, "Dovid Bergelsons Berliner Erzählungen. Ein vergessenes Kapitel der jiddischen Literatur," in *Jiddische Philologie: Festschrift für Erika Timm,* ed. Walter Röll and Simon Neuberg (Tübingen: Max Niemeyer, 1999), 257–72.

18. Lev Bergelson, "Erinnerungen an mainem Vater: Die Berliner Jahre," in David Bergelson, *Leben ohne Früling* (Berlin: Aufbau, 2001), 283–85.

19. Nakhman Meisel, "Mir forn farbay Berlin," *Literarishe bleter* 43 (1937): 689–90.

20. David G. Roskies, "The Re-education of Der Nister: 1922–29," in *Jews and Jewish Life in Russia and the Soviet Union,* ed. Yaacov Ro'i (Ilford: F. Cass, 1995), 201.

21. See *Bikher-velt* no. 2 (1922): 223–24. On Edouard Bernstein's and Karl Kautski's attitude to *Forverts,* see Jack Jacobs, *On Socialists and "the Jewish Question" after Marx* (New York: New York Univ. Press, 1992), 26–28, 67.

22. Elias Schulman, *Leksikon fun Forverts shrayber zint 1897* (New York: Forward, 1986), 12.

23. "Ekonomicheskoe polozhenie evreev v Bessarabii," *Rul',* 1 Jan. 1925; Leon Shapiro, *The History of ORT: A Jewish Movement for Social Change* (New York: Schocken Books, 1980), 143.

24. "Khronika," *Rul',* 24 Dec. 1924.

25. Rapoport, *Zoymen in vint,* 381; Bal-Makhshoves, *Geklibene verk* (New York: Tsiko, 1953), 77–111.

26. Rapoport, *Zoymen in vint,* 384.

27. Leon Shapiro, *History of ORT,* 144.

28. Mordechai Altshuler, ed., *Briv fun yidishe sovetishe shraybers,* 478.

29. See Shlomo Belis, *Portretn un problemen* (Warsaw: Yidish bukh, 1964), 22.

30. For the early history of *Frayhayt,* see Tony Michels, "Socialism with a Jewish Face: The

Origins of the Yiddish-Speaking Communist Movement in the United States, 1907–23," in *Yiddish and the Left,* ed. Estraikh and Krutikov, 24–55.

31. Charney, *A yortsendlik aza,* 291–93; Raphael Abramovitsh, *In tsvey revolutsyes* (New York: Workmen's Circle, 1944), 398–99.

32. Cf. Hirshbein, *In gang fun lebn,* 147.

33. Moshe Olgin, *In der velt fun gezang: a bukh vegn poezye un poetn* (New York: Forward, 1919).

34. "A Morris Winchevsky-vokh in Moskve," *Yidishe ilustrirte tsaytung,* 25 July 1924.

35. Ber Green, *Fun dor tsu dor: literarishe eseyen* (New York: Ikuf, 1971), 148–49.

36. Moshe Nadir, *Humor, kritik, lirik* (Buenos Aires: YIVO, 1971), 258.

37. Alexander Pomerantz, *Proletpen: etyudn un materyaln tsu der geshikhte fun dem kamf far proletarisher literatur in amerike (f.sh.a.)* (Kiev: All-Ukrainian Academy of Science, 1935), 173.

38. RCPSDCH, f. 515, op. 1, d. 1180, p. 6.

39. S. B. Dzhimbinov, ed., *Literaturnye manifesty: ot simvolizma do nashikh dnei* (Moscow: XXI vek-Soglasie, 2000), 419–46.

40. M. Basin, ed., *Antologye: Finf hundert yor yidisher poezye* (New York: Dos yidishe bukh, 1917), 2: 85.

41. Estraikh, *Soviet Yiddish,* 139–40.

42. Pomerantz, *Proletpen,* 44.

43. R. M. Iangirov, "Marginal'nye temy v tvorcheskoi praktike LEFa," in *Tynianovskii sbornik,* ed. Marietta Chudakova (Riga: Zinatne, 1994), 230, 236; see also J. Hoberman, *Bridge of Light: Yiddish Film Between Two Worlds* (New York: Schocken Books, 1991), 125.

44. Benjamin Harshav and Barbara Harshav, *American Yiddish Poetry: A Bilingual Anthology* (Berkeley: Univ. of California Press, 1986), 41.

45. See Benjamin Hrushovski, "On Free Rhythms in Yiddish Poetry," in *The Field of Yiddish: Studies in Yiddish Language, Folklore, and Literature,* ed. Uriel Weinreich (Philadelphia: Institute for the Study of Human Issues, 1954), 265.

46. Stephen Stepanchev, "Walt Whitman in Russia," in *Whitman and the World,* ed. Gay W. Allen and Ed Folsom (Iowa City: Univ. of Iowa Press, 1995), 300–13.

47. Isaac E. Rontch, *Amerike in der yidisher literatur* (New York: I. E. Rontch bukh-komitet, 1945), 155–56.

48. Steven Cassedy, *To the Other Shore: The Russian Jewish Intellectuals Who Came to America* (Princeton, N.J.: Princeton Univ. Press, 1997), 151.

49. Nokhum Oyslender, *Veg-ayn-veg-oys: literarishe epizodn* (Kiev: Kultur-lige, 1924), 173.

50. "A banket dem kh[aver] Leyvik," *Der emes,* 27 Sept. 1925.

51. Peretz Markish, "Shpan-tsedek," *Literarishe bleter* 106 (1926).

52. For Khalyastre, see in particular Ravitsh, *Dos mayse-bukh fun mayn lebn,* 353–59, 387–90; Rachel Ertel, ed., *Khalyastre/La bande: Revue littéraire, Varsovie 1922–Paris 1924* (Paris: Lachenal et Ritter, 1989).

53. Niger, *Lezer, dikhter, kritiker,* 1: 121–29.

54. David Bergelson, "An entfer Sh. Nigern," *Frayhayt,* 22 Aug. 1926.

55. *Literarishe bleter* 81 (1925): 260. Bergelson was among the fifteen people briefly detained by the Riga police after his lecture at the local Communist Winchevsky Club; "Verhaftung David Bergelsons in Riga," *Jüdische Rundschau,* 1 Apr. 1931.

56. Bergelson, "An entfer Sh. Nigern."

57. Cf. Boris Groys, "The Birth of Socialist Realism from the Spirit of the Russian Avant-Garde," in *Laboratory of Dreams: The Russian Avant-Garde and Cultural Experiment,* ed. John E. Bowlt and Olga Matich (Stanford, Calif.: Stanford Univ. Press, 1996), 194. Evgenii Dovrenko in his book *Formovka sovetskogo pisatelia: sotsial'nye i esteticheskie istoki sovetskoi literaturnoi kul'tury* (St. Petersburg: Akademicheskii proekt, 1999) (see in particular pp. 69 and 102) corrects Groys's conclusions. According to Dovrenko, socialist realism was a product of the whole revolutionary culture rather than of the avant-garde alone.

58. Dobrushin, *Gedankengang,* 11.

59. Groys, "Birth of Socialist Realism," 198.

60. Yakov Shternberg, *Vegn literatur un teater* (Tel Aviv: H. Leivik, 1987), 145, 147.

61. Ilya Ehrenburg, *Zhizn' i gibel' Nikolaia Kurbova* (Berlin: Gelikon, 1923).

62. In fact, Marx never used the term "dialectical materialism," which was later introduced by Josef Dietzgen and G. V. Plekhanov. See Gregor McLennan, *Marxism and the Methodologies of History* (London: NLB, 1981), 4.

63. Cf. Gershon Scholem, *The Messianic Idea in Judaism* (New York: Schocken Books, 1971), 18.

64. Susan Ann Slotnick, "The Novel Form in the Works of David Bergelson" (Ph.D. diss., Columbia Univ., 1978), 332.

65. Y. Zilbergelt, "A groyser Bergelson ovnt in Moskve," *Frayhayt,* 8 Oct. 1926; Abraham Novershtern, "Hundert yor Dovid Bergelson: materyaln tsu zayn lebn un shafn," *Di goldene keyt* 115 (1986): 46–57.

66. Peretz Markish, "Mayn parol!" *Der emes,* 28 Dec. 1926.

67. Peretz Markish, "Gut iz tsu dir kumen," *Frayhayt,* 12 Nov. 1926.

68. Hirsh Bloshtein, "Tsum ratnfarband," *Frayhayt,* 26 Nov. 1926.

69. Shimen Lozovski, "Moyshe Nadir ovnt in Kiev," *Frayhayt,* 30 Sept. 1926.

70. Alla Chernykh, *Stanovlenie Rossii sovetskoi: 20-e gody v zerkale sotsiologii* (Moscow: Pamiatniki istoricheskoi mysli, 1998), 16.

71. E. N. Danilova, "Immigratsionaia politika i sozdanie trudovykh kommun iz emigrantov i reemigrantov v SSSR v 1920-e gody," *Vestnik Moskovskogo universiteta. Seriia 8, istoriia* no. 1 (2002): 7.

72. Ermolaev, *Soviet Literary Theories,* 48.

73. See for example N. Osinskii, "K voprosu o 'literaturnoi' politike partii," *Pravda,* 11 Feb. 1925; I. Vareikis, "O nashei linii v khudozhestvennoi literature i o proletarskikh pisateliakh," *Pravda,* 12 Feb. 1925; I. Zhiga, "Proletarskie pisateli i ikh organizatsii," *Pravda,* 18 June 1925.

74. Mikhail Kalinin, "Di aynordnung fun yidn af erd," *Frayhayt*, 22 Aug. 1926. This is, interestingly, the same issue in which Bergelson's answer to Niger was published.

75. RCPSDCH, f. 445, op. 1, d. 86, p. 115.

76. Quoted in Nora Levin, *The Jews of the Soviet Union since 1917: Paradox of Survival* (New York: New York Univ. Press, 1988), 1: 146–47.

77. Iu. Golde, *Evrei-zemledel'tsy v Krymu* (Moscow: Komzet, 1931), 74.

78. *Istochnik* no. 4 (1994): 115; Ivanov, *Russkie sezony teatra Gabima*, 145–50.

79. A. Merezhin, "Tsvey yor yidishe erd-aynordnung in sovetn-farband," *Frayhayt*, 19 Sept. 1926.

80. See Mikhail Koltsov, "Ahin un tsurik," *Der emes*, 3 Nov. 1925.

81. Estraikh, *Soviet Yiddish*, 28.

82. Mikhail Kalinin, "Evrei-zemledel'tsy v soiuze narodov SSSR," *Izvestiia*, 17 Nov. 1926.

83. David Bergelson, "Af der shvel fun 'der velt' un 'yener velt,' " *Frayhayt*, 19 Sept. 1926 (published as a feuilleton under Merezhin's article; see note 78). This piece first appeared in *Der emes*, 29 Aug. 1926.

84. David Bergelson, "Moskve," *Frayhayt*, 5 Sept. 1926; and *Der emes*, 19 Sept. 1926.

85. See Iehuda Erez, ed., *My nachinali eshche v Rossii: vospominaniia* (Jerusalem: Biblioteka-Aliia, 1990), 276–77.

86. David Bergelson, "Dray pretendentn afn 'veg' keyn Krim," *Der emes*, 29 Sept. 1926; and *Frayhayt*, 2 Oct. 1926.

87. Walter Benjamin, *Selected Writings* (Cambridge, Mass.: Belknap Press of Harvard Univ. Press, 1999), 2: 30.

88. Ibid., 22.

89. Israel Joshua Singer, *Nay-Rusland* (Vilna: B. Kletzkin, 1928); in particular pp. 22–23, 164, 166.

90. Erez, ed., *My nachinali eshche v Rossii*, 288–89.

91. RCPSDCH, f. 445, op. 1, d. 86, p. 126.

92. Aron Singalowsky, "Aufbau und Umbau: Zum Problem des jüdischen Wirtschaftsleben in Osteuropa," *Der Morgen* 3, no. 4 (1927): 382.

93. Daniel Soyer, "Abraham Cahan's Travels in Jewish Homelands: Palestine in 1925 and the Soviet Union in 1927," in *Yiddish and the Left*, ed. Estraikh and Krutikov, 56–79.

94. See Gennady Estraikh, "Soviet Yiddish Vernacular of the 1920s: Avrom Abchuk's *Hershl Shamaj* as a Socio-linguistic Source," *Slovo* 7, no. 1 (1994): 1–12.

95. See David Bergelson, *Tsugvintn* (Vilna: B. Kletzkin, 1930). For more on "Hershl Toker," see Joseph Sherman, "From Isolation to Entrapment: Bergelson and the Party Line, 1919–27," *Slavic Almanach* 6, no. 9 (2000): 211–18.

96. Reisen, *Leksikon*.

97. Ibid., 4: 200–201.

98. *Bol'shaia sovetskaia entsiklopediia* (Moscow: Sovetskaia entsiklopediia, 1927), 5: 574.

99. *Literaturnaia entsiklopediia* (Moscow: Izdatel'stvo Kommunisticheskoi akademii, 1930), 1: 455–56.

100. Isaac Nusinov, "D. Bergel'son—sozdatel' evreiskogo impressionizma," in David Bergelson, *Burnye dni* (Moscow and Leningrad: Khozhestvennaia literatura, 1930), 3.

101. Abraham Wieviorka, "Problema tvorchoï metody v evreis'kii proletars'kii literaturi," *Krytyka* no. 7–8 (1931): 138.

102. Zalman Libinzon, "Dovid Bergelsons dramaturgie," *Sovetish heymland* no. 12 (1984): 151.

103. Nakhman Meisel, "Dovid Bergelson's 'Der toyber' in vaysrusishn yidishn melukhe-teater," *Literarishe bleter* no. 4 (1929).

104. See in particular Pesakh Novick, "Der opklang fun der Reyzen-Leyvik geshikhte in ratn-farband," *Morgn-frayhayt*, 15 Oct. 1929.

105. *Jüdische Rundschau*, 24 Apr. 1928.

106. Nakhman Meisel, "Dovid Bergelson tsugast in Varshe," *Literarishe bleter* no. 22 (1930).

107. Ravitsh, *Dos mayse-bukh fun mayn lebn*, 376.

108. Litvakov, *In umru* (1926), 9.

109. Nokhum Oislender, *Grunt-shtrikhn fun yidishn realizm* (Vilna: B. Kletzkin, 1928).

110. David Bergelson, "Problemen fun der yidisher literatur," *Literarishe bleter* no. 24 (1930).

111. Nakhman Meisel, "A por verter," *Literarishe bleter* no. 24 (1930).

112. "Afn Bergelson ovnt," *Der emes*, 22 Nov. 1931.

113. "Literatur un kultur-khronik," *Berliner bleter far dikhtung un kunst* 1 (1931): 22; "Literatur un kultur-khronik," *Berliner bleter far dikhtung un kunst* 3–4 (1932): 31. Issue 3–4 of this short-lived publication, edited by Y. Rapoport, came out in Soviet spelling, addressing Bergelson as "comrade [*khaver*]"—a signal of its shifting to the pro-Soviet camp.

114. Alexander (pseudonym), "Di debate vegn proletarisher literatur," *Frayhayt*, 20 Oct. 1926.

115. Moshe Olgin, *Havrile and Yoel* (New York: Frayhayt, 1927).

116. Irving Howe, *World of Our Fathers: The Journey of the East European Jews to America and the Life They Found and Made* (New York: Harcourt Brace Jovanovich, 1976), 344.

117. Pomerantz, *Proletpen*, 49.

118. Ibid., 50.

119. Ibid., 51.

120. Cf. Itche Goldberg, *Eseyen* (New York: Ikuf, 1981), 204–5.

121. Moshe Litvakov, "A klap in tish un a lek dem shtivl," *Der emes*, 30 June 1929 and 3 July 1929.

122. For the Yiddish PEN Club, see for example Nakhman Meisel, *Geven amol a lebn*, 278–90.

123. See Lawrence H. Schwartz, *Marxism and Culture: The CPUSA and Aesthetics in the 1930s* (Port Washington, N.Y.: Kennikat Press, 1980), 41.

124. "Rezolyutsye vegn der yidisher literatur fun der tsvishnfelkerlekher konferents fun revolutsyonerer literatur," *Prolit* no. 12 (1930): 88–91.

125. Cited in Alexander Pomerantz, "Yidishe proletarishe literatur," in *Almanakh: Baytrog fun yidn tsu dem oyfboy fun Amerike: 10-yoriker yubiley fun internatsyonaln arbeter ordn* (New York: Kooperativer folks-farlag, 1940), 396.

126. See in particular Israel Serebriani, "Vizit-kartlekh," *Sovetish heymland* no. 11 (1974): 129–37.

127. D. Kurland and S. Rokhkind, eds., *Di haynttsaytike proletarishe yidishe dikhtung in Amerike* (Minsk: Melukhe-farlag, 1932); Abraham Wieviorka, ed., *In shotn fun tlies: almanakh fun der yidisher proletarisher literatur in di kapitalistishe lender* (Kiev: Melukhisher natsmind-farlag, 1932).

128. Abraham Wieviorka, "Fremds un eygns," *Farmest* nos. 2–3 (1923): 174–82.

129. Henry Hart, ed., *American Writers' Congress* (London: Martin Lawrence, 1935), 153–56.

130. See Olgin's "farewell" to Leivick in Moshe Olgin, *Folk un kultur* (New York: Alveltlekher yidisher kultur-farband, 1939), 75–80.

131. Gennadii Kostyrchenko, *Tainaia politika Stalina: vlast' i antisemitizm* (Moscow: Mezhdunarodnye otnosheniia, 2001), 134–35.

132. See in particular Shira Gorshman, "Ziskind Levs goyrl," *Oysdoyer* (Tel Aviv: Yisroel-bukh, 1992), 208–21.

133. Leyzer Ran, "Der umbakanter yung-vilner dertseyler Henekh Soloveichik," *Di goldene keyt* 101 (1980): 96–101.

134. See Mikhail Krutikov, "Meir Wiener in yor 1925: naye materyaln tsu zayn biographye," *Forverts*, 5 Sept. 2003.

135. Esther Rosenthal-Shneiderman, *Oyf vegn un umvegn* (Tel Aviv: Ha-Menorah, 1978), 2: 201–9.

136. See his letters to Pomerantz published in Alexander Pomerantz, *Di sovetishe hatuge-malkhes* (Buenos Aires: YIVO, 1962), 398–413.

137. Kurland and Rokhkind, *Di haynttsaytike proletarishe yidishe dikhtung in Amerike*, 37.

138. See Gennady Estraikh, "Metamorphoses of *Morgn-frayhayt*," in *Yiddish and the Left*, ed. Estraikh and Krutikov, 144–66.

Chapter Four: The New Growth

1. Nicholas P. Vakar, *Belorussia: The Making of a Nation* (Cambridge, Mass.: Harvard Univ. Press, 1956), 142.

2. B. Ignatovskii and A. Smolich, *Belorussiia* (Minsk: n.p., 1925), 49.

3. A. Yuditski, "Yidishe arbeter-bavegung af Ukrayne," *Di royte velt* no. 3 (1926): 78–82; *Prakticheskoe razreshenie natsional'nogo voprosa v Belorusskoi Sovetskoi Sotsialisticheskoi Respublike* (Minsk: Gosizdat, 1928), 2: 20.

4. Cf. Mishkinsky, "Regional Factors," 78–100.

5. RCPSDCH, f. 17, op. 60, d. 1005, p. 25.

6. Gregory Aronson et al., eds., *Vitebsk amol* (New York: Waldon Press, 1956), 587–92.

7. Abchuk, *Etyudn un materyaln,* 84–89.

8. Abraham Dobrinki, "Di yidishe dikhtung in der prese fun di ershte revolutsye-yirn," *Sovetish heymland* no. 6 (1962): 102.

9. S. Dimanshtein, ed., *Itogi razresheniia natsional'nogo voprosa v SSSR* (Moscow: Gosizdat, 1936), 13.

10. *Historyia belaruskai literatury* (Minsk: Mastatskaia literatura, 1999), 1: 239.

11. Sh. Plavnik and N. Rubinshtein, *Yidish-vaysrusisher tashn-verterbukh* (Minsk: Belorussian Academy of Science, 1932).

12. V. M. Zharkov et al., *Kniga: Entsiklopediia* (Moscow: Bol'shaia rossiiskaia entsiklopedii, 1999), 296.

13. I. V. Iashunskii, *Evreiskaia periodicheskaia pechat' v 1917 i 1918 g.g.* (Petrograd: Rossiiskaia knizhnaia palata, 1920), 6.

14. Charney, "Tsu der kharakteristik fun der yidisher literatur," 75.

15. Bal-Dimeyn, "Der yidisher komunist," 34.

16. Abchuk, *Etyudn un materyaln,* 253; Ber Orshanskii, "Zachatki evreiskoi proletarskoi poezii v Belorussii," *Literatura i marksizm* no. 4 (1931): 95–116.

17. Alfred Abraham Greenbaum, *Jewish Scholarship and Scholarly Institutions in Soviet Russia, 1918–53* (Jerusalem: Hebrew Univ., 1978), 30, 32.

18. Abchuk, *Etyudn un materyaln,* 253–64.

19. "Goset Belorussii," *Literaturnaia gazeta,* 7 Apr. 1930. See also Alfred Abraham Greenbaum, "The Belorussian State Jewish Theatre in the Interwar Period," *Jews in Eastern Europe* no. 2 (2000): 56–75.

20. Nokhum Oislender, "Mit Ezra Fininberg," *Sovetish heymland* no. 2 (1981): 131.

21. On his Kiev period, see Hersh Smolyar, *Vu bistu khaver Sidorov?* (Tel Aviv: I. L. Peretz, 1975), 25–27.

22. Abchuk, *Etyudn un materyaln,* 259.

23. Bronshtein, "Der stiln-kamf," 64–65; Abchuk, *Etyudn un materyaln,* 268.

24. I. E. Bahdanovich, ed., *Belaruskiia pis'menniki* (Minsk: Belaruskaia entsyklapedyia, 1995), 6: 174.

25. Abchuk, *Etyudn un materyaln,* 268.

26. Orshanski, *Di yidishe literatur in Vaysrusland,* 229–30.

27. Irving Howe, Ruth R. Wisse, and Khone Shmeruk, eds., *The Penguin Book of Modern Yiddish Verse* (New York: Viking, 1988), 530–31.

28. Itsik Fefer, *Lider, balades, poemes: oysderveylts* (Moscow: Sovetskii pisatel', 1967), 192–93.

29. Abchuk, *Etyudn un materyaln,* 162–65.

30. Itsik Fefer, "Ideolohichna borot'ba v evreiskii literaturi," *Krytyka* no. 12 (1930): 63.

31. B. Tsukker, "Do henezy evreiskoï proletars'koï literatury," *Krytyka* no. 11 (1928): 48, 50.

32. G. Meisel, *Eseyen,* 116–17.

33. Cf. Jacob Glatstein, *Oyf greyte temes* (Tel Aviv: I. L. Peretz, 1967), 392.

34. Estraikh, *Soviet Yiddish,* 57.

35. Abchuk, *Etyudn un materyaln,* 97; Dobrenko, *Formovka sovetskogo pisatelia,* 303.

36. RCPSDCH, f. 445, op. 1, d. 149, pp. 8, 18, 27. For more on Hofshtein's case, see the articles in *Der emes*: "Yidishe kultur-tuer kegn kemfndikn hebraizm," 12 Feb. 1924, and "Yidishlekher ongrif un Dovid Hofshteyn," 29 Feb. 1924.

37. RCPSDCH, f. 445, op. 1, d. 149, pp. 45–47.

38. See in particular Charney, "Tsu der kharakteristic fun der yidisher literatur," 81.

39. Vasyl' Atamaniuk, *Nova evreis'ka poeziia: Antolohiia* (Kiev: n.p., 1923).

40. Dzhimbinov, ed., *Literaturnye manifesty,* 428.

41. Isaac Nusinov, "Fun baobakhtn tsu onteylnemen," *Di royte velt* no. 12 (1925): 58.

42. Irme Druker, *Literarishe eseyen.* Supplement to *Sovetish heymland* no. 1 (1981): 6.

43. Abchuk, *Etyudn un materyaln,* 182–83. Cf. Luckyj, *Literary Politics,* 47–52.

44. See for example Zhiga, "Proletarskie pisateli i ikh organizatsii"; Nikolai Bukharin, *Proletariat i voprosy khudozhestvennoi politiki* (Letchworth: Prideaux Press, 1979).

45. Sheila Fitzpatrick, *The Cultural Front: Power and Culture in Revolutionary Russia* (Ithaca, N.Y.: Cornell Univ. Press, 1992), 109.

46. Abchuk, *Etyudn un materyaln,* 192–99.

47. Moshe Litvakov, "Arbkorn-shafung," *Der emes,* 4 May 1924.

48. Quoted in Abchuk, *Etyudn un materyaln,* 201.

49. Liptzin, *History of Yiddish Literature,* 224.

50. Fefer, *Lider, balades, poemes,* 6.

51. Gennady Estraikh, "Yiddish Literary Life in Soviet Moscow, 1918–24," *Jews in Eastern Europe* no. 2 (2000): 48.

52. Reisen, *Leksikon,* 3: 127; Rosenthal-Shneiderman, *Oyf vegn un umvegn,* 3: 59.

53. Leyb Bravarnik, "Vos hot men geleyent in Kiever Vinchevsky-bibliotek in 1930 yor," *Di royte velt* nos. 1–2 (1931): 218–23.

54. Remenik, *Shtaplen,* 85.

55. Itsik Fefer, *Geklibene verk* (Kiev: Melukhe-farlag, 1929), 19.

56. Howe, Wisse, and Shmeruk, eds., *Modern Yiddish Verse,* 546–47.

57. Mordechai Yushkovsky, "Leivick un di sovetishe publitsistik," in *Shtudyes in Leivick,* ed. Gershon Winer (Ramat Gan: Univ. Bar-Ilan, 1992), 104.

58. Fefer, *Geklibene verk.*

59. See in particular George Z. Patrick, *Popular Poetry in Soviet Russia* (Berkeley: Univ. of California Press, 1929), 142–51.

60. L. Leintes, "O stikhakh Fefera," *Literaturnaia gazeta,* 28 Dec. 1931.

61. Maxim D. Shrayer, *Russian Poet/Soviet Jew: The Legacy of Eduard Bagritskii* (Lanham, Md.: Rowman and Littlefield, 2000), 120.

62. Mordechai Altshuler, ed., *Briv fun yidishe sovetishe shraybers*, 109.

63. "Khronika," *Rul'*, 5 Mar. 1928.

64. Remenik, *Shtaplen*, 86.

65. Howe, Wisse, and Shmeruk, eds., *Modern Yiddish Verse*, 548–49.

66. Khone Shmeruk, ed., *A shpigl oyf a shteyn* (Jerusalem: The Magnes Press, 1987), 682–83.

67. Smolyar, *Fun ineveynik*, 153.

68. Singer, *Nay-Rusland*, 109.

69. Mordechai Altshuler, ed., *Briv fun yidishe sovetishe shraybers*, 184.

70. *Di yidishe velt*, no. 6 (1913): 156.

71. See Gideon Shimoni, *The Zionist Ideology* (Hanover and London: Univ. Press of New England for Brandeis Univ. Press, 1995), 35–37.

72. Abraham Golomb, *A halber yorhundert yidishe dertsiung* (Rio de Janeiro: Monte Skopus, 1957), 49–52.

73. L. M. Spirin, *Rossia 1917 god: iz istorii bor'by politicheskikh partii* (Moscow: Mysl', 1987), 273–328.

74. Ratner and Kvitni, *Yidishe bukh in f.s.s.r.*, 16.

75. For the Jewish sections, see the classic study, Zvi Y. Gitelman, *Jewish Nationality and Soviet Politics: The Jewish Sections of the CPSU, 1917–30* (Princeton, N.J.: Princeton Univ. Press, 1972).

76. Charney, "Tsu der geshikhte," 135.

77. "Di shprakh-baratung in Kharkiv," *Di yidishe shprakh* nos. 4–5 (1930): 85–90.

78. Nakhman Meisel, "Der krizis fun yidishn bukh"; Shmuel Niger, "Der yidisher lezer in Amerike," *Di tsukunft* no. 1 (1930): 55–59.

79. Cf. L. Abram, "An ernster gefar," *Der emes*, 11 Jan. 1925.

80. George Liber, *Soviet Nationality Policy, Urban Growth, and Identity Change in the Ukrainian SSR, 1932–34* (Cambridge: Cambridge Univ. Press, 1992), 189.

81. Aleksandr Leibfreid and Iuliana Poliakova, *Kharkov: ot kreposti do stolitsy* (Kharkov: Folio, 1998), 213.

82. A. L. Tsukernik, ed., *Trud i profsoiuzy na Ukraine* (Kharkiv: Spilka, 1928), 114–15.

83. RCPSDCH, f. 445, op. 1, d. 37, p. 10.

84. Smolyar, *Fun ineveynik*, 249.

85. Ibid., 249.

86. Kvitko and Petrovskii, *Zhizn' i tvorchestvo L'va Kvitko*, 131, 135–36; Pavlo Tychina, *Zibrannia tvoriv* (Kiev: Naukova dumka, 1990), 12.1: 145, 350. Tsentralfarlag is the Yiddish name of the Central Publishing House of the Soviet Peoples with offices in Moscow, Kharkiv, and Minsk. It was the most significant publisher of Yiddish books in the late 1920s. See Khone Shmeruk, ed., *Pirsumim yehudiyim be-vrit ha-mo'atsot* (Jerusalem: Hebrew Univ., 1961), lxxix.

87. A. Makagon, "Dray yor *Royte velt*," *Di royte velt* nos. 8–9 (1927): 176–80.

88. Mordechai Altshuler, ed., *Briv fun yidishe sovetishe shraybers*, 67.

89. Nusinov, "Fun baobakhtn tsu onteylnemen," 58–59.

90. Isaac Nusinov, "Di sotsyale trayb-kreftn fun undzer literatur," *Di royte velt* no. 13 (1925): 74; Isaac Nusinov, "Di sotsyale trayb-kreftn fun undzer literatur," *Di royte velt* no. 1 (1926): 124–25. See also Mikhail Krutikov, "Soviet Yiddish Scholarship in the 1930s: From Class to *Folk*," *Slavic Almanach: The South African Year Book for Slavic, Central, and East European Studies* 7, no. 10 (2001): 231–35.

91. Bukharin, *Proletariat i voprosy khudozhestvennoi politiki*, 9.

92. Yekhezkel Dobrushin, "A briv in redaktsye," *Der emes*, 16 Jan. 1925.

93. Shakhne Epshtein, ed., *Di yidishe kinstlerishe literatur*, 24.

94. RCPSDCH, f. 445, op. 1, d. 172, pp. 28–37.

95. Abchuk, *Etyudn un materyaln*, 207, 209, 212, 225. See also Luckyj, *Literary Politics*, 59–61, 74–75.

96. "Di ershte alukrainishe baratung fun di yidishe revolutsyonere proletarishe shrayber in Ukraine," *Di royte velt* no. 1 (1928): 122–26.

97. Mordechai Altshuler, ed., *Briv fun yidishe sovetishe shraybers*, 48.

98. Shakhne Epshtein, "Di yidishe proletarishe literatur un di proletarishe shrayber-organizatsyes," *Di royte velt* no. 3 (1930): 113.

99. Shmuel Niger, "In der sovetish-yidisher literatur," *Di tsukunft* no. 2 (1930): 103–8.

100. Itsik Fefer, *Di ufgabes fun der yidisher proletarisher literatur in rekonstruktivn period* (Kiev: Ukrmelukhenatsmindfarlag, 1932), 11.

101. Fefer, *Di ufgabes*, 43–44.

102. Vitaly Shentalinsky, *The KGB's Literary Archive* (London: Harvill Press, 1995), 140.

103. Moshe Litvakov, "Keyn shaykhes tsu literatur," *Der emes*, 4 Apr. 1929; Estraikh, *Soviet Yiddish*, 65–66.

104. Novick, "Der opklang fun der Reyzen-Leyvik geshikhte in ratn-farband."

105. Mordechai Altshuler, ed., *Briv fun yidishe sovetishe shraybers*, 276–77.

106. See for example Moshe Litvakov, "Litkomandes un litrekhiles," *Der emes*, 13 July 1929; Fefer, "Ideolohichna borot'ba," 61; William Abrams, "Kleynbirgerlekhe nokhveyenishn in sovetisher yidisher literatur," *Morgn-frayhayt*, 10 Feb. 1930.

107. Ravitsh, *Dos mayse-bukh fun mayn lebn*, 412.

108. Mordechai Altshuler, ed., *Briv fun yidishe sovetishe shraybers*, 278. See also Smolyar, *Fun ineveynik*, 249.

109. Litvakov, "Litkomandes un litrekhiles."

110. Lipe Reznik, "A briv in redaktsye," *Der emes*, 16 Feb. 1926.

111. Shmeruk, ed., *A shpigl oyf a shteyn*, 768.

112. Cited in Schulman, *Di sovetish-yidishe literatur*, 164–65.

113. Mikhail Krutikov, "Mistishe vortslen fun sovetisher yidisher literatur," *Forverts*, 9 Aug. 2002.

114. Central State Archive, f. 296, op. 1, d. 539, p. 67.

115. Fefer, "Ideolohichna borot'ba," 65.

116. Kvitko and Petrovskii, *Zhizn' i tvorchestvo L'va Kvitko*, 136.

117. Shakhne Epshtein, ed., *Di yidishe kinstlerishe literatur*, 44.

118. "Kegn dem rekht opnoyg in der literatur," *Der emes,* 21 Sept. 1929.

119. Litvakov, "Litkomandes un litrekhiles."

120. Moshe Altshuler, "Fun leninistisher onfirung veln mir zikh nit opzogn!" *Der emes,* 22 Oct. 1929.

121. Shakhne Epshtein, "Vos lernt undz der inyen 'Kvitko,' " *Der emes,* 24 Oct. 1929.

122. *Der emes,* 19 Nov. 1929.

123. Motl Kiper, "A vort tsu der ordenung," *Di royte velt* no. 6 (1930): 94–111.

124. Bravarnik, "Vos hot men geleyent in Kiever Vinchevsky-bibliotek," 220.

125. S. Zhukovski, "Tsu der itstiker literarisher situatsye," *Prolit* nos. 11–12 (1929): 139–46. Kahan would later recall Hofshtein's and Kipnis's "nationalist relapses" and "mistakes." See Abraham Kahan, "Evreiska radians'ka literatura USRR za dva roky," *Literaturna hazeta,* 1 May 1934.

126. Moshe Litvakov, *Af tsvey frontn* (Moscow: Tsentr-farlag, 1931), 102–3, 110.

127. I. S. Rabinovich, ed., *Sbornik evreiskoi poezii* (Moscow and Leningrad: Gosizdat, 1931).

128. Leyb Kvitko, *Tsvey khaveyrim* (Moscow: Emes, 1933), 5.

129. Kvitko and Petrovskii, *Zhizn' i tvorchestvo L'va Kvitko,* 137–38.

130. David Markish, *Tovaryshi kustari* (Kharkov: Spilka, 1930).

131. Itsik Kipnis, *Mesiatsy i dni* (Moscow: Gosizdat, 1930).

132. Sholem Asch, *Sobranie sochinenii,* 7 vols. (Moscow: Gosizdat, 1929).

133. Aleksandr Khashin, "Front kriticheskii," *Literaturnaia gazeta,* 4 Aug. 1934.

134. Nusinov, "Af farfestikte pozitsyes," 105–6.

135. Isaac Nusinov, "Vuhin geyt undzer literatur?" *Di royte velt* no. 5 (1930): 116.

Chapter Five: Toward Socialist Realism

1. Cf. Igor Krupnik, "Soviet Cultural and Ethnic Policies Towards Jews: A Legacy Reassessed," in *Jews and Jewish Life in Russia and the Soviet Union,* ed. Yaacov Ro'i (Ilford: F. Cass, 1995), 75–76.

2. Gennady Estraikh, "Pyrrhyc Victories of Soviet Yiddish Language Planners," *East European Jewish Affairs* 23, no. 2 (1993): 25–37.

3. Note Lurye, "Tsuzamen mit Gorkin," *Sovetish heymland* no. 5 (1964): 157. Apart from the delegates, a number of Yiddish literati were invited as guests of the congress.

4. I. K. Luppol, M. M. Rozental', and S. M. Tret'akov, eds., *Pervyi Vsesoiuznyi s ezd sovetskikh pisatelei, 1934: stenograficheskii otchet* (Moscow: Sovetskii pisatel', 1990), 219–21, 444–47.

5. Shakhne Epshtein, "Di yidishe marksistishe kritik," *Di royte velt* nos. 4–5 (1931): 154–65, 165–69, 181.

6. "Po povodu diskussii o stat'akh Litvakova," *Literaturnaia gazeta,* 12 May 1930.

7. See "Evreiskie gazety," *Krasnaia pechat'* no. 25 (1925): 40–41; David Shneer, "The His-

tory of 'The Truth': Soviet Jewish Activists and the Moscow Yiddish Daily Newspaper," in *Yiddish and the Left,* ed. Estraikh and Krutikov, 129–43.

8. "Nakanune pervogo Vsesoiuznogo s'ezda evreiskikh proletarskikh pisatelei," *Literaturnaia gazeta,* 22 Nov. 1931.

9. Abraham Abchuk, "Di problemen fun yerushe bam kh[aver] Litvakov," *Di royte velt* no. 5 (1932): 128–52; Khaim Gildin, "Tsayt-fragn," *Di royte velt* nos. 1–3 (1933): 18.

10. Del'man, "Soveshchanie evreiskikh pisatelei," *Literaturnaia gazeta,* 11 Dec. 1933.

11. See also Osip Kolychev, "Vegn mayne fraynt," *Sovetish heymland* no. 3 (1967): 148–54.

12. "Ot natsional'noi skorbi k klassovoi bor'be," *Literaturnaia gazeta,* 4 Aug. 1934.

13. Kolychev, "Vegn mayne fraynt," 150.

14. Moshe Litvakov, "Novaia literature," *Literaturnaia gazeta,* 4 Aug. 1934.

15. David Bergelson, "Cherta itoga," *Literaturnaia gazeta,* 18 Aug. 1934.

16. Luppol, Rozental', and Tret'akov, eds., *Pervyi Vsesoiuznyi s"ezd sovetskikh pisatelei, 1934,* 446.

17. Ibid., 166.

18. Ibid., 220.

19. See in particular Dalia Kaufman, "Fir gilgulim fun Bergelson's dertseylung 'Batshka,' " *Yerusholayemer almanakh* 4 (1974): 216–21.

20. For a contemporary Soviet criticism of Hamsun, see N. Sobolevskii, "Poslednii roman Knuta Gamsuna," *Novyi mir* no. 5 (1934): 256–60.

21. David Bergelson, "Trud, vozvedennyi v stepen' iskusstva," *Literaturnaia gazeta,* 26 Aug. 1934; Luppol, Rozental', and Tret'akov, eds., *Pervyi Vsesoiuznyi s"ezd sovetskikh pisatelei, 1934,* 270–71.

22. Brianski, *Bergelson in shpigl,* 72. This pronouncement echoes Aleksey Tostoy's "Oktaibr'skaia revoliutsiia dala mne vse," *Literaturnaia gazeta,* 11 Jan. 1933.

23. Jacob Lvavi, *Ha-hityashvut ha-yahudit be-Birobig'an* (Jerusalem: Hebrew Univ., 1965), 376–77.

24. Khaim Sloves, *Sovetishe yidishe melukheshkayt* (Paris: H. Sloves, 1979), 203; Rabin, "Hert mikh oys," 153.

25. Nakhman Meisel, "M. Goldshteyn," in M. Goldshteyn, *Biro-bidzhaner afn Amur un andere dertseylungen* (New York: Ikuf, 1944), 8.

26. See Estraikh, *Soviet Yiddish,* 164.

27. See Grigorii Kobets and Iogann Zel'tser, "Iskateli schast'ia," *God za godom* 4 (1988): 204–40.

28. Sloves, *Sovetishe yidishe melukheshkayt,* 138.

29. Moshe Alberton, *Birobidzhan* (Kharkov: Tsentralfarlag, 1929).

30. Shmuel Niger, *Yidishe shrayber in sovet-rusland* (New York: Alveltlekher yidisher kultur-kongres, 1958), 312.

31. David Bergelson and Emanuel Kazakevich, *Birobidzhan: an algemeyner iberblik fun*

der yidisher avtonomer gegnt (Moscow: Emes, 1939), 13–14. Kazakevich was the only Soviet Yiddish writer who later became a significant Russian writer.

32. Fefer, *Lider, balades, poemes,* 120.

33. Aron Kushnirov, *Geklibene lider* (Moscow: Sovetskii pisatel', 1975), 16.

34. Ibid., 26.

35. David Khait, "Storona Birobidzhanskaia," *Bezbozhnik* no. 6 (1936): 8–9.

36. Joseph Leftwich, ed., *The Way We Think: A Collection of Essays from the Yiddish* (South Brunswick, N.J.: T. Yoseloff, 1969), 1: 92.

37. Nakham Meisel, "Dovid Bergelson tsugast in Varshe"; Brianski, *Bergelson in shpigl,* 73.

38. Nakhman Meisel, "Bamerkungen fun a lezer," in *Yidisher almanakh,* ed. Shmarayhu Gorelik (Kiev: Kunst-farlag, 1910), 37–48. A reproduction of this and a few other literary relics are included in Nakhman Meisel, *Onhoybn: Dovid Bergelson* (Kibbutz Alonim: n.p., 1977).

39. David Bergelson, *Bam Dnyeper* (Moscow: Emes, 1932), 447.

40. See Bergelson's letter to Niger, written in January 1913 and published in *Zamlbikher* 8 (1952): 103.

41. A 1932 letter to Opatoshu, in Shlomo Bikl, ed., *Pinkes far der forshung fun der yidisher literatur un prese* (New York: Alveltlekher yidisher kultur-kongres, 1965), 345.

42. Lamed Shapiro, *Der shrayber geyt in kheyder* (Los Angeles: Aleyn, 1945), 63–64.

43. Of all Soviet Yiddish novels, *Lyam un Petrik* had arguably the largest number of editions in Yiddish and other languages. See Aba Finkel'shtein, "Bibliografiia," in Kvitko and Petrovskii, *Zhizn' i tvorchestvo L'va Kvitko,* 271–86.

44. Klaus Mehnert, *The Russians and Their Favorite Books* (Stanford, Calif.: Hoover Institution, 1983), 241.

45. Meir Wiener, "O nekotorykh voprosakh sotsialisticheskogo realizma," *Oktiabr'* no. 1 (1935): 239.

46. See Evgenii Dobrenko, *Metafora vlasti: Literatura stalinskoi epokhi v istoricheskom osveshchenii* (Munich: Otto Sagner, 1993), 74.

47. Cf. Rivka Rubin, "Izi Kharik," *Literaturnaia gazeta,* 8 June 1934.

48. "Ba di yidishe sovetishe shrayber in sovetn-farband," *Morgn-frayhayt,* 15 Dec. 1933.

49. Luppol, Rozental', and Tret'akov, eds., *Pervyi Vsesoiuznyi s"ezd sovetskikh pisatelei, 1934,* 3, 709; Luckyj, *Literary Politics,* 228–29.

50. Abraham Wieviorka, *Revizye* (Kiev and Kharkov: Literatur un kunst, 1931).

51. Niger, *Yidishe shrayber,* 172–88.

52. Peretz Markish, *Eyns af eyns* (Kharkov and Kiev: Ukrmelukhenatsmindfarlag, 1934); Peretz Markish, *Vozvrashchenie Neitana Bekera* (Moscow: Goslit, 1934).

53. Mordechai Altshuler, ed., *Briv fun yidishe sovetishe shraybers,* 244–45.

54. Leyb Kvitko, *Riogrander fel: dertseylungen funem arbeter-lebn in Daytshland* (Kharkov: Melukhe-farlag, 1928). See also Delphine Bechtel, "Leyb Kvitko à Hambourg: entre politique, science-fiction et espionnage," in *Le yiddish: langue, culture, société: Mélanges du*

Centre de Recherche Français de Jérusalem, ed. Jean Baumgarten and David Bunis (Jerusalem: CNRS Editions, 1999), 247–71.

55. Moshe Kulbak, *Geklibene verk* (New York: Tsiko, 1953), 233.

56. Yasha Bronshtein, "The Literature of the White Russian Socialist Soviet Republic," *Literature of the Peoples of the USSR,* nos. 7–8 (1934): 65.

57. See Hoberman, *Bridge of Light,* 170–74; Jeffrey Veidlinger, *The Moscow State Yiddish Theater: Jewish Culture on the Soviet Stage* (Bloomington: Indiana Univ. Press, 2000), 132–33.

58. Fefer, *Di ufgabes,* 15; I. Veitsblit, *Vegn altn un nayem shtetl* (Moscow, Kharkov, and Minsk: Tsentrfarlag, 1930).

59. Estraikh, "Soviet Yiddish Vernacular."

60. Druker, *Literarishe eseyen,* 10.

61. Cf. Scholem, *Messianic Idea in Judaism,* 1–36.

62. N. Gergel, "Yidn in der ruslendisher komunistisher partey un in komunistishn yudnt-farband," *YIVO Bleter* 1, no. 1 (1931): 63–69.

63. Joseph Roth, *The Wandering Jews* (London: Granta, 2001), 107.

64. Shmuel Godiner, *Figurn afn rand* (Kiev: Kultur-lige, 1929), 133–45.

65. See David E. Fishman, "Religioznye lidery sovetskogo evreistva (1917–34)," in *Is-toricheskie sud'by evreev v Rossii i SSSR: nachalo dialoga,* ed. Igor Krupnik (Moscow: Evreiskoe istoricheskoe obshchestvo, 1992), 189–99; David E. Fishman, "Judaism in the USSR, 1917–30: The Fate of Religious Education," in *Jews and Jewish Life in Russia and the Soviet Union,* ed. Yaacov Ro'i (Ilford: F. Cass, 1995), 251–62.

66. Yudel Yoffe, *Afn glaykhn veg* (Moscow: Emes, 1941).

67. Veidlinger, *Moscow State Yiddish Theater,* 130.

68. Moshe Alberton, *Shakhtes* (Moscow: Emes, 1934), 252–55. While both Alberton and Frumkin used *(tsapn)lager* for "bearing," the Yiddish newspaper, published in 1934–35 at the Moscow-based First State Bearing Factory, was titled *Far a sovetishn podshipnik* (For a Soviet Bearing), using the Russianism *podshipnik.*

69. Iakov Kantor, *Nathional'noe stroitel'stvo sredi evreev v SSSR* (Moscow: Vlast' Sove-tov, 1935), 142, 148.

70. Itsik Fefer, ed., *Almanakh fun yidishe sovetishe shrayber: tsum alfarbandishn shrayber-tsuzamenfor* (Kharkov and Kiev: Ukrmelukhenatsmindfarlag, 1934).

71. Luppol, Rozental', and Tret'akov, eds., *Pervyi Vsesoiuznyi s"ezd sovetskikh pisatelei, 1934,* 167.

72. See Otto Shmidt, ed., *The Voyage of the Chelyuskin* (New York: Macmillan, 1935).

73. Marina Tsvetaeva, *Sochineniia* (Moscow: Sovetskii pisatel', 1980), 1: 320–21.

74. John McCannon, "Positive Heroes at the Poles: Celebrity Status, Socialist-Realist Ideals, and the Soviet Myth of the Arctic, 1932–39," *The Russian Review* 56, no. 3 (1997): 348.

75. Yekhezkel Dobrushin, "Fefer der dikhter," *Di royte velt* no. 1 (1929): 102.

76. McCannon, "Positive Heroes at the Poles," 352–53.

77. Tsvetaeva, *Sochineniia,* 320.

78. Régine Robin, *Socialist Realism: An Impossible Aesthetic* (Stanford, Calif.: Stanford Univ. Press, 1992), 52–54.

79. Barry P. Scherr, *Russian Poetry: Meter, Rhythm, and Rhyme* (Berkeley: Univ. of California Press, 1986), 70.

80. The light in Stalin's window was a common symbol of the leader's fatherly concern for his people. See Rosalind Marsh, *Images of Dictatorship: Portraits of Stalin in Literature* (London: Routledge, 1989), 29.

81. David L. Hoffmann, *Stalinist Values: The Cultural Norms of Soviet Modernity, 1917–41* (Ithaca, N.Y.: Cornell Univ. Press, 2003), 156.

82. Abraham Gontar, *Heler tog* (Kiev: Ukrmelukhenatsmindfarlag, 1938), 26–27.

83. Dobrenko, *Metafora vlasti*, 50.

84. Fayvl Sito, *Ot dos zaynen mir* (Kharkov and Kiev: Ukrmelukhenatsmindfarlag, 1932), 75.

85. *Sovetish heymland* no. 5 (1974): 160.

86. "Ba di yidishe sovetishe shrayber in sovetn-farband." See also Andrei Khvylia, "Literatura—osnovnaia chast' stroitel'stva unkrainskoi sovetskoi kul'tury," *Literaturnaia gazeta,* 29 July 1933.

87. "120 pisatelei na Belomorsko-Baltiiskom kanale," *Literaturnaia gazeta,* 29 Aug. 1933.

88. S. I. Andreeva, "O p'ese Pogodina 'Aristokraty,' " *Uchenye zapiski Leningradskogo gosudarstvennogo universiteta* 230 (1957): 188.

89. Michael Heller, *Kontsentratsionnyi mir i sovetskaia literatura* (London: Overseas Publications Interchange, 1974), 95.

90. J. Otto Pohl, *The Stalinist Penal System: A Statistical History of Soviet Repression and Terror, 1930–53* (Jefferson, Mo., and London: McFarland, 1997), 12–13.

91. V. G. Makurov, ed., *Gulag v Karelii* (Petrozavodsk: Karel'skii nauchnyi tsentr RAN, 1992), 78–79. On Firin's "achievements," see also Joseph Kamenetski, "Der Volge-Moskver kanal," *Der emes,* 12 June 1934.

92. Maxim Gorki, Leopold Auerbach, and Semen Firin, eds., *The White Sea Canal* (London: John Lane, 1935).

93. Dobrenko, *Metafora vlasti,* 35.

94. See Nikolai Pogodin, *Sobranie dramaticheskikh proizvedenii* (Moscow: Iskusstvo, 1960), 3: 85–171; Mikhas' Lyn'kov, *Rasskazy* (Leningrad: Khudozhestvennaia literatura, 1961), 117–43; see also Yasha Bronshtein, "Pevets romanticheskoi real'nosti," *Literaturnaia gazeta,* 8 June 1934.

95. Tsodek Dolgopolski, *Zayd* (Minsk: Melukhe-farlag, 1933), 182.

96. Gitelman, *Jewish Nationality and Soviet Politics, 355.*

97. Edward Hallett Carr, *Socialism in One Country 1924–25* (Harmondsworth: Penguin, 1970), 2: 342–43.

98. Gennady Estraikh, "The Soviet Shtetl in the 1920s," *Polin* (forthcoming).

99. Anna Shternshis, "Soviet and Kosher in the Ukrainian Shtetl," in *The Shtetl: Image and Reality,* ed. Estraikh and Krutikov, 145.

100. Iurii Druzhinikov, *Donoschik 001, ili voznesenie Pavlika Morozova* (Moscow: Moskovskii rabochii, 1995).

101. Abraham Kahan, *A khazer* (Kharkov: Ukrmelukhenatsmindfarlag, 1928). See also Gennady Estraikh, "Pig-breeding, *Shiksas,* and Other *Goyish* Themes in Soviet Yiddish Literature and Life," *Symposium* 57, no. 3 (2003): 157–74.

102. Tsodek Dolgopolski, *Mit mayn pen in hant* (Minsk: Melukhe-farlag, 1932), 19.

103. See Estraikh, *Soviet Yiddish,* 83.

104. For statistics on pig-breeding by Jewish peasants, see Kantor, *Nathional'noe stroitel'stvo sredi evreev v SSSR,* 52, 81–82.

105. M. Druyanov, *Krolik-tsukht in der yidisher kolektiver virtshaft* (Moscow: Tsentrfarlag, 1930); M. Druyanov, *Hodevanye fun khazeyrim* (Moscow: Tsentrfarlag, 1931); M. Druyanov, *Khazeyrim-fermes* (Moscow: Emes, 1933).

106. On Yudel Yoffe, who was criticized for this fault, see L. Polonskaia, "Iz evreiskoi literatury," *Novyi mir* no. 3 (1931): 173.

107. David Bergelson, "Leksik-problemen."

108. Aron Raskin, *Literarishe eseyen* (Jerusalem: Bar-Ilan Univ., 1989), 245; Birgit Mai, *Satire im Sowjetsozialismus* (Bern: P. Lang, 1993), 11, 15, 17.

109. Niger, *Yidishe shrayber,* 62–68.

110. "Ba di yidishe sovetishe shrayber in sovetn-farband."

111. Khatskl Dunets, *Far magnitboyen fun der literatur* (Minsk: Belorussian Academy of Science, 1932).

112. Shmuel Halkin, *Far dem nayem fundament* (Moscow: Emes, 1932), 3–10.

Epilogue

1. Lvavi, *Ha-hityashvut ha-yahudit be-Birobig'an,* 309.

2. Rabin, "Hert mikh oys," 153.

3. Sloves, *Sovetishe yidishe melukheshkayt,* 194.

4. S. Dimanshtein, "Problemy natsional'noi kultury i kul'turnogo stroitel'stva v natsional'nykh respublikakh," *Vestnik Kommunisticheskoi Akademii* no. 1 (1929): 119.

5. Fefer, *Lider, balades, poemes,* 134.

6. Gennady Estraikh, "Yiddish Language Conference Aborted," *East European Jewish Affairs* 25, no. 2 (1995): 91–96.

7. It appeared in 1988, in issues 4 and 5 of *Sovetish heymland*. The next year it came out in a Russian translation; see *God za godom 5*.

8. Kostyrchenko, *Tainaia politika Stalina,* 135–36.

9. Eli Shekhtman, *Ringen oyf der neshome* (Tel Aviv: Yisroel-bukh, 1981), 373–75.

10. For an attempt to chronicle the repression in Ukraine, see George S. N. Luckyj, *Keeping a Record: Literary Purges in Soviet Ukraine, 1930s: A Bio-Bibliography* (Edmonton: Canadian Institute of Ukrainian Studies, 1988).

11. Cf. in particular Viacheslav Selimenev and Arkadii Zeltser, "The Jewish Intelligentsia

and the Liquidation of Yiddish Schools in Belorussia, 1938," *Jews in Eastern Europe* no. 3 (2000): 78–97.

12. See Smolyar, *Vu bistu khaver Sidorov?* 157–64; Sfard, *Mit zikh un mit andere*, 100–119.

13. Sfard, *Mit zikh un mit andere*, 119.

14. Eli Gordon, Peretz Markish, and Aron Kushnirov, eds., *Komyug* (Moscow: Emes, 1938); Fayvl Sito and Hershl Polyanker, eds., *Komsomolye* (Kiev: Ukrmelukhenatsmindfarlag, 1938).

15. Abraham Kahan and Abraham Gontar, eds., *Onheyb* (Kiev: Ukrmelukhenatsmindfarlag, 1940).

16. See in particular Kostyrchenko, *Tainaia politika Stalina*; Joshua Rubenstein and Vladimir P. Naumov, eds., *Stalin's Secret Pogrom: The Postwar Inquisition of the Jewish Anti-Fascist Committee* (New Haven, Conn., and London: Yale Univ. Press, 2001).

17. David Bergelson, *Tsvey veltn* (New York: Ikuf, 1953).

18. Aleksandr Borshchagovskii, *Obviniaetsia krov'* (Moscow: Gruppa Progress, 1994).

19. Fefer, *Lider, balades, poemes*, 221.

20. For *Sovetish heymland* see, for instance, my articles "The Era of *Sovetish Heymland*: Readership of the Yiddish Press in the Former Soviet Union," *East European Jewish Affairs* 25, no. 1 (1995): 17–22; " 'Jewish Street' or Jewish Cul-de-Sac? From *Sovetish Heymland* to *Di Yidishe Gas*," *East European Jewish Affairs* 26, no. 1 (1996): 25–33; "Aron Vergelis: The Perfect Jewish *Homo Sovieticus*," *East European Jewish Affairs* 27, no. 2 (1997): 3–20; "The Shtetl Theme in *Sovetish heymland*," in *The Shtetl: Image and Reality*, ed. Estraikh and Krutikov, 152–68.

Bibliography

"A banket dem kh[aver] Leyvik." *Der emes,* 27 Sept. 1925.

"A Morris Winchevsky-vokh in Moskve." *Yidishe ilustrirte tsaytung,* 25 July 1924.

Abchuk, Abraham. "Di problemen fun yerushe bam kh[aver] Litvakov." *Di royte velt* no. 5 (1932): 128–52.

———. *Etyudn un materyaln tsu der geshikhte fun der yidisher literatur-bavegung in fssr, 1917–1927.* Kharkov: Literatur un kunst, 1934.

Abram, Leyb "An ernster gefar." *Der emes,* 11 Jan. 1925.

Abramovitsh, Raphael. *In tsvey revolutsyes.* New York: Workmen's Circle, 1944.

Abrams, William. "Kleynbirgerlekhe nokhveyenishn in sovetisher yidisher literatur." *Morgn-frayhayt,* 10 Feb. 1930.

Abramskii, I. "Eto bylo v Vitebske." *Iskusstvo* no. 10 (1964): 69–71.

"Afn Bergelson ovnt." *Der emes,* 22 Nov. 1931.

Agranovskii, Genrikh. "Evreiskoe knigopechatanie v Vil'ne v 60-70-e gody XIX sto-letiia." *Vestnik Evreiskogo universiteta v Moskve* 15 (1995): 110–25.

Agurski, Shmuel. "Di antshteyung un antviklung fun der yidisher komunistisher prese." *Der veker,* 3 Mar. 1923.

———. "Di antshteyung fun der ershter komunistisher tsaytung in yidish." *Komunistishe fon,* 7 Mar. 1923.

———. *Der yidisher arbeter in der komunistisher bavegung, 1917–21.* Minsk: Melukhe-farlag, 1925.

———. "Di ershte yidishe sovetishe tsaytung." *Folks-shtime,* 7 Nov. 1967.

A.K. "Yidishe kunst-oysshtelung." *Der emes,* 8, 9, and 11 Aug. 1918.

Alberton, Moshe. *Birobidzhan.* Kharkov: Tsentralfarlag, 1929.

———. *Shakhtes.* Moscow: Emes, 1934.

Albom lekoved dem yoyvl fun progresivn yidishn vort in Argentine. Buenos Aires: n.p., 1973.

Alexander (pseudonym). "Di debate vegn proletarisher literatur." *Frayhayt,* 20 Oct. 1926.

Altshuler, Mordechai, ed. *Briv fun yidishe sovetishe shraybers.* Jerusalem: Hebrew Univ., 1979.

Altshuler, Moshe. "Fun leninistisher onfirung veln mir zikh nit opzogn!" *Der emes*, 22 Oct. 1929.

Amishai-Maisels, Ziva. "The Jewish Awakening: A Search for National Identity." In *Russian Jewish Artists in a Century of Change, 1890–1990*, edited by Susan Tumarkin Goodman, 45–65. Munich: Prestel, 1995.

Anderson, Barbara A. *Internal Migration During Modernization in Late Nineteenth-Century Russia*. Princeton, N.J.: Princeton Univ. Press, 1980.

Andreeva, S. I. "O p'ese Pogodina 'Aristokraty.' " *Uchenye zapiski Leningradskogo gosudarstvennogo universiteta* 230 (1957): 184–203.

Anilowicz, J., and M. Joffe. "Yidishe lernbikher un pedagogik, 1900–30." *Shriftn far psikhologye un pedagogik* 1 (1931): 483–88.

Antokol'skii, L. M. "Evreiskaia khudozhestvennaia vystavka v Moskve." *Evreiskaia nedelia* no. 25 (1917): 33.

Aronson, Gregory. *Rusish-yidishe inteligents*. Buenos Aires: Yidbukh, 1962.

Aronson, Gregory, et al., eds. *Vitebsk amol*. New York: Waldon Press, 1956.

Asch, Sholem. *Sobranie sochinenii*. 7 vols. Moscow: Gosizdat, 1929.

Assmann, Jan. *Religion und kulturelles Gedächtnis*. Munich: C. H. Beck, 2000.

Atamaniuk, Vasyl'. *Nova evreis'ka poeziia: antolohiia*. Kiev: Drukar, 1923.

Az. "Zhargonnaia literatura v 1905 g." *Voskhod* 26, no. 1 (1906): 40–48.

"Ba di yidishe sovetishe shrayber in sovetn-farband." *Morgn-frayhayt*, 15 Dec. 1933.

Bachelis, Shomer Rose. *Undzer tate Shomer*. New York: Ikuf, 1950.

Bahdanovich, I. E., ed. *Belaruskiia pis'menniki*. Vol. 6. Minsk: Belaruskaia entsyklapedyia, 1995.

Bal-Dimyen [Nokhum Shtif]. *Yidn un yidish, oder ver zaynen "yidishistn" un vos viln zey? Poshete verter far yedn yidn*. Kiev: Onhoyb, 1919.

———. *Humanizm in der elterer yidisher literatur: a kapitl literatur-geshikhte*. Kiev: Kultur-lige, 1920.

———. "An ekspeditsye fun aeroplan oyf di gimalayen fun undzer moyekh." *Dos fraye vort* 3 (1923): 32–36.

———. "Der yidisher komunist, di kultur-lige un dos yidishe bukh." *Di tsukunft* 28, no. 1 (1923): 32–34.

Bal-Makhshoves [I. Z. Eliashev]. "Narodno-evreiskaia literatura s XIX-go veka." In *Otechestvo. Puti i dostizheniia natsional'nykh literatur Rossii. Natsional'nyi vopros*, edited by J. N. Baudoin de Courtenay et al., 1: 325–35. Petrograd: M. V. Petrov, 1916.

———. *Shriftn*. Vol. 4. Vilna: B. Kletzkin, 1928.

———. *Geklibene verk*. New York: Tsiko, 1953.

Basin, Morris, ed. *Antologye: Finf hundert yor yidisher poezye*. Vol. 2. New York: Dos yidishe bukh, 1917.

Bathrick, David. "Die Berliner Avantgarde der 20er Jahre: Das Beispiel Franz Jung."

In *Literarisches Leben in Berlin, 1871–1933,* edited by Peter Wruck, 2: 45–65. Berlin: Akademie, 1987.

Baytrog fun yidn tsu dem oyfboy fun Amerike: 10-yoriker yubiley fun internatsyonaln arbeter ordn. New York: Kooperativer folks-farlag, 1940.

Bechtel, Delphine. *Der Nister's Work 1907–1929: A Study of a Yiddish Symbolist.* Bern: P. Lang, 1990.

———. "Dovid Bergelsons Berliner Erzählungen. Ein vergessenes Kapitel der jiddischen Literatur." In *Jiddische Philologie: Festschrift für Erika Timm,* edited by Walter Röll and Simon Neuberg, 257–72. Tübingen: Max Niemeyer, 1990.

———. "Leyb Kvitko à Hambourg: entre politique, science-fiction et espionnage." In *Le yiddish: langue, culture, société: Mélanges du Centre de Recherche Français de Jérusalem,* edited by Jean Baumgarten and David Bunis, 247–71. Jerusalem: CNRS Editions, 1999.

———. *La Renaissance culturelle juive: Europe centrale et orientale, 1897–1930.* Paris: Belin, 2002.

Beider, Khaim. "Fun Yekhezkl Dobrushins arkhiv." *Sovetish heymland* no. 1 (1976): 128–32.

Beizer, Michael, and Vladlen Izmozik. "Dzerzhinskii's Attitude Toward Zionism." *Jews in Eastern Europe* no. 1 (1994): 64–70.

Belen'kii, Moisei. "Put' pisatelia." In *Izbrannoe,* by Joseph Rabin, 3–7. Moscow: Khudozhestvennaia literatura, 1984.

Belis, Shlomo. *Portretn un problemen.* Warsaw: Yidish bukh, 1964.

Ben Adir. *Undzer shprakh-problem.* Kiev: Kultur-lige, 1918.

Benjamin, Walter. *Selected Writings.* Vol. 2. Cambridge, Mass.: Belknap Press of Harvard Univ. Press, 1999.

Ben-Yakov [Kalman Zingman]. *In der tsukunft-shtot Edenya.* Kharkov: Yidish, 1918.

Bergelson, David. "An entfer Sh. Nigern." *Frayhayt,* 22 Aug. 1926.

———. "Af der shvel fun 'der velt' un 'yener velt.' " *Der emes,* 29 Aug. 1926; *Frayhayt,* 19 Sept. 1926.

———. "Moskve." *Frayhayt,* 5 Sept. 1926; *Der emes,* 19 Sept. 1926.

———. "Dray pretendentn afn 'veg' keyn Krim." *Der emes,* 29 Sept. 1926; *Frayhayt,* 2 Oct. 1926.

———. *Tsugvintn.* Vilna: B. Kletzkin, 1930.

———. "Problemen fun der yidisher literatur." *Literarishe bleter* 24 (1930).

———. *Bam Dnyeper.* Moscow: Emes, 1932.

———. *Birebidzhaner.* Moscow: Emes, 1934.

———. "Trud, vozvedennyi v stepen' iskusstva." *Literaturnaia gazeta,* 26 Aug. 1934.

———. "Leksik-problemen in der yidisher literatur." *Forpost* no. 2 (1937): 140–53.

———. "A zun-bashaynter riz." In *Osher Shvartsman: zamlung gevidmet dem XX yortog fun zayn heldishn toyt,* edited by Aron Kushnirov, 10–14. Moscow: Emes, 1940.

———. *Tsvey veltn.* New York: Ikuf, 1953.

———. *Autour de la Gare; suivi de, Joseph Shur.* Lausanne: L'Age d'homme, 1982.

———. *Leben ohne Früling.* Berlin: Aufbau, 2001.

Bergelson, David, and Emanuel Kazakevich. *Birobidzhan: an algemeyner iberblik fun der yidisher avtonomer gegnt.* Moscow: Emes, 1939.

Bikl, Shlomo, ed. *Pinkes far der forshung fun der yidisher literatur un prese.* New York: Alveltlekher yidisher kultur-kongres, 1965.

Birnbaum, Nathan. "Di absolute idee fun yidntum un di yidishe shprakh." *Di yidishe velt* no. 1 (1912): 45–52.

Blium, Arlen. *Evreiskii vopros pod sovetskoi tsenzuroi, 1917–91.* St. Petersburg: Peterburgskii evreiskii universitet, 1996.

Bloshtein, Hirsh. "Tsum ratnfarband." *Frayhayt,* 26 Nov. 1926.

Bol'shaia sovetskaia entsiklopediia. Vol. 5. Moscow: Sovetskaia entsiklopediia, 1927.

Bondarenko, Iv. "Z istorii natsional'noho pytannia: K. Marksa Zur Judenfrage." *Literaturno-naukovyi vistnyk* (June 1909): 483–88.

Borokhov, Ber. *Shprakh-forshung un literatur-geshikhte.* Tel Aviv: I. L. Peretz, 1966.

Borshchagovskii, Aleksandr. *Obviniaetsia krov'.* Moscow: Gruppa Progress, 1994.

Brainin, Reuven. *Fun mayn lebns-bukh.* New York: Ikuf, 1946.

Bramson-Alperniene, Esfir. "Der Vilner yidisher farlag un zayn grinder Boris Kletzkin." *Jiddistik-Mitteilungen* 27 (2002): 3–6.

Braude, Kh. "Iz evreiskoi rabochei statistiki." *Novyi put'* nos. 26–27 (1917): 9–14.

Bravarnik, Leyb. "Vos hot men geleyent in Kiever Vinchevsky-bibliotek in 1930 yor." *Di royte velt* nos. 1–2 (1931): 218–23.

Brianski, Sh. *D. Bergelson in shpigl fun der kritik, 1909–32.* Kiev: Institut far yidisher proletarisher kultur, 1934.

Brodsky, Alexandra Fanny. *Smoke Signals: From Eminence to Exile.* London and New York: Radcliffe Press, 1997.

Bronshtein, Yasha. "Der stiln-kamf inem period fun militerishn komunizm." *Prolit* nos. 11–12 (1929): 64–66.

———. "The Literature of the White Russian Socialist Soviet Republic." *Literature of the Peoples of the USSR* nos. 7–8 (1934): 65.

———. "Pevets romanticheskoi real'nosti." *Literaturnaia gazeta,* 8 June 1934.

Bukharin, Nikolai. *Proletariat i voprosy khudozhestvennoi politiki.* Letchworth: Prideaux Press, 1979.

Carr, Edward Hallett. *Socialism in One Country, 1924–25.* Vol. 2. Harmondsworth: Penguin, 1970.

Cassedy, Steven. *To the Other Shore: The Russian Jewish Intellectuals Who Came to America*. Princeton, N.J.: Princeton Univ. Press, 1997.

Charney, Daniel. "Tsu der geshikhte fun der yidisher komunistisher prese." *In shpan* no. 1 (1926): 131–38.

———. "Tsu der kharakteristik fun der yidisher literatur inem ratnfarband." *Fraye shriftn farn yidishn sotsyalistishn gedank* no. 6 (1929): 74–79.

———. *A yortsendlik aza, 1914–24*. New York: Tsiko, 1943.

Cherepakhov, M., and E. Fingerit. *Russkaia periodicheskaia pechat', 1895–1917*. Moscow: Gosudarstvennoe izdatel'stvo politicheskoi literatury, 1957.

Chernykh, Alla. *Stanovlenie Rossii sovetskoi: 20-e gody v zerkale sotsiologii*. Moscow: Pamiatniki istoricheskoi mysli, 1998.

Connor, Walker. *The National Question in Marxist-Leninist Theory and Strategy*. Princeton, N.J.: Princeton Univ. Press, 1984.

Corrsin, Stephen D. *Warsaw Before the First World War: Poles and Jews in the Third City of the Russian Empire, 1880–1914*. New York: Boulder, 1989.

Cummy, Justin D. "Tsevorfene bleter: The Emergence of Yung Vilne." *Polin: Studies in Polish Jewry* 14 (2001): 170–91.

Danilova, E. N. "Immigratsionaia politika i sozdanie trudovykh kommun iz emigrantov i reemigrantov v SSSR v 1920-e gody." *Vestnik Moskovskogo universiteta. Seriia 8, istoriia* no. 1 (2002): 3–20.

Del'man. "Soveshchanie evreiskikh pisatelei." *Literaturnaia gazeta*, 11 Dec. 1933.

"Der mishpet iber Yungvald." *Der emes*, 1 Nov. 1925.

Der Nister. "Moskve: a shvere dermonung." *Di royte velt* nos. 7–8 (1932): 125–33.

"Di ershte alukrainishe baratung fun di yidishe revolutsyonere proletarishe shrayber in Ukraine." *Di royte velt* no. 1 (1928): 122–26.

"Di shprakh-baratung in Kharkiv." *Di yidishe shprakh* nos. 4–5 (1930): 85–90.

Dimanshtein, Semen. "Problemy natsional'noi kultury i kul'turnogo stroitel'stva v natsional'nykh respublikakh." *Vestnik Kommunisticheskoi Akademii* no. 1 (1929): 115–19.

———, ed. *Itogi razresheniia natsional'nogo voprosa v SSSR*. Moscow: Gosizdat, 1936.

Dovrenko, Evgenii. *Metafora vlasti: Literatura stalinskoi epokhi v istoricheskom osveshchenii*. Munich: Otto Sagner, 1993.

———. *Formovka sovetskogo pisatelia: sotsial'nye i esteticheskie istoki sovetskoi literaturnoi kul'tury*. St. Petersburg: Akademicheskii proekt, 1999.

Dobrinki, Abraham. "Di yidishe dikhtung in der prese fun di ershte revolutsyeyorn." *Sovetish heymland* no. 6 (1962): 100–105.

Dobrushin, Yekhezkel. "Yidisher kunst-primitiv un dos kunst-bukh far kinder." *Bikher-velt* nos. 4–5 (1919).

———. *Gedankengang*. Kiev: Kutur-lige, 1922.

———. "Sholem-Aleichem's alie." *Shtrom* 2 (1922): 57–61.

———. "A briv in redaktsye." *Der emes,* 15 Jan. 1925.

———. "Fefer der dikhter." *Di royte velt* no. 1 (1929): 80–89.

Dolgopolski, Tsodek [Horodoker]. *Mit mayn pen in hant.* Minsk: Melukhe-farlag, 1932.

Dolgopolski, Tsodek. *Zayd.* Minsk: Melukhe-farlag, 1933.

Draudin, T. *Ocherki izdatel'skogo dela v SSSR.* Moscow and Leningrad: Gosudarstvennoe sotsial'no-ekonomicheskoe izdatel'stvo, 1934.

Druker, Irme. *Literarishe eseyen.* Supplement to *Sovetish heymland* no. 1 (1981).

Druyanov, M. *Krolik-tsukht in der yidisher kolektiver virtshaft.* Moscow: Tsentrfarlag, 1930.

———. *Hodevanye fun khazeyrim.* Moscow: Tsentrfarlag, 1931.

———. *Khazeyrim-fermes.* Moscow: Emes, 1933.

Druzhinikov, Iurii. *Donoschik 001, ili voznesenie Pavlika Morozova.* Moscow: Moskovskii rabochii, 1995.

Dubnov, Shimen [Kritikus]. "Literaturnaia letopis'." *Voskhod* 7, no. 5 (1887): 6–21.

———. "Literaturnaia letopis'." *Voskhod* 7, no. 7 (1887): 12–15.

———. "O zhargonnoi literature voobshche i o nekotorykh noveishikh ee proizvedeniiakh v chastnosti." *Voskhod* 8, no. 10 (1888): 21.

Dubnov, Shimen. *Fun 'zhargon' tsu yidish un andere artiklen: literarishe zikhroynes.* Vilna: B. Kletzkin, 1929.

———. "Zhitlovskis avtonomism." In *Zhitlovski-zamlbukh,* 190–95. Warsaw: H. Bzshozo, 1929.

Dubnov-Erlich, Sofia. "Yosef Leshtshinsky (Y. Khmurner): zayn lebn un shafn." In *Kmurner-bukh,* 64–76. New York: Unzer tsayt, 1958.

Dunets, Khatskl. *Far magnitboyen fun der literatur.* Minsk: Belorussian Academy of Science, 1932.

Dzhimbinov, S. B., ed. *Literaturnye manifesty: ot simvolizma do nashikh dnei.* Moscow: XXI vek-Soglasie, 2000.

Ehrenburg, Ilya. *Zhizn' i gibel' Nikolaia Kurbova.* Berlin: Gelikon, 1923.

"Ekonomicheskoe polozhenie evreev v Bessarabii." *Rul',* 1 Jan. 1925.

Elyashevich, Dmitry A. *Pravitel'stvennaia politika i evreiskaia pechat' v Rossii, 1797–1917.* St. Petersburg and Jerusalem: Gesharim, 1999.

Epshtein, Shakhne. "Vos lernt undz der inyen 'Kvitko.' " *Der emes,* 24 Oct. 1929.

———. "Di yidishe proletarishe literatur un di proletarishe shrayber-organizatsyes." *Di royte velt* no. 3 (1930): 112–24.

———. "Di yidishe marksistishe kritik." *Di royte velt* nos. 4–5 (1931): 148–81.

———, ed. *Di yidishe kinstlerishe literatur un di partey-onfirung.* Kharkov: Melukhe-farlag, 1929.

Erez, Iehuda, ed. *My nachinali eshche v Rossii: vospominaniia.* Jerusalem: Biblioteka-Aliia, 1990.

Ermolaev, Herman. *Soviet Literary Theories 1917–34: The Genesis of Socialist Realism.* Berkeley: Univ. of California Press, 1963.

Ertel, Rachel, ed. *Khalyastra/La bande: Revue littéraire, Varsovie 1922–Paris 1924.* Paris: Lachenal et Ritter, 1989.

Esenin, Sergei. *Sobranie sochinenii v trekh tomakh.* Moscow: Sovetskii pisatel', 1987.

Estraikh, Gennady. "Languages of 'Yehupets' Students." *East European Jewish Affairs* 21, no. 1 (1991): 63–71.

———. "Pyrrhyc Victories of Soviet Yiddish Language Planners." *East European Jewish Affairs* 23, no. 2 (1993): 25–37.

———. "Soviet Yiddish Vernacular of the 1920s: Avrom Abchuk's *Hershl Shamaj* as a Socio-linguistic Source." *Slovo* 7, no. 1 (1994): 1–12.

———. "The Era of *Sovetish Heymland*: Readership of the Yiddish Press in the Former Soviet Union." *East European Jewish Affairs* 25, no. 1 (1995): 17–22.

———. "Yiddish Language Conference Aborted." *East European Jewish Affairs* 25, no. 2 (1995): 91–96.

———. " 'Jewish Street' or Jewish Cul-de-Sac? From *Sovetish Heymland* to *Di Yidishe Gas.*" *East European Jewish Affairs* 26, no. 1 (1996): 25–33.

———. "Aron Vergelis: The Perfect Jewish Homo Sovieticus." *East European Jewish Affairs* 27, no. 2 (1997): 3–20.

———. "A Touchstone of Socialist Realism: The 1934 *Almanac* of Soviet Yiddish Writers." *Jews in Eastern Europe* no. 3 (1998): 24–37.

———. *Soviet Yiddish: Language Planning and Linguistic Development.* Oxford: Oxford Univ. Press, 1999.

———. "From Yehupets Jargonists to Kiev Modernists: The Rise of a Yiddish Literary Centre, 1880s–1914." *East European Jewish Affairs* 30, no. 1 (2000): 17–38.

———. "The Shtetl Theme in *Sovetish heymland.*" In *The Shtetl: Image and Reality,* edited by Gennady Estraikh and Mikhail Krutikov, 152–68. Oxford: Legenda, 2000.

———. "Yiddish Literary Life in Soviet Moscow, 1918–1924." *Jews in Eastern Europe* no. 2 (2000): 25–55.

———. "David Bergelson: From Fellow Traveller to Soviet Classic." *Slavic Almanach: The South African Year Book for Slavic, Central and East European Studies* 7, no. 10 (2001): 191–222.

———. "Metamorphoses of *Morgn-frayhayt.*" In *Yiddish and the Left,* edited by Gennady Estraikh and Mikhail Krutikov, 144–66. Oxford: Legenda, 2001.

———. "Itsik Fefer: A Yiddish *Wunderkind* of the Bolshevik Revolution." *Shofar* 20, no. 3 (2002): 14–31.

———. "The Kharkiv Yiddish Literary World, 1920s–Mid-1930s." *East European Jewish Affairs* 32, no. 2 (2002): 70–88.

————. "Pig-breeding, *Shiksas,* and Other *Goyish* Themes in Soviet Yiddish Literature and Life." *Symposium* 57, no. 3 (2003): 157–74.

————. "The Soviet Shtetl in the 1920s." *Polin* forthcoming (2004).

"Evreiskie gazety." *Krasnaia pechat'* no. 25 (1925): 40–41.

Fefer, Itsik. *Geklibene verk.* Kiev: Melukhe-farlag, 1929.

————. "Ideolohichna borot'ba v evreiskii literaturi." *Krytyka* no. 12 (1930): 59–67.

————. *Di ufgabes fun der yidisher proletarisher literatur in rekonstruktivn period.* Kiev: Ukrmelukhenatsmindfarlag, 1932.

————. *Lider, balades, poemes: oysderveylts.* Moscow: Sovetskii pisatel', 1967.

————, ed. *Almanakh fun yidishe sovetishe shrayber: tsum alfarbandishn shrayber-tsuzamenfor.* Kharkov and Kiev: Ukrmelukhenatsmindfarlag, 1934.

Finkel, Uri. "Moyshe Khashchevatsky." *Folks-shtime,* 8 June 1957.

Finkelshtein, Abe. "Vegn eynem a briv." *Sovetish heymland* no. 8 (1973): 167–68.

Fishman, David E. "Religioznye lidery sovetskogo evreistva (1917–34)." In *Istoricheskie sud'by evreev v Rossii i SSSR: nachalo dialoga,* edited by Igor Krupnik, 189–99. Moscow: Evreiskoe istoricheskoe obshchestvo, 1992.

————. "Judaism in the USSR, 1917–30: The Fate of Religious Education." In *Jews and Jewish Life in Russia and the Soviet Union,* edited by Yaacov Ro'i, 251–62. Ilford: F. Cass, 1995.

Fishman, Joshua A. *Yiddish: Turning to Life.* Amsterdam: J. Benjamins, 1991.

Fitzpatrick, Sheila. *The Cultural Front: Power and Culture in Revolutionary Russia.* Ithaca, N.Y.: Cornell Univ. Press, 1992.

Flynn, James T. *The University Reform of Tsar Alexander 1, 1802–35.* Washington, D.C.: Catholic Univ. of America Press, 1988.

Freitag, Gabriele. "Evreiskoe naselenie Moskvy v fokuse politiki kommunisticheskoi partii v otnoshenii natsional'nykh men'shinstv." *Tirosh* 3 (1999): 170–90.

Frenkel, Jonathan. "The Dilemmas of Jewish National Autonomism: The Case of Ukraine, 1917–20." In *Ukrainian-Jewish Relations in Historical Perspective,* edited by Howard Aster and Peter J. Potichnyj, 263–76. Edmonton: Canadian Institute of Ukrainian Studies, 1990.

Frieden, Ken. *Classic Yiddish Fiction: Abramovitsh, Sholem Aleichem, and Peretz.* Albany: State Univ. of New York Press, 1995.

Fuks, Leo, and Renate Fuks. "Yiddish Publishing Activities in the Weimar Republic, 1920–33." *Leo Baeck Institute Year Book* 33 (1988): 420–42.

Gassenschmidt, Christoph. *Jewish Liberal Politics in Tsarist Russia, 1900–14: The Modernization of Russian Jewry.* Basingstoke: Macmillan, 1995.

Geller, Ewa. *Warschauer Jiddisch.* Tübingen: Max Niemeyer, 2001.

Gergel, N. "Yidn in der ruslendisher komunistisher partey un in komunistishn yudntfarband." *YIVO Bleter* 1, no. 1 (1931): 63–69.

Gets, F. "Shkol'noe obuchenie u russkikh evreev." *Zhurnal Ministerstva narodnogo prosveshcheniia* 51 (1914): 1–29.

Gildin, Khaim. "Tsayt-fragn." *Di royte velt* nos. 1–3 (1933): 1–29.

Gitelman, Zvi Y. *Jewish Nationality and Soviet Politics: The Jewish Sections of the CPSU, 1917–30.* Princeton, N.J.: Princeton Univ. Press, 1972.

Glatstein, Jacob. *In tokh genumen: eseyen 1945–1947.* New York: Matones, 1947.

———. *Oyf greyte temes.* Tel Aviv: I. L. Peretz, 1967.

Godiner, Shmuel. *Figurn afn rand.* Kiev: Kultur-lige, 1929.

Goldberg, Itche. *Eseyen.* New York: Ikuf, 1981.

Golde, Iu. *Evrei-zemledel'tsy v Krymu.* Moscow: Komzet, 1931.

Gol'del'man, Solomon I. *Zhidivs'ka natsional'na avtonomiia na Ukraïni.* Munich: Institut zur Erforschung der UdSSR, 1963.

Goldenveizer, A. A. "Iz kievskikh vospominanii, 1917–21." *Arkhiv russkoi revoliutsii* 4 (1922): 170–85.

Goldovskii, O. B. *Evrei v Moskve: stranitsy iz istorii sovremennoi Rossii.* Berlin: n.p., 1904.

Goldsmith, Emanuel S. *Modern Yiddish Culture: The Story of the Yiddish Language Movement.* New York: Fordham Univ. Press, 1997.

Golomb, Abraham. *A halber yorhundert yidishe dertsiung.* Rio de Janeiro: Monte Skopus, 1957.

Gontar, Abraham. *Heler tog.* Kiev: Ukrmelukhenatsmindfarlag, 1938.

Gordon, Eli, Peretz Markish, and Aron Kushnirov, eds. *Komyug.* Moscow: Emes, 1938.

Gordon Mlotek, Khana [Eleanor]. "Der toyt fun A. Vayter un zayne nokhfolgn." *YIVO Bleter* 2 (1994): 49–56.

Gorelik, Shmarayhu. "Kunst un natsyonale oyslebn." In *Der yidisher almanakh,* 85. Kiev: Kunst-farlag, 1910.

Gorin, B. "Di oyfbliung fun der yidisher literatur in Amerike." *Di tsukunft* 7, no. 7 (1902): 340–43.

Gorki, Maxim, Leopold Auerbach, and Semen Firin, eds. *The White Sea Canal.* London: John Lane, 1935.

Gornfel'd, A. "Zhargonnaia literatura na russkom knizhnom rynke." *Evreiskii mir* (Jan. 1909): 68–69.

Gorshman, Shira. *Oysdoyer.* Tel Aviv: Yisroel-bukh, 1992.

"Goset Belorussii." *Literaturnaia gazeta,* 7 Apr. 1930.

Green, Ber. *Fun dor tsu dor.* New York: Ikuf, 1971.

Greenbaum, Alfred Abraham. *Jewish Scholarship and Scholarly Institutions in Soviet Russia, 1918–1953.* Jerusalem: Hebrew Univ., 1978.

———. *Tenu'at ha-tehiyah ("vozroz'denyah") u-mifleget ha-poalim ha-yehudit-sotsyalistit.* Jerusalem: Merkaz Dinur, 1988.

———. "The Belorussian State Jewish Theatre in the Interwar Period." *Jews in Eastern Europe* no. 2 (2000): 56–75.

Gritsenko, Adelina. *Politychni syly u borot'bi za vladu v Ukraïni.* Kiev: Institut istoriã Ukraïny AN Ukraïny, 1993.

Groys, Boris. "The Birth of Socialist Realism from the Spirit of the Russian Avant-Garde." In *Laboratory of Dreams: The Russian Avant-Garde and Cultural Experiment,* edited by John E. Bowlt and Olga Matich, 190–211. Stanford, Calif.: Stanford Univ. Press, 1996.

Gudzhiev, Nikolai. *Stat'i ob avangarde.* Vol. 1. Moscow: RA, 1997.

Gurevitsh, G. "Di kiever yidishe kehile in di yorn 1906–16." *Shriftn far ekonomik un statistik* 1 (1928): 100–108.

Halkin, Shmuel. *Far dem nayem fundament.* Moscow: Emes, 1932.

Halpern, Menashe. *Parmetn: zikhroynes un shilderungen.* Saõ Paolo: Alveltlekher yidisher kultur-kongres, 1952.

Hamm, Michael F. *Kiev: A Portrait, 1800–1917.* Princeton, N.J.: Princeton Univ. Press, 1993.

Harshav, Benjamin, and Barbara Harshav. *American Yiddish Poetry: A Bilingual Anthology.* Berkeley: Univ. of California Press, 1986.

Hart, Henry, ed. *American Writers' Congress.* London: Martin Lawrence, 1935.

Heller, Michael. *Kontsentratsionnyi mir i sovetskaia literatura.* London: Overseas Publications Interchange, 1974.

Hertsman, Nosn. "Der vald hot oysgeshpign a ban." *Folks-shtime,* 5 Dec. 1959.

Hirshbein, Peretz. *In gang fun lebn.* New York: Tsiko, 1948.

Hoberman, J. *Bridge of Light: Yiddish Film Between Two Worlds.* New York: Schocken Books, 1981.

Hoffmann, David L. *Stalinist Values: The Cultural Norms of Soviet Modernity, 1917–41.* Ithaca, N.Y.: Cornell Univ. Press, 2003.

Howe, Irving. *World of Our Fathers: The Journey of the East European Jews to America and the Life They Found and Made.* New York: Harcourt Brace Jovanovich, 1976.

Howe, Irving, Ruth R. Wisse, and Khone Shmeruk, eds. *The Penguin Book of Modern Yiddish Verse.* New York: Viking, 1988.

Hrigor'ev, Hrihorii. *U staromu Kievi.* Kiev: Dumka, 1961.

Hrushovski [Harshav], Benjamin. "On Free Rhythms in Yiddish Poetry." In *The Field of Yiddish: Studies in Yiddish Language, Folklore, and Literature,* edited by Uriel Weinreich, 219–66. Philadelphia: Institute for the Study of Human Issues, 1954.

Hurvits, Kh. D. *Yidishe klasn un parteyen.* Petrograd: Geule, 1918.

Iangirov, R. M. "Marginal'nye temy v tvorcheskoi praktike LEFa." In *Tynianovskii sbornik,* edited by Marietta Chudakova, 225–40. Riga: Zinatne, 1994.

Iashunskii, I. V. *Evreiskaia periodicheskaia pechat' v 1917 i 1918 g.g.* Petrograd: Rossiiskaia knizhnaia palata, 1920.

Ignatovskii, B., and A. Smolich. *Belorussiia.* Minsk: n.p., 1925.

Ivanov, Vladislav. *Russkie sezony teatra Gabima.* Moscow: Artist. Rezhiser. Teatr, 1999.

Jacobs, Jack. *On Socialists and "the Jewish Question" after Marx.* New York: New York Univ. Press, 1992.

Johansson, Kurt. *Aleksej Gastev: Proletarian Bard of the Machine Age.* Stockholm: Almqvist and Wiksell International, 1983.

Kahan, Abraham. *A khazer.* Kharkov: Ukrmelukhenatsmindfarlag, 1928.

———— "Evreiska radians'ka literatura URSR za dva roky." *Literaturna hazeta,* 1 May 1934.

Kahan, Abraham, and Abraham Gontar, eds. *Onheyb.* Kiev: Ukrmelukhenatsmindfarlag, 1940.

Kahan, Arcadius. "Vilne—a sotsial-kultureler profil fun a yidisher kehile tsvishn beyde velt-milkhomes." *YIVO Bleter* 2 (1994): 27–42.

Kalinin, Mikhail. "Di aynordnung fun yidn af erd." *Frayhayt,* 22 Aug. 1926.

————. "Evrei-zemledel'tsy v soiuze narodov SSSR." *Izvestiia,* 17 Nov. 1926.

Kalmanson, Elhanan. *Dos lebedike vort.* Kiev: n.p., 1910.

Kamenetski, Joseph. "Der Volge-Moskver kanal." *Der emes,* 12 June 1934.

Kamensky, Aleksandr. *Chagall: The Russian Years, 1907–22.* London: Thames and Hudson, 1989.

Kantor, Iakov. *Nathional'noe stroitel'stvo sredi evreev v SSSR.* Moscow: Vlast' Sovetov, 1935.

Kas'ianov, Heorhii. *Ukraïnska intelihentsiia na rubezhi XIX–XX stolit'.* Kiev: Lybid', 1933.

Karalnik, A. D. "Evreiskaia problema vlasti." *Novyi put'* no. 32 (1917): 10.

Kaufman, Dalia. "Fir gilgulim fun Bergelson's dertseylung 'Batshka.'" *Yerusholayemer almanakh* 4 (1974): 216–21.

Kazdan, Khaim. "Undzer literatur far kinder." *Bikher-velt* nos. 4–5 (1919): 29.

————. *Fun kheyder un "shkoles" biz tsisho.* Mexico: Shlomo Mendelson fond, 1956.

Kazovsky, Hillel. *Artists from Vitebsk: Yehuda Pen and His Pupils.* Moscow: Imidzh, 1992.

————. "The Art Section of the Kultur Lige." *Jews in Eastern Europe* no. 3 (1993): 6–7.

————. "Vospominaniia Leo Keniga." *Vestnik Evreiskogo universiteta* 2 (1999): 331.

————. "Jewish Art Between *yidishkayt* and Civilization." In *The Shtetl: Image and Reality,* edited by Gennady Estraikh and Mikhail Krutikov, 80–90. Oxford: Legenda, 2000.

————. "Shtetl versus megapolis v tvorchestve evreiskikh poetov i khudozhnikov v Amerike." *Zerkalo* 17–18 (2002): 171–83.

————. *The Artists of the Kultur-Lige.* Jerusalem and Moscow: Gesher, 2003.

"Kegn dem rekht opnoyg in der literatur." *Der emes,* 21 Sept. 1929.

Kel'ner, Viktor, and Dmitrii Eliashevich. *Literatura o evreiakh na russkom iazyke, 1890–1947.* St. Petersburg: Akademicheskii proekt, 1995.

Kenig, Leo. *Shrayber un verk.* Vilna: B. Kletzkin, 1929.

Khait, David. "Storona Birobidzhanskaia." *Bezbozhnik* no. 6 (1936): 8–9.

Khashin, Aleksandr. "Front kriticheskii." *Literaturnaia gazeta,* 4 Aug. 1934.

Khodos, M. P. *Materialy po statistike naseleniia Kieva.* Kiev: n.p., 1926.

Khorol, Dvoire. "Lirishe heftn." *Sovetish heymland* no. 9 (1975): 150–55.

"Khronik fun der yidisher sovetisher literatur." *Sovetish heymland* no. 11 (1966): 141–46; no. 12 (1966): 134–40; no. 4 (1967): 139–45.

Khvylia, Andrei. "Literatura—osnovnaia chast' stroitel'stva unkrainskoi sovetskoi kul'tury." *Literaturnaia gazeta,* 29 July 1933.

Kiper, Motl. "A vort tsu der ordenung." *Di royte velt* no. 6 (1930): 94–112.

Kipnis, Itsik. *Mesiatsy i dni.* Moscow: Gosizdat, 1930.

Kirzhnits, Abraham. *Der yidisher arbeter: khrestomatye tsu der geshikhte fun der yidisher arbeter, revolyutsionerer un sotsialistisher bavegung in Rusland.* Moscow: Tsentrfarlag, 1927.

Kleinman, Moshe. "Der kumendiker yid." In *Untervegs,* 158–70. Odessa: Moria, 1917.

Kobets, Grigorii, and Iogann Zel'tser. "Iskateli schast'ia." *God za godom* 4 (1988): 204–40.

Koltsov, Mikhail. "Ahin un tsurik." *Der emes,* 3 Nov. 1925.

Kol'tsova, V. A., et al. "I. N. Shpil'rein i sovetskaia psikhotekhnika." *Psikhologicheskii zhurnal* 11, no. 2 (1990): 111–33.

Kolychev, Osip. "Vegn mayne fraynt." *Sovetish heymland* no. 3 (1967): 148–54.

Korsyna, S., and E. Shabad. "Ob izdanii detskoi literatury na razgovorno-evreiskom iazyke." *Vestnik Obshchestva rasprostraneniia prosveshcheniia mezhdu evreiami v Rossii* 22 (1913): 55–62.

Kostyrchenko, Gennadii. *Tainaia politika Stalina: vlast' i antisemitizm.* Moscow: Mezhdunarodnye otnosheniia, 2001.

Krüger, Maren. "Buchproduktion im Exil: Der Klal-Verlag." In *Juden in Kreuzberg: Fundstücke, Fragmente, Erinnerungen,* 421–26. Berlin: Berliner Geschichtswerkstatt, 1991.

Krupnik, Igor. "Soviet Cultural and Ethnic Policies Towards Jews: A Legacy Reassessed." In *Jews and Jewish Life in Russia and the Soviet Union,* edited by Yaacov Ro'I, 70–82. Ilford: F. Cass, 1995.

Krutikov, Mikhail. "Soviet Literary Theory in the Search for a Yiddish Canon: The Case of Moshe Litvakov." In *Yiddish and the Left,* edited by Gennady Estraikh and Mikhail Krutikov, 226–41. Oxford: Legenda, 2000.

———. "Soviet Yiddish Scholarship in the 1930s: From Class to Folk." *Slavic Al-*

manach: The South African Year Book for Slavic, Central, and East European Studies 7, no. 10 (2001): 223–51.

———. Yiddish Fiction and the Crisis of Modernity, 1905–1914. Stanford, Calif.: Stanford Univ. Press, 2001.

———. "Mistishe vortslen fun sovetisher yidisher literatur." Forverts, 9 Aug. 2002.

———. "Meir Wiener in yor 1925: naye materyaln tsu zayn biographye." Forverts, 5 Sept. 2003.

Kulbak, Moshe. Geklibene verk. New York: Tsiko, 1953.

Kupovetskii, Mark. "Evreiskoe naselenie Moskvy, XV–XX vv." In Etnicheskie gruppy v gorodakh evropeiskoi chasti SSSR, edited by Igor' Krupnik, 58–71. Moscow: Geographicheskoe obshchestvo, 1987.

Kurland, D., and S. Rokhkind, eds. Di haynttsaytike proletarishe yidishe dikhtung in Amerike. Minsk: Melukhe-farlag, 1932.

Kushnirov, Aron. Vent. Kiev: Melukhe-farlag, 1921.

———. Geklibene lider. Moscow: Sovetskii pisatel', 1975.

———, ed. Osher Shvarstman: zamlung gevidmet dem XX yortog fun zayn heldishn toyt. Moscow: Emes, 1940.

Kvitko, B., and M. Petrovskii. Zhizn' i tvorchestvo L'va Kvitko. Moscow: Detskaia literatura, 1976.

Kvitko, Leyb. Riogrander fel: dertseylungen funem arbeter-lebn in Daytshland. Kharkov: Melukhe-farlag, 1928.

———. Tsvey khaveyrim. Moscow: Emes, 1933.

Lapitskaia, Sara. "Publitsisticheskaia deiatel'nost' Bera Gal'perina v Parizhe." In Evrei Rossii—immigranty Frantsii, edited by W. Moskovich, V. Khazan, and S. Breuillard, 144–51. Jerusalem and Moscow: Mosty kul'tury, 2000.

Lapshin, Vladimir. Khudozhestvennaia zhizn' Moskvy i Petrograda v 1917 godu. Moscow: Sovetskii khudozhnik, 1983.

Leftwich, Joseph, ed. The Way We Think: A Collection of Essays from the Yiddish. Vol. 1. South Brunswick, N.J.: T. Yoseloff, 1969.

Leibfreid, Aleksandr, and Iuliana Poliakova. Kharkov: ot kreposti do stolitsy. Kharkov: Folio, 1998.

Leintes, L. "O stikhakh Fefera." Literaturnaia gazeta, 28 Dec. 1931.

Leksikon fun der nayer yidisher literatur. Vols. 1–8. New York: Tsiko, 1956–81.

Lenin. Troyer-tog. 27 yanvar 1924. Moscow: Kultur-lige, 1924.

Levin, Nora. The Jews of the Soviet Union since 1917: Paradox of Survival. Vol. 1. New York: New York Univ. Press, 1988.

Liber, George. Soviet Nationality Policy, Urban Growth, and Identity Change in the Ukrainian SSR, 1932–34. Cambridge: Cambridge Univ. Press, 1992.

Libinzon, Zalman. "Dovid Bergelsons dramaturgie." Sovetish heymland no. 12 (1984): 151–59.

Liptzin, Sol. *A History of Yiddish Literature*. New York: Jonathan David, 1985.

Lissitzky-KÅppers, Sophie. *El Lissitzky: Life, Letters, Texts*. London: Thames and Hudson, 1968.

"Literarish-kinstlerishe khronik." *Literarishe monatsshriftn* no. 3 (1912): 96–97.

Literaturnaia entsiklopediia. Vol. 1. Moscow: Izdatel'stvo Kommunisticheskoi akademii, 1930.

"Literaturnaia khronika." *Novyi put'* no. 7 (1917): 31.

Litvak, A. *Vos geven*. Vilna: B. Kletzkin, 1925.

———. *Geklibene shriftn*. New York: Veker, 1945.

Litvakov, Moshe [M. Lirov]. "Sholom-Aleikhem." *Kievskaia mysl'*, 9 May 1916.

Litvakov, Moshe. *In umru*. Kiev: Kiever farlag, 1919.

———. "Nayes fun der yidisher literatur." *Der emes*, 26 Apr. 1924.

———. "Arbkorn-shafung." *Der emes*, 4 May 1924.

———. *In umru*. Moscow: Shul un bukh, 1926.

———. "A klap in tish un a lek dem shtivl." *Der emes*, 30 June, 3 July 1929.

———. "Litkomandes un litrekhiles." *Der emes*, 13 July 1929.

———. *Af tsvey frontn*. Moscow: Tsentr-farlag, 1931.

———. "Novaia literature." *Literaturnaia gazeta*, 4 Aug. 1934.

Liubomirsky, Yeshue. "Farblibn in zikorn: a bleter zikhroynes vegn Osher Shvarts-man." *Sovetish heymland* no. 1 (1965): 135–36.

Lozovski, Shimen. "Moyshe Nadir ovnt in Kiev." *Frayhayt*, 30 Sept. 1926.

Luckyj, George S. N. *Keeping a Record: Literary Purges in Soviet Ukraine, 1930s: A Bio-Bibliography*. Edmonton: Canadian Institute of Ukrainian Studies, 1988.

———. *Literary Politics in the Soviet Ukraine, 1917–34*. Durham, N.C.: Duke Univ. Press, 1990.

Lunacharskii, Anatolii. "Svoboda knigi i revoliutsiia." *Pechat' i revoliutsiia* no. 1 (1921): 3–12.

Luppol, I. K., M. M. Rozental', and S. M. Tret'akov, eds. *Pervyi Vsesoiuznyi s ezd sovetskikh pisatelei, 1934: stenograficheskii otchet*. Moscow: Sovetskii pisatel', 1990.

Lurye, Note. "Tsuzamen mit Gorkin." *Sovetish heymland* no. 5 (1964): 157.

Lvavi, Jacob. *Ha-hityashvut ha-yahudit be-Birobig'an*. Jerusalem: Hebrew Univ., 1965.

Lyn'kov, Mikhas'. *Rasskazy*. Leningrad: Khudozhestvennaia literatura, 1961.

Mai, Birgit. *Satire im Sowjetsozialismus*. Bern: P. Lang, 1993.

Makagon, Aron. "Dray yor *Royte velt*." *Di royte velt* nos. 8–9 (1927): 176–80.

Makurov, V. G., ed. *Gulag v Karelii*. Petrozavodsk: Karel'skii nauchnyi tsentr RAN, 1992.

Markish, Peretz. "Af di vegn fun yidisher dikhtung." In *Trep*, 37. Ekaterinoslav: Kultur-lige, 1921.

———. *Nakht-royb*. Moscow: Lirik, 1922.

———. "Shpan-tsedek." *Literarishe bleter* 106 (1926).

———. "Gut iz tsu dir kumen." *Frayhayt,* 12 Nov. 1926.

———. "Mayn parol!" *Der emes,* 28 Dec. 1926.

———. "Khaveyrim kustarn." *Di royte velt* no. 10 (1928): 26–42; no. 11 (1928): 10–34.

———. *Tovaryshi kustari.* Kharkov: Spilka, 1930.

———. *Eyns af eyns.* Kharkov and Kiev: Ukrmelukhenatsmindfarlag, 1934.

———. *Vozvrashchenie Neitana Bekera.* Moscow: Goslit, 1934.

Marsh, Rosalind. *Images of Dictatorship: Portraits of Stalin in Literature.* London: Routledge, 1989.

Marten-Finnis, Susanne. "Wilna als Zentrum der jüdischen Parteiliteratur 1896 bis 1922." *Aschkenas* 10, no. 1 (2000): 208–9.

Marten-Finnis, Susanne, and Heather Valencia. *Sprachinseln: Jiddische Publizistik in London, Wilna, und Berlin, 1880–1930.* Cologne: Böhlau, 1999.

"Materyaln tsu D. Bergelsons bio-bibliografye." *Visnshaft un revolutsye* nos. 1–2 (1934): 60–80.

McCannon, John. "Positive Heroes at the Poles: Celebrity Status, Socialist-Realist Ideals, and the Soviet Myth of the Arctic, 1932–39." *The Russian Review* 56, no. 3 (1997): 344–72.

McLennan, Gregor. *Marxism and the Methodologies of History.* London: NLB, 1981.

Mehnert, Klaus. *The Russians and Their Favorite Books.* Stanford, Calif.: Hoover Institution, 1983.

Meisel, Gitl. *Eseyen.* Tel Aviv: I. L. Peretz, 1974.

Meisel, Nakhman. "Bamerkungen fun a lezer." In *Yidisher almanakh,* 37–48. Kiev: Kunst-farlag, 1910.

———. "Der krizis fun yidishn bukh." *Literarishe bleter* 56 (1925).

———. "Dos yidishe bukh in 1925." *Literarishe bleter* 87 (1926).

———. "Dovid Bergelson's 'Der toyber' in vaysrusishn yidishn melukhe-teater." *Literarishe bleter* 4 (1929).

———. "Dovid Bergelson tsugast in Varshe." *Literarishe bleter* 22 (1930).

———. "A por verter." *Literarishe bleter* 24 (1930).

———. "Mir forn farbay Berlin." *Literarishe bleter* 43 (1937).

———. *Dovid Bergelson.* New York: Kooperativer folks-farlag, 1940.

———. "M. Goldshteyn." In *Biro-bidzhaner afn Amur un andere dertseylungen,* by M. Goldshteyn, 3–15. New York: Ikuf, 1944.

———. *Forgeyer un mittsaytler.* New York: Ikuf, 1946.

———. *Geven amol a lebn: dos yidishe kultur-lebn in Poyln tsvishn beyde velt-milkhomes.* Buenos Aires: Tsentral farband fun poylishe yidn, 1951.

———. *Dos yidishe shafn un der yidisher shrayber in sovetnfarband.* New York: Ikuf, 1959.

———. *Undzer Sholem Aleykhem*. Warsaw: Yidish bukh, 1959.

———. *Kegnzaytike hashpoes in velt-shafn*. Warsaw: Ikuf, 1965.

———. *Onhoybn: Dovid Bergelson*. Kibbutz Alonim: n.p., 1977.

———. *Bleter zikhroynes*. Kibbutz Alonim: n.p., 1978.

———, ed. *Briv un redes fun Y. L. Peretz*. New York: Ikuf, 1944.

Merezhin, A. "Tsvey yor yidishe erd-aynordnung un [sic] sovetn-farband." *Frayhayt*, 19 Sept. 1926.

Michels, Tony. "Socialism with a Jewish Face: The Origins of the Yiddish-Speaking Communist Movement in the United States, 1907–1923." In *Yiddish and the Left*, edited by Gennady Estraikh and Mikhail Krutikov, 24–55. Oxford: Legenda, 2001.

Miron, Dan. *Sholem Aleykhem: Person, Persona, Presence*. New York: Columbia Univ., 1972.

———. *A Traveler Disguised: The Rise of Modern Yiddish Fiction in the Nineteenth Century*. New York: Syracuse Univ. Press, 1996.

Mishkinsky, Moshe. "Regional Factors in the Formation of the Jewish Labor Movement in Czarist Russia." In *Essential Papers on Jews and the Left*, edited by Ezra Mendelsohn, 78–100. New York: New York Univ. Press, 1997.

Myer, Morris. *A yidishe utopye: a plan fun rekonstruktsye farn yidishn folk*. London: Tsayt, 1918.

Nadir, Moshe. *Humor, kritik, lirik*. Buenos Aires: YIVO, 1971.

"Nakanune pervogo Vsesoiuznogo s'ezda evreiskikh proletarskikh pisatelei." *Literaturnaia gazeta*, 22 Nov. 1931.

Naumov, Vladimir, ed. *Nepravednyi sud: Poslednii stalinskii rasstrel*. Moscow: Mezhdunarodnye otnosheniia, 1994.

Niger, Shmuel. *Shmuesn vegn bikher*. New York: Yidish, 1922.

———. *Lezer, dikhter, kritiker*. Vol. 1. New York: Yidisher kultur farlag, 1928.

———. "Der yidisher lezer in Amerike." *Di tsukunft* 35, no. 1 (1930): 55–59.

———. "In der sovetish-yidisher literatur." *Di tsukunft* 35, no. 2 (1930): 103–8.

———. "Briv fun Dovid Bergelson." *Zamlbikher* 8 (1952): 80–95.

———. *Yidishe shrayber in sovet-rusland*. New York: Alveltlekher yidisher kultur-kongres, 1958.

———, ed. *Der pinkes: yorbukh far der geshikhte fun der yidisher literatur un shprakh, far folklor, kritik un bibliografye*. Vilna: B. Kletzkin, 1913.

Notovich, Moshe. "Yugnt—zayn oytser." *Sovetish heymland* no. 1 (1967): 69–73.

Novershtern, Abraham. "Sholem-Aleykhem un zayn shtelung tsu der shprakhn-frage." *Di goldene keyt* 74 (1971): 164–88.

———. "Hundert yor Dovid Bergelson: materyaln tsu zayn lebn un shafn." *Di goldene keyt* 115 (1986): 46–57.

Novick, Pesakh. "Der opklang fun der Reyzen-Leyvik geshikhte in ratn-farband." *Morgn-frayhayt*, 15 Oct. 1929.

Nusinov, Isaac. "Fun baobakhtn tsu onteylnemen." *Di royte velt* no. 12 (1925): 58–68.

———. "Di sotsyale trayb-kreftn fun undzer literatur." *Di royte velt* no. 13 (1925): 74–78.

———. "Af farfestikte pozitsyes." *Di royte velt* no. 9 (1926): 105–6.

———. "D. Bergel'son—sozdatel' evreiskogo impressionizma." In *Burnye dni*, by David Bergelson, 3–7. Moscow and Leningrad: Khuzhestvennaia literatura, 1930.

———. "Vuhin geyt undzer literatur?" *Di royte velt* no. 5 (1930): 102–16.

Oislender, Nokhum. *Veg-ayn-veg-oys.* Kiev: Kultur-lige, 1924.

———. *Grunt-shtrikhn fun yidishn realizm.* Vilna: B. Kletzkin, 1928.

———. "In 1917." *Sovetish heymland* no. 9 (1969): 130–33.

———. "Yugnt, yugnt! Vi a shpilndike vel." *Sovetish heymland* no. 2 (1980): 118–40.

———. "Mit Ezra Fininberg." *Sovetish heymland* no. 2 (1981): 119–33.

Olgin, Moshe. *In der velt fun gezang: a bukh vegn poezye un poetn.* New York: Forward, 1919.

———. *Havrile and Yoel.* New York: Frayhayt, 1927.

———. *Folk un kultur.* New York: Alveltlekher yidisher kultur-farband, 1939.

Olgin, Moshe [J. Moissaye]. *A Guide to Russian Literature, 1820–1917.* New York: Harcourt, Brace, and Howe, 1920.

"120 pisatelei na Belomorsko-Baltiiskom kanale." *Literaturnaia gazeta,* 29 Aug. 1933.

Orshanski, Ber. *Di yidishe literatur in Vaysrusland nokh der revolutsye.* Minsk: Tsentr-farlag, 1931.

———. "Zachatki evreiskoi proletarskoi poezii v Belorussii." *Literatura i marksizm* no. 4 (1931): 95–116.

Osinskii, N. "K voprosu o 'literaturnoi' politike partii." *Pravda,* 11 Feb. 1925.

"Ot natsional'noi skorbi k klassovoi bor'be." *Literaturnaia gazeta,* 4 Aug. 1934.

Patkin, A. L. *The Origins of the Russian-Jewish Labour Movement.* Melbourne: F. W. Cheshire Pty, 1947.

Patrick, George Z. *Popular Poetry in Soviet Russia.* Berkeley: Univ. of California Press, 1929.

Pennell, Joseph. *The Jew at Home.* London: William Heinemann, 1892.

Peretz, Y. L. *Di verk fun Yitskhok Leybush Perets.* Vol. 1. New York: Yidish, 1920.

Perlmann, Joel. "Russian Jewish Literacy in 1897: A Reanalysis of Census Data." In *Papers in Jewish Demography in Memory of U. O. Schmelz,* edited by Sergio DellaPergola and Judith Even, 123–37. Jerusalem: Hebrew Univ., 1997.

Pinkus, Benjamin. "La participation des minorités nationales extra-territoriales à la vie politique et république de l'Union Soviétique, 1917–39." *Cahiers du monde russe* 36, no. 3 (1995): 290–318.

Pivovar, E. I., et al., eds. *Rossiia v izgnanii: sud'by russkikh emigrantov za rubezhom.* Moscow: Institut vseobshchei istorii RAN, 1999.

"Po povodu diskussii o stat'akh Litvakova." *Literaturnaia gazeta,* 12 May 1930.

Pogodin, Nikolai. *Sobranie dramaticheskikh proizvedenii.* Vol. 3. Moscow: Iskusstvo, 1960.

Pohl, J. Otto. *The Stalinist Penal System: A Statistical History of Soviet Repression and Terror, 1930–53.* Jefferson, Mo., and London: McFarland, 1997.

Polonskaia, L. "Iz evreiskoi literatury." *Novyi mir* no. 3 (1931): 171–75.

Pomerantz, Alexander. *Proletpen: etyudn un materyaln tsu der geshikhte fun dem kamf far proletarisher literatur in Amerike (f.sh.a.).* Kiev: All-Ukrainian Academy of Science, 1935.

———. "Yidishe proletarishe literatur." In *Almanakh: Baytrog fun yidn tsu dem oyfboy fun Amerike: 10-yoriker yubiley fun internatsyonaln arbeter ordn,* 390–405. New York: Kooperativer folks-farlag, 1940.

———. *Di sovetishe hatuge-malkhes.* Buenos Aires: YIVO, 1962.

Rabin, Joseph. "Hert mikh oys: fun mayne zikhroynes." *Sovetish heymland* no. 8 (1984): 137–53.

Rabinovich, I. S., ed. *Sbornik evreiskoi poezii.* Moscow and Leningrad: Gosizdat, 1931.

Ran, Leyzer. "Der umbakanter yung-vilner dertseyler Henekh Soloveichik." *Di goldene keyt* 101 (1980): 96–101.

Rapoport, Y. *Zoymen in vint.* Buenos Aires: Alveltlekher yidisher kultur-kongres, 1962.

Raskin, Aron. *Literarishe eseyen.* Jerusalem: Bar-Ilan Univ., 1989.

Ratner, Z., and Y. Kvitni. *Dos yidishe bukh in f.s.s.r. far di yorn 1917–1921.* Kiev: Tsentrfarlag, 1930.

Ravitsh, Melekh. *Dos mayse-bukh fun mayn lebn: yorn in Varshe, 1921–34.* Tel Aviv: I. L. Peretz, 1975.

Reisen, Zalman. *Leksikon fun der yidisher literatur, prese un filologye.* Vols. 1–4. Vilna: B. Kletzkin, 1928–29.

———. "Tsu der statistik fun yidishn bukh." *YIVO Bleter* 1, no. 2 (1931): 182–84.

Remenik, Hersh. *Shtaplen: portretn fun yidishe shrayber.* Moscow: Sovetskii pisatel', 1982.

Reznik, Lipe. "A briv in redaktsye." *Der emes,* 16 Feb. 1926.

"Rezolyutsye vegn der yidisher literatur fun der tsvishnfelkerlekher konferents fun revolutsyonerer literatur." *Prolit* no. 12 (1930): 88–91.

Rivkin, B. *Grunt-tendentsn fun der yidisher literatur in Amerike.* New York: Ikuf, 1948.

Robin, Régine. "L'itinéraire de David Bergelson." In *Autour de la Gare suivi de Joseph Shur,* by David Bergelson, 3–35. Lausanne: L'Age d'homme, 1982.

———. *Socialist Realism: An Impossible Aesthetic.* Stanford, Calif.: Stanford Univ. Press, 1992.

Rontch, Isaac E. *Amerike in der yidisher literatur.* New York: I. E. Rontch bukh-komitet, 1945.

Rosenthal-Shneiderman, Esther. *Oyf vegn un umvegn: zikhroynes, gesheenishn, perzenlekhkaytn.* Vol. 2. Tel Aviv: Ha-Menorah, 1978.

———. *Oyf vegn un umvegn: zikhroynes, gesheenishn, perzenlekhkaytn.* Vol. 3. Tel Aviv: I. L. Peretz, 1982.

Roskies, David G. "Ayzik-Meyer Dik and the Rise of Yiddish Popular Literature." Ph.D. diss., Brandeis Univ., 1974.

———. "The Re-education of Der Nister: 1922–1929." In *Jews and Jewish Life in Russia and the Soviet Union,* edited by Yaacov Ro'i, 201–11. Ilford: F. Cass, 1995.

Roth, Joseph. *The Wandering Jews.* London: Granta, 2001.

Rozier, Gilles. *Moyshe Broderzon: Un écrivain yiddish d'avant-garde.* Saint-Denis: Presses Universitarires de Vincennes, 1999.

Rubin, Burton. "Plekhanov and Soviet Literary Criticism." *The American Slavic and East European Review* 15, no. 4 (1956): 527–42.

Rubin, Israel. "Bay di tishlekh fun romanishn kafe." *Literarishe bleter* 3 (1930).

Rubin, Rivka. "Izi Kharik." *Literaturnaiia gazeta,* 8 June 1934.

———. *Shrayber un verk.* Warsaw and Moscow: Yidish bukh, 1968.

Rubenstein, Joshua, and Vladimir P. Naumov, eds. *Stalin's Secret Pogrom: The Postwar Inquisition of the Jewish Anti-Fascist Committee.* New Haven, Conn., and London: Yale Univ. Press, 2001.

Rybakov, Mikhailo, ed. *Pravda istorii. Diial'nist' evreiskoï kul'turno-prosvitnyts'koï organizatsiï "Kul'turna Liha" u Kievi, 1918–25.* Kiev: Kyi, 2001.

Sakwa, Richard. *Soviet Communists in Power: A Study of Moscow During the Civil War, 1918–21.* Basingstoke: Macmillan, 1988.

Scherr, Barry P. *Russian Poetry: Meter, Rhythm, and Rhyme.* Berkeley: Univ. of California Press, 1986.

Scholem, Gershon. *The Messianic Idea in Judaism.* New York: Schocken Books, 1971.

Schulman, Elias. *Di sovetish-yidishe literatur.* New York: Bikher, 1971.

———. *Leksikon fun Forverts shrayber zint 1897.* New York: Forward, 1986.

Schwartz, Lawrence H. *Marxism and Culture: The CPUSA and Aesthetics in the 1930s.* Port Washington, N.Y.: Kennikat Press, 1980.

Selimenev, Viacheslav, and Arkadii Zeltser. "The Jewish Intelligentsia and the Liquidation of Yiddish Schools in Belorussia, 1938." *Jews in Eastern Europe* no. 3 (2000): 78–97.

Serebriani, Israel. "Vizit-kartlekh." *Sovetish heymland* no. 11 (1974): 129–37.

Sfard, David. *Mit zikh un mit andere.* Jerusalem: Yerusholayimer almanakh, 1984.

Shapiro, Lamed. *Der shrayber geyt in kheyder.* Los Angeles: Aleyn, 1945.

Shapiro, Leon. *The History of ORT: A Jewish Movement for Social Change.* New York: Schocken Books, 1980.

Shavit, David. "The Emergence of Jewish Public Libraries in Tsarist Russia." *Journal of Library History* 20, no. 3 (1985): 239–52.

Sheikevitsh, N. M. *Di amerikanishe glikn: a roman fun yidishn lebn in Amerike.* Vilna: Katsenelson, 1912.

Shekhtman, Eli. *Ringen oyf der neshome.* Tel Aviv: Yisroel-bukh, 1981.

Shentalinsky, Vitaly. *The KGB's Literary Archive.* London: Harvill Press, 1995.

Sherman, Joseph. "With Perfect Faith: The Life and Work of Leibl Feldman." In *Oudtshoorn: Jerusalem of Africa,* by Leibl Feldman, 1–25. Johanessburg: Univ. of the Witwatersrand, 1989.

———. "From Isolation to Entrapment: Bergelson and the Party Line, 1919–1927." *Slavic Almanach* 6, no. 9 (2000): 211–18.

Shevelov, George Y. *The Ukrainian Language in the First Half of the Twentieth Century, 1900–41.* Cambridge, Mass.: Harvard Univ. Press, 1989.

Shimeni [Shimen Dobin]. "Di geshikhte fun a shul." *Literatur un lebn* no. 3 (1914): 142–36.

Shimoni, Gideon. *The Zionist Ideology.* Hanover and London: Univ. Press of New England for Brandeis Univ. Press, 1995.

Shmeruk, Khone. "Sholem-Aleykhem un di onheybn fun der yidisher literatur far kinder." *Di goldene keyt* 112 (1984): 48.

———. "Aspects of the History of Warsaw as a Yiddish Literary Centre." In *From Shtetl to Socialism,* edited by Antony Polonsky, 120–33. London: Littman Library of Jewish Civilization, 1993.

———. "Nokhem Shtif, Mark Shagal, un di yidishe kinder-literatur in vilner kletskin farlag." *Di pen* 26 (1996): 1–19.

———, ed. *Pirsumim yehudiyim be-vrit ha-mo'atsot.* Jerusalem: Hebrew Univ., 1961.

———, ed. *A shpigl oyf a shteyn.* Jerusalem: The Magnes Press, 1987.

Shmidt, Otto, ed. *The Voyage of the Chelyuskin.* New York: Macmillan, 1935.

Shneer, David. "The History of 'The Truth': Soviet Jewish Activists and the Moscow Yiddish Daily Newspaper." In *Yiddish and the Left,* edited by Gennady Estraikh and Mikhail Krutikov, 129–43. Oxford: Legenda, 2001.

———. "An Ambivalent Revolutionary: Izi Khari's Image of the Shtetl." *East European Jewish Affairs* 32, no. 1 (2002): 117.

Sholem Aleichem. *Shomers mishpet, oder der sud prisyazhnikh oyf ale romanen fun Shomer.* Berdichev: n.p., 1888.

———. *Ale verk.* Vols. 4, 12, and 16. New York: Sholem Aleichem folksfond, 1925.

———. *Oysgeklibene briv, 1883–1916.* Moscow: Emes, 1941.

Shrayer, Maxim D. *Russian Poet/Soviet Jew: The Legacy of Eduard Bagritskii.* Lanham, Md.: Rowman and Littlefield, 2000.

Shternberg, Yakov. *Vegn literatur un teater.* Tel Aviv: H. Leivik, 1987.

Shternshis, Anna. "Soviet and Kosher in the Ukrainian Shtetl." In *The Shtetl: Image and Reality,* edited by Gennady Estraikh and Mikhail Krutikov, 133–51. Oxford: Legenda, 2000.

Shulman, M. "Vos iz azoyns proletarishe poezye?" *Di komunistishe velt* no. 2 (1919): 18–22.

Shvartsman, Osher. *Ale lider.* Moscow: Sovetskii pisatel', 1961.

Singalowsky, Aron. "Aufbau und Umbau: Zum Problem des jüdischen Wirtschaftsleben in Osteuropa." *Der Morgen* 3, no. 4 (1927): 355–85.

Singer, Israel Joshua. *Nay-Rusland.* Vilna: B. Kletzkin, 1928.

———. "A briv fun Amerike." *Forverts,* 7 June 1942.

Sito, Fayvl. *Ot dos zaynen mir.* Kharkov and Kiev: Ukrmelukhenatsmindfarlag, 1932.

Sito, Fayvl, and Hershl Polyanker, eds. *Komsomolye.* Kiev: Ukrmelukhenatsmindfarlag, 1938.

Slotnick, Susan Ann. "The Novel Form in the Works of David Bergelson." Ph.D. diss., Columbia Univ., 1978.

Sloves, Khaim. *Sovetishe yidishe melukheshkayt* Paris: H. Sloves, 1979.

Slutskii, A. "Detskaia literatura na razgovorno-evreiskom iazyke." *Vestnik Obshchestva rasprostraneniia prosveshcheniia mezhdu evreiami v Rossii* 13 (1912): 29–45.

Smolyar, Hersh. *Vu bistu khaver Sidorov?* Tel Aviv: I. L. Peretz, 1975.

———. *Fun ineveynik.* Tel Aviv: I. L. Peretz, 1978.

Sobolevskii, N. "Poslednii roman Knuta Gamsuna." *Novyi mir* no. 5 (1934): 256–60.

Soyer, Daniel. "Abraham Cahan's Travels in Jewish Homelands: Palestine in 1925 and the Soviet Union in 1927." In *Yiddish and the Left,* edited by Gennady Estraikh and Mikhail Krutikov, 56–79. Oxford: Legenda, 2001.

Spengler, Oswald. *The Decline of the West.* London: G. Allen and Unwin, 1959.

Spirin, L. M. *Rossia 1917 god: iz istorii bor'by politicheskikh partii.* Moscow: Mysl', 1987.

Stampfer, Shaul. "What Did 'Knowing Hebrew' Mean in Eastern Europe?" In *Hebrew in Ashkenaz: A Language in Exile,* edited by Lewis Glinert, 129–40. Oxford: Oxford Univ. Press, 1993.

"Statistika evreiskoi literatury v 1915 g." *Novyi put'* no. 18 (1916): 7–9.

Stencl, Abrahan-Nokhum. "Arop funem yarid . . ." *Loshn un lebn* nos. 10–11 (1968): 25.

Stepanchev, Stephen. "Walt Whitman in Russia." In *Whitman and the World,* edited by Gay W. Allen and Ed Folsom, 300–13. Iowa City: Univ. of Iowa Press, 1995.

Strazh, Sh. "Der ufshtand fun masnleyener." *Oktyabr* 1 (1925): 107–8.

Syrkin, Nakhman. *Geklibene tsionistish-sotsyalistishe shriftn.* New York: Central Committee Poale Zion, 1925.

Tager, Alexander B. *The Decay of Czarism: The Beiliss Trial.* Philadelphia: The Jewish Publication Society of America, 1935.

Tamarkin, Khaim. "Durkh yorn un gesheenishn." *Sovetish heymland* no. 4 (1983): 118–20.

———. "Moskve in di tsvantsiker yorn." *Sovetish heymland* no. 8 (1985): 125–33.

Tenenbaum, Joseph. "Di yidishe shprakh oyf der tog-ordenung fun der sholem-konferents in Paris, 1919." *YIVO Bleter* 41 (1957–58): 217–29.

Timenchik, Roman, and Zoia Kopel'man. "Viacheslav Ivanov i poeziia Kh.N. Bialika." *Novoe literaturnoe obozrenie* 14 (1995): 105–22.

Tolstoy, Aleksey. "Oktaibr'skaia revoliutsiia dala mne vse." *Literaturnaia gazeta,* 11 Jan. 1933.

Trotskii, Lev. *K istorii russkoi revoliutsii.* Moscow: Izdatel'stvo politicheskoi literatury, 1990.

Tsivyon. "Di ershte yidishe sotsialistishe teglekhe tsaytung in Vilne." In *Vilne,* edited by Ephraim H. Jeshurin, 190–205. New York: Vilner Brentsh 367 Arbeter Ring, 1935.

Tsukernik, A. L., ed. *Trud i profsoiuzy na Ukraine.* Kharkiv: Spilka, 1928.

Tsukker, B. "Do henezy evreiskoï proletars'koï literatury." *Krytyka* no. 11 (1928): 45–53.

Tsvetaeva, Marina. *Sochineniia.* Vol. 1. Moscow: Sovetskii pisatel', 1980.

Tychina, Pavlo. *Zibrannia tvoriv.* Vol. 12.1. Kiev: Naukova dumka, 1990.

Vakar, Nicholas P. *Belorussia: The Making of a Nation.* Cambridge, Mass.: Harvard Univ. Press, 1956.

Vareikis, I. "O nashei linii v khudozhestvennoi literature i o proletarskikh pisateliakh." *Pravda,* 12 Feb. 1925.

Veidlinger, Jeffrey. "Let's Perform a Miracle: The Soviet Yiddish State Theatre in the 1920s." *Slavic Review* 52, no. 2 (1998): 380–84.

———. *The Moscow State Yiddish Theater: Jewish Culture on the Soviet Stage.* Bloomington: Indiana Univ. Press, 2000.

Veitsblit, I. *Vegn altn un nayem shtetl.* Moscow: Tsentrfarlag, 1930.

Vergelis, Aron. "Di goldene keyt fun der yidisher literatur." *Sovetish heymland* no. 4 (1963): 100–15.

"Verhaftung David Bergelsons in Riga." *Jüdische Rundschau,* 1 Apr. 1931.

Vermel', S. *Moskovskoe izgnanie.* Moscow: Mir, 1924.

Vidmantas, Edvardas. "Sotsial-demokraticheskaia pechat' i rabochee dvizhenie v Litve v 1895–1907 gg." Candidate diss., Vilnius Univ., 1976.

Volfson, I. V. *Adresnaia i spravochnaia kniga: gazetnyi mir.* St. Petersburg: n.p., 1910–11.

"Vystavka evreev-khudozhnikov." *Novyi put'* nos. 13–15 (1917): 32.

Weinreich, Max. "Yidish." In *Algemeyne entsiklopedye,* Yidn/B: 25–47. Paris: Dubnov-fond, 1940.

Wendroff, Zalmen. "Di 70-yorike milkhome." *Sovetish heymland* no. 3 (1966): 149–53.

Wiener, Leo. *The History of Yiddish Literature in the Nineteenth Century.* New York: C. Scribner's Sons, 1899.

Wiener, Meir. "O nekotorykh voprosakh sotsialisticheskogo realizma." *Oktiabr'* no. 1 (1935): 239.

Wiener, Norbert. *I Am a Mathematician.* London: Gollancz, 1956.

Wieviorka, Abraham. *Revizye.* Kiev and Kharkov: Literatur un kunst, 1931.

———. "Problema tvorchoï metody v evreis'kii proletars'kii literaturi." *Krytyka* nos. 7–8 (1931): 129–45.

———. "Fremds un eygns." *Farmest* nos. 2–3 (1933): 174–82.

———, ed. *In shotn fun tlies: almanakh fun der yidisher proletarisher literatur in di kapitalistishe lender.* Kiev: Melukhisher natsmindfarlag, 1932.

Wolitz, Seth. "The Kiev-Grupe (1918–1920) Debate: The Function of Literature." *Yiddish* 3, no. 3 (1978): 97–106.

Yerusalimski, Aron. "Di 'mayrevke'—undzer 'kleyner internatsional.' " *Sovetish heymland* no. 2 (1974): 168–73.

"Yidishe kultur-tuer kegn kemfndikn hebraizm." *Der emes,* 12 Feb. 1924.

"Yidishlekher ongrif un Dovid Hofshteyn." *Der emes,* 29 Feb. 1924.

Yoffe, Yudel. *Afn glaykhn veg.* Moscow: Emes, 1941.

Yuditski, A. "Yidishe arbeter-bavegung af Ukrayne." *Di royte velt* no. 3 (1926): 78–82.

Yushkovsky, Mordechai. "Leivick un di sovetishe publitsistik." In *Shtudyes in Leivick,* edited by Gershon Winer, 100–15. Ramat Gan: Univ. Bar-Ilan, 1992.

Zaslavsky, David. "Materyaln tsu der geshikhte fun kiever organizatsye fun Bund." *Royter pinkes* 1 (1920): 27–35.

Zharkov, V. M., et al. *Kniga: Entsiklopediia.* Moscow: Bol'shaia rossiiskaia entsiklopedii, 1999.

Zhiga, I. "Proletarskie pisateli i ikh organizatsii." *Pravda,* 18 June 1925.

Zhitlovsky, Khaim. *Yidn un yidishkayt.* New York: Kh. Zhitlovsky farlag-komitet, 1939.

Zhukovski, S. "Tsu der itstiker literarisher situatsye." *Prolit* nos. 11–12 (1929): 139–46.

Zilbergelt, Z. "A groyser Bergelson ovnt in Moskve." *Frayhayt,* 8 Oct. 1926.

Zitron, Shmuel Leyb. *Dray literarishe doyres.* Vol. 1. Vilna: S. Sreberk, 1920.

Index

231